Elena Furlanetto, Dietmar Meinel (eds.)
A Poetics of Neurosis

I0812159

Culture & Theory | Volume 161

Elena Furlanetto, Dietmar Meinel (eds.)

A Poetics of Neurosis

Narratives of Normalcy and Disorder in Cultural and Literary Texts

[transcript]

The volume was supported by the main research area "Transformation of Contemporary Societies" at the University of Duisburg-Essen, the Faculty of Humanities at the University of Duisburg-Essen, the Department of Anglophone Studies at the University of Duisburg-Essen, and the University Library of the University of Duisburg-Essen.

The electronic version of this book is freely available due to funding by OGeSoMo, a BMBF-project to support and analyse open access book publications in the humanities and social sciences (BMBF: Federal Ministry of Education and Research). The project is led by the University Library of Duisburg-Essen. For more information see https://www.uni-due.de/ogesomo.

Bibliographic information published by the Deutsche Nationalbibliothek
The Deutsche Nationalbibliothek lists this publication in the Deutsche Nationalbibliografie; detailed bibliographic data are available in the Internet at http://dnb.d-nb.de

This work is licensed under the Creative Commons Attribution 4.0 (BY) license, which means that the text may be be remixed, transformed and built upon and be copied and redistributed in any medium or format even commercially, provided credit is given to the author. For details go to http://creativecommons.org/licenses/by/4.0/.

Creative Commons license terms for re-use do not apply to any content (such as graphs, figures, photos, excerpts, etc.) not original to the Open Access publication and further permission may be required from the rights holder. The obligation to research and clear permission lies solely with the party re-using the material.

First published in 2018 by transcript Verlag
© Elena Furlanetto, Dietmar Meinel (eds.), chapters by respective authors

Cover layout: Maria Arndt, Bielefeld
Printed by docupoint GmbH, Magdeburg
Print-ISBN 978-3-8376-4132-5
PDF-ISBN 978-3-8394-4132-9

Table of Contents

Acknowledgements

On October 8-10, 2015, a group of young scholars gathered at the University of Duisburg-Essen for the third Postgraduate Forum of the Association for Anglophone Postcolonial Studies (GAPS) under the title "Empire and Neurosis." GAPS, the DokForum, the Dekanat der Geisteswissenschaften, and the Gesellschaft von Freunden und Förderern of the University of Duisburg-Essen generously supported the event. As many questions remained unanswered and many discussions unresolved, the organizers opted for a follow-up conference a year later, on February 18-19, 2016, which promised to investigate "Neurosis and Social Transformations." As the negotiations for the publication of a volume had already started, this second event, which pursued an expanded and more open-ended version of the original topic, was designed as a conference as well as a writing workshop, where the invited speakers presented more elaborate versions of their papers with an eye on publication. That was the beginning of a long process of editing and of an intensive multilateral dialogue that has resulted in this volume. We would like to thank our contributors and acknowledge their commendable resilience and long-term commitment to the project, without which this publication would not have seen the light.

The editors also thank the Profilschwerpunkt Wandeln von Gegenwartsgesellschaften of the University of Duisburg-Essen (UDE), which provided generous funding for both the "Neurosis and Social Transformation" workshop and the book publication. We are grateful to the Faculty of the Humanities (UDE), to the Department of Anglophone Studies (UDE), and to the University Library of the University of Duisburg-Essen for their generous financial assistance and for their enthusiastic response to our publication ambitions. And we are greatly indebted to our mentor Prof. Dr. Barbara Buchenau for her endless advice and encouragement: she has been and continues to be a crucial influence in our academic trajectories.

Introduction

A Cultural History of Neurosis, From Diagnostics to Poetics

DIETMAR MEINEL

In 1994, the handbook of the American Psychology Association – the *Diagnostic and Statistical Manual* – dropped neurosis from its medical vocabulary. This deletion constituted the end of a psychoanalytical concept that had shaped medical discourse for the better part of the twentieth century but became obsolete and deemed too elusive for a proper diagnosis of psychological disorders. In "Where Have All the Neurotics Gone?" (2012), journalist Benedict Carey explains that, as "scientists […] began to slice neurosis into ever finer pieces, like panic disorder, social anxiety and obsessive-compulsive disorder" (Carey), the concept lost its analytical value. Subsequently, Carey recalls its broader cultural relevance for postwar middle-class Americans when, instead of indicating "merely being anxious" or "exhibiting […] hysteria," neurosis actually designated a person as "being interesting (if sometimes exasperating)" (Carey). In the end, however, neurosis may not have vanished as completely as present-day medical discourse and nostalgia for the past may imply.

After all, Carey reasons, people continue to experience their everyday life as disquieting and distressing, while the five-factor model of personality indicates that among college students the "neuroticism levels have increased by as much as 20 percent" (Carey) since the 1950s. Similarly, some of the features of neurosis, and particularly the use of talk therapy for its treatment, may have simply been absorbed into mainstream since "[p]eople of all ages […] are awash in self-confession, not only in the reality-show of pop culture but in the increasingly public availability of almost every waking thought, through Facebook, Twitter and other social media" (Carey). In this view, neurosis did not disappear but came to be an integral, often unnoticed part of contemporary daily life.

Whereas neurosis slowly disappeared from medical and public discourse, trauma and trauma narratives rapidly gained prominence after the terrorist attacks on September 11, 2001. To understand the events of that day, a plethora of journalistic as well as popular and literary texts adopted the notion of trauma as their predominant frame of reference.[1] Neither journalists nor writers, artists, politicians, or even scholars, however, appropriated trauma in its narrow medical definition, as the adaptation of a vague notion of trauma allowed for a larger variety of cultural narratives, Susan Faludi asserts in *The Terror Dream* (2007). Trauma became a trope in popular and scholarly attempts to understand September 11 as well as the cultural and literary productions in its wake. Even when texts did not explicitly refer to the collapse of the World Trade Center, the portrayal of emotional distance or numbness, for example, was read in light of a 'September 11 trauma.' According to Didier Fassin and Richard Rechtman in *The Empire of Trauma* (2007), the general idea guiding most post-9/11 publications presumed that "both survivors and witnesses, but also television viewers and residents of the United States in general were suffering from exposure to a traumatic event" (2).[2] The study of trauma eventually helped to develop a lan-

1 Initially, trauma studies developed out of scholarship interest in understanding the (psychological) consequences of the Holocaust. Later, trauma also became an essential concept to think through the trans-Atlantic slave trade, the experience of slavery, and its aftermath in the twentieth century.

2 In *Trauma Culture: The Politics of Terror and Loss in Media and Literature* (2005), for example, E. Ann Kaplan introduces a broad, ubiquitous notion of trauma to bring together a wide variety of texts from World War II representations to Hitchcock films, media images of Rwanda and the Iraq War, indigenous cinema, and narratives of September 11. For Kaplan, trauma extends from an immediate to a highly mediated experience: "At one extreme there is the direct trauma victim while at the other we find a person geographically far away, having no personal connection to the victim. In between are a series of positions: for example, there's the relative of trauma victims or the position of workers coming in after a catastrophe, those who encounter trauma through accounts they hear, or clinicians who may be vicariously traumatized now that increasingly counseling is offered to people who survive catastrophes. People encounter trauma by being a bystander, by living near to where a catastrophe happened, or by hearing about a crisis from a friend. But most people encounter trauma through the media, which is why focusing on so-called mediatized trauma is important" (2). Fritz Breithaupt labeled this mediatization "the plot of trauma" (72), in which the staging of September 11, 2001 as a trauma in the media "serves as the central axis of organizing the diverse information material in such a way to bring about the said response in the audience. In short, the media themselves responded to the attack by creating that which they perceived as the outcome of the attacks: 'a trauma.' At the same

guage and establish a discourse about the events of September 11 in the American public. Whether this suffering was understood in the psycho-analytical sense of "traces left in the psyche" or in the popular notion of "an open wound in the collective memory" (2), the prevalent mainstream narratives initially tended to frame the collapse of the World Trade Center as an exceptional rupture and trauma as an inhibition of daily life that necessitates healing and closure (see Däwes 1-5).[3]

The animation film *Finding Nemo* (2003) follows trauma narratives of the kind gestured to above in the underwater world of the Great Barrier Reef. If the personal journey of one character, Marlin, unfolds a narrative of healing, however, the film includes a plethora of psychologically wounded minor characters who have learnt to coexist with their disorders and, unlike Marlin, are offered no closure. The presence of these characters marked by quirks and eccentricities make *Finding Nemo* as much a story about neurosis as about trauma, and one that invites questions about preponderant fictions of normalcy.

The film opens with the clownfish father Marlin moving into the coral reef equivalent of a suburban home with his wife Coral. When a barracuda ravages their home killing his wife and almost all of their brood, Marlin develops a fearful attitude about life because of "the traumatic attack" (Whitley 130). Consequentially, Marlin raises his only surviving son, Nemo, on the idea that life outside the anemone and in the ocean "is not safe" (*Finding Nemo*). *Finding Nemo* underscores this traumatized view of the world when other parents ask Marlin to tell a joke, presuming that he, as a clownfish, has to be particularly humorous.

---

time, the media recommend themselves as therapist, as the agent of national healing" (67).

3 In trauma studies, the aspiration to heal the (psychological) wound or pain similarly presupposes a wholeness of identity and – as Allan Young maintains in *The Harmony of Illusions: Inventing Post-Traumatic Stress Disorder* (1995) – is expressive of late nineteenth-century Western views informing 'trauma.' For Stef Craps, this notion of healing can privilege forms of psychological restoration "over the transformation of a wounding political, social, or economic system," as normative trauma discourse may disavow "the need for taking collective action towards systemic change [and] […] serve as a political palliative to the socially disempowered" (50). In *Ground Zero Fiction* (2011), Birgit Däwes offers a nuanced reading of the American 9/11 novel not only as perpetuating narratives of national hubris, American heroism, and xenophobic fear. Instead, the genre "provides the narrative agency to name and possibly replace the semantic absences that the Trade Center Towers left behind, but it also resists the authority of closure" (7).

As Marlin stammers and mumbles erratically and eventually fails to deliver the punchline, the scene captures his social anxieties about the world outside his home; Marlin is unable to function within expected social parameters. The Pixar film portrays him as a traumatized figure, in the words of Ruth Leys, "unable to recollect and integrate the hurtful experience in normal consciousness" (2). Instead, the murder of his family has frozen Marlin in time as the memories of the event continue to shape his behavior in the present. In this sense, Marlin exemplifies the notion of trauma as "a disorder of memory" ensuing from "emotions of terror and surprise caused by a certain event," in which the mind "is unable to register the wound to the psyche because the ordinary mechanisms of awareness and cognition are destroyed" (2). It is when a scuba diver captures Nemo that Marlin decides to conquer his anxieties and venture into the ocean, beyond his coral home, to find his son. As he meets numerous benevolent and supportive sea animals on his journey, Marlin eventually comes to appreciate the necessity to listen to and work with others and eventually changes from an angst-ridden into an assured, poised, even humorous father. In this sense, *Finding Nemo* offers a narrative of healing trauma through communal, transspecies cooperation.[4]

At the same time, this trauma narrative of closure or healing also includes a variety of characters who do not mend their emotional or psychological wounds.[5] In its emphasis on learning to live *with* their impulses, the narrative of neurosis in *Finding Nemo* deviates from early trauma schemas. For example, the surgeonfish Dory lives with a severe condition of short-term memory loss as she cannot remember any immediate information. As her amnesia allows Dory to be-

---

4 With its narrative about an unprovoked assault on the home(land), the killing of the innocent, and the psychological pain the father endures, *Finding Nemo* animates a trauma script prevalent in post-September 11 narratives. By portraying the white suburban family as an innocent victim of a villainous assault for which the surviving but traumatized father Marlin eventually finds closure, *Finding Nemo* participates in what Breithaupt labeled the "fabrication and ritualization of 'trauma' in September 11" (67). However, as Marlin also befriends a variety of fish, birds, and mammals who help him find his son, the film suggests that neither fear nor anxiety should guide Marlin in his approach to life after the shocking event.

5 *Finding Nemo* also introduces characters with physical disability. The young clownfish Nemo is born with one very small fin and the Moorish Idol Gill possess one several injured fin. The film portrays both as courageous, persevering, and witty in their attempt to escape human captivity.

friend even the most threatening sea creatures,[6] she becomes essential for Marlin in finding Nemo. As she embraces threatening sharks or gigantic whales with an open mind, for Jack Halberstam in *The Queer Art of Failure* (2011), Dori embodies "a new version of selfhood" (80) founded on transspecies trust and cooperation. Similarly, the three sharks Bruce, Anchor, and Chum desire to adhere to a vegetarian diet. Yet, their exuberant grinning as well as the extensive display of their teeth indicates the psychological tensions and aggression underneath their excessively cordial behavior. On the other hand, the young clownfish Nemo encounters a variety of compassionate and urbane fish after his abduction from the coral reef brings him to the aquarium of a dentist in Sidney. In their highly technologized environment, the fish tank inhabitants developed an obsession with their mirror image, a preoccupation with bubbly water, or an intense fear of germs. Since all characters with neurosis have learned to live with their impulses and manage their daily life with some ease, the animation of neurosis in *Finding Nemo* appears to challenge narratives of normalcy. However, even as the (involuntary) expressions of their neurosis renders these characters often charming, amiable, and complex, *Finding Nemo* also uses their non-conforming behavior for cheap laughter. Dory's short-term amnesia furthermore leaves her vulnerable to the manipulation by others who coerce her into life threatening situations. As characters with neurosis remain vulnerable to abuse and suffering or function as targets of ridicule and violence, their animation asks us to explore the notion of normalcy informing the portrayal of neurosis – particularly in contrast to the depiction of the innocent father mastering the trauma of an exceptional assault.

Seen in this light, we understand neither trauma nor neurosis in this volume as primarily medical or psychoanalytical concepts. This introduction and the following contributions address neurosis as an analytical category that builds on, but eventually moves away from the premises of trauma studies. Following the adaptation of trauma theory for cultural and literary study, this book aims to disentangle neurosis from its medical, psychoanalytical, and psychiatric context and entangle it in debates about culture and literature. Since neurosis in its psychoan-

6 Since for Freud, a person with neurosis may turn from its "exciting cause" and "consign […] it to amnesia" ("The Loss of Reality in Neurosis and Psychosis" 4095), Dory's chronic forgetfulness may similarly exemplify her attempt to manage neurosis. The sequel *Finding Dory* (2016) sheds further light on the history of Dory's forgetfulness showing that she experienced short-term memory loss from a very young age. The sequel, however, documents the neurotic behavior resulting from the memory loss and the emotional toll exerted on Dory in even greater detail. Finding closure for (the origins of) her neurotic behavior becomes the main narrative device of the plot.

alytical or even Freudian understanding has been substituted with a host of anxiety disorders anchored in biogenetic research and has virtually disappeared from medical discourse, this volume aims to re-visit neurosis as a cultural rather than a medical concept. Since the 1970s, neurosis proved to be less and less useful in psychological research as denominations that are more specific supplanted a concept many considered too elusive for an exact medical diagnosis and unhelpful for therapeutic treatment. Particularly discoveries in neuroscience and an increasing knowledge of genetic processes contributed to the demise of neurosis in psychological, medical, and eventually popular discourse (see Carey). However, this volume posits that what has been considered too elusive in the fields of medicine and psychology may have not ceased to matter in textual analyses.

In cultural and literary studies, texts and images hardly ever lend themselves to neuroscientific or genetic analyses. Even an exact or detailed medical diagnosis of anxiety disorders such as post-traumatic stress disorder or obsessive-compulsive behavior may often be impossible when analyzing fictional texts. Fiction, in fact, shows very little concern for diagnostic exactness, as mental disorders are routinely romanticized or vilified, bent to suit aesthetic and narrative choices. Questions about a character's mental well-being or the portrayal and function of anxiety disorders in a text, nonetheless, continue to offer analytical paths to understanding literary and cultural texts. Debates about what qualifies as mental well-being, furthermore, question and highlight the social constructedness of the narratives of normalcy embedded in psychological discourses. As the close reading of *Finding Nemo* and the contributions to this volume demonstrate, the elusiveness of neurosis allows analyzing the portrayal of psychological conditions and notions of mental well-being beyond medical diagnoses.

Moving beyond (exclusively) psychoanalytical notions of neurosis in *Human Experience: Philosophy, Neurosis, and the Elements of Everyday Life* (2003), John Russon grounds neurosis in a (Western European) philosophy of embodiment, temporality, and intersubjectivity (see 1-2). The experiences, the expectations, and the tensions of everyday life, Russon asserts, contribute to the formation of neurosis as an expression of moments "when some sector of a person's life cannot function compatibly with the demands of intersubjective life [...] in other sectors of that person's life" (81). This incompatibility finds its expression in everyday practices of walking, sleeping, eating, remembering, toileting, and sex – or telling a joke, we could add, thinking of Marlin – so much so that neurosis prohibits the individual from participating in "patterns of behavior that stand at odds with the patterns one would otherwise choose" and are generally considered "normal" (85). This assumption about what a culture deems normal is eventually at the heart of his re-interpretation of neurosis as a cultural and social phenomenon. For Russon, "the very existence of neurosis gives the lie to the narrative of the normal self" (85) because the latter presupposes a rational subject able to function entirely in compliance with cultural expectations, and without questioning the validity of social norms. Seen in this light, neurosis speaks to the tension between the individual (corporeal and emotional) experience of daily life and the pressures to conform. Rather than manifesting an illness that necessitates medical or psychological care, then, expressions of neurosis ask us to question the narratives of normalcy that function to brand patterns, behaviors, and individuals as neurotic (see 91).

Against the foil of trauma as an exceptional event and the notion of restoring an ideal status quo, this introduction sets out to address two apparently contradictory aspects of neurosis. In the first place, it aims to demonstrate the empowering potential of neurosis by looking at *Finding Nemo.* As various characters with neurosis help Marlin to overcome his trauma, *Finding Nemo* animates neurosis as a routine, even valiant form of daily life. Since the film marginalizes the vulnerability and the precarious life of its characters with neurosis and exploits their situation for cheap laughs, however, the introduction also aspires to highlight the ways in which *Finding Nemo* animates narratives of normalcy. The following passages provide a broad sketch of the historical development of neurosis from medical to psychological to cultural concept, exemplarily animated in *Finding Nemo*.

OF TOXIC VAPORS, AMERICANITIS, AND FAILED SUBLIMATIONS

In *Historical Origins of the Concept of Neurosis* (1983), Jose M. Lopez Pinero traces the contemporary use of neurosis back to the development of medical discourses and science at the beginning of the eighteenth century. The concept emerged "as an alternative to the Galenic doctrine that considered hysteria as caused by vapours that emanated from corrupt humours in the womb and hypochondria as resulting from vapours originating from 'atrabilis'" (4),[7] and functioned as a neologism for "nervous disease." While speculative medical science continued to shape notions of neurosis in the late eighteenth and early nineteenth

7 Galen of Pergamon (129 AD – c. 200/c. 216) was a Greek physician. Meaning "black bile" in Latin, "atrabilis" was one of the four bodily humors that were believed to trigger different emotions: this one was responsible for melancholy or irritability (see *Merriam Webster,* "atrabilious").

century, Pinero locates a shift in the medical perception of neurosis in the advent of the Anatomoclinical School of Paris and its practice of anatomical lesion in the middle of the nineteenth century. The first neurological or pre-psychological notions of neurosis developed parallel to this physiological perspective. With his work on the psychogenetic origins of hysteria in the late nineteenth century, Jean-Martin Charcot eventually "started a new period in the history of neurosis" (x).

In his history of neurosis, Pinero not only chronicles its shift from a physiological to a proto-psychological phenomenon in the eighteenth and nineteenth century, but also suggests that neurosis never functioned as a purely medical concept. On the contrary, neurosis needs to be considered in its historical contexts as its meaning altered with cultural, legal, medical, political, or social changes. In the United States, for example, George Miller Beard popularized the idea of tired nerves as a consequence of modern, industrial life under the name neurasthenia. In the late nineteenth century, Andrea Tone explains in *The Age of Anxiety* (2009), the idiom functioned as "a catchall diagnosis for a range of nonpsychotic emotional problems that included worry, headache, fatigue, indigestion, muscle pain, inability to concentrate, and more" (8). Due to the absence of coherent medical diagnosis at the time, neurasthenia indicated a presumed fatigue and exhaustion of nerves. Its popular name "Americanitis," however, speaks to the narrow cultural context Beard and his followers ascribed to the diagnosis. Although similar diagnoses were popular in Germany, England, and Russia, they framed neurasthenia in an explicitly national context.[8] For Beard, the idea that nerve diseases plagued Americans in particular illustrated the cultural and technological superiority of the country since the United States was "an empire in which neurasthenia was not just a disease but a 'possession'" (Campbell 163). In this logic, (white) upper-class Americans were particularly vulnerable to nerve diseases because of their immediate exposure to the consequences of

8 In his essay "From Shock to Schreck: Psychiatrists, Telephone Operators and Traumatic Neurosis in Germany, 1900-26" (2003), Andreas Killen examines the emergence of "traumatic neurosis" in the early twentieth century within "the context of contemporaneous debates in Germany about work, social insurance, gender, and the accidents, shocks and afflictions of industrial society" (201). After its diagnosis in 1889 and its subsequent introduction to German insurance law, which entitled patients to financial compensation, "traumatic neurosis" developed into a widespread disease in the early twentieth century. With increasing financial expenses and monetary compensations particularly for female telephone operators, the German state eventually "legislated [the illness] out of existence in 1926" (201).

modernity from the steam engine, and the telegraph to innovations in science, media, and education. Neurasthenia, thus, played a fundamental role in the formation of American national identity in the nineteenth century: "Much more than a simple disease," Brad Campbell writes, "neurasthenia was a veritable force of Americanization" (164) as its diagnosis eventually linked modernity to (a particular form of) nerve disease and citizenship. Popular view considered neurasthenia "as the price Americans paid for their stunning success" (Tone 9). These notions continued to inform widespread understanding and medical scholarship even as the physiological approach of the nineteenth century yielded to psychoanalytical perspectives in the twentieth, and neurasthenia to neurosis (see Campbell 164, 168, 175).

In his early work, Sigmund Freud proposed to separate those disorders linked to the body and those he attributed to entirely psychological origins. In his essay "On the Grounds for Detaching a Particular Syndrome from Neurasthenia under the Description 'Anxiety Neurosis'" (1895), he distinguishes anxiety neurosis from neurasthenia as the latter originates in situations "when normal coiton, carried out in the most favourable conditions, is replaced by masturbation or spontaneous emission" while the former "is the product of all those factors which prevent the somatic sexual excitation from being worked over *psychically*" (109; emphasis added). This essay and his *Studies on Hysteria* (1895) both helped to establish modern notions of neurosis as distinctively detached from physical conditions for which "[r]est cures, diets, electric gadgets, and other somatic therapies would not help [...] [since neurosis] was a disorder rooted in the workings of the mind" (Tone 16). Although Jean-Martin Charcot and Pierre Janet had already associated neurosis with "intrapsychic process," Freud popularized the notion of neurosis as a psychological disorder and "established psychoanalysis as a mainstream therapeutic approach" (16).

Particularly his distinction between neurosis and psychosis helped to dissipate widespread worries about psychological disorders and legitimize their treatment. Whereas psychosis referred to "schizophrenia (also called *dementia praecox*) and manic-depressive disorder" (18), neurosis illustrated for Freud "the everyday worries and character foibles that troubled his otherwise normal patients" (15). In contrast to the often delusional and hallucinating behavior observed in psychosis, neurosis produced a sense of emotional or psychological "turmoil" (18) but allowed for daily life otherwise. With his conception of neurosis as anxiety disorder and its therapeutic treatment, Freud shaped the field of psychology for decades to come. "Freud," Tone explains, "had his greatest impact in the United States, where psychoanalytic teachings (based on the work of Freud and his many disciples) became fashionable in the 1920s and 1930s and became a staple of psychiatric medical training from the 1940s to the 1970s" (19). The *Diagnostic and Statistical Manual* from 1952 attests to the popularity of his views:

> The chief characteristic of these disorders is 'anxiety' which may be directly felt and expressed or which may be unconsciously and automatically controlled by the utilization of various psychological defense mechanisms [...]. In contrast to those with psychoses, patients with psychoneurotic disorders do not exhibit gross distortion or falsification of external reality (delusions, hallucinations, illusions) and they do not present gross disorganization of the personality. Longitudinal (lifelong) studies of individuals with such disorders usually present evidence of periodic or constant maladjustment of varying degree from early life. Special stress may bring about acute symptomatic expression of such disorders. (*DSM* 31)

Not only did Freud shape psychological and medical discourse of the twentieth century, his vocabulary also transitioned into popular culture and became part of everyday language. Multitudes of 'neurotic' New Yorkers, for example, populate Woody Allen's films, each of them endowed with a colorful array of phobias and obsessions. The figure of the urban neurotic, mostly played by Allen himself, contributed to the self-fashioning of a recognizable persona and to the constitution of a Woody Allen character type. Allen's oeuvre, or at least his Manhattan stories, connect life in New York to the development of low-intensity, essentially comical forms of neurosis that never become impairing, neither for the subject nor for the characters that gravitate around him. In fact, Allen's Manhattan neurotics show the resilience of neurosis understood as a metropolitan disease. The aquarium inhabitants in *Finding Nemo* exhibit a similar urban habitus and reveal a rebellious spirit when the clownfish boy Nemo strands in their fish tank.

The aquarium inhabitants, Gill, Bloat, Peach, Gurgle, Bubbles, Deb, and Jacques, express a profound understanding of their technologized environment and human conduct (and engage in detailed considerations of dental procedures). Their knowledge allows them to anticipate and manipulate the dentist's behavior to help Nemo escape the fish tank. Their plan consists of tempering with the computerized laser scanner that monitors water temperature and pH level in the aquarium, and then polluting the water so that the dentist will be forced to place the fish outside of the aquarium and provide them with an opportunity for escape. While their strategy to sabotage the high-tech machinery and anticipate the dentist's behavior suggests deep knowledge of human culture, life in this technologically mediated space has left its marks on the animals in the form of irrepressible ticks, impulses, and obsessions: Deb obsesses over her mirror image, Bubbles stares mesmerized into bubbly water, and Gurgle panics at the slightest mention of germs.

In a nod to Freudian notions of psychoanalysis and to early notions of neurosis as the price to pay for modernity, *Finding Nemo* links neurosis to life in a highly technologized, yet alienating environment. While neurosis develops out of "a conflict between the ego and its id" (Freud, "Neurosis and Psychosis" 4065), particularly the ability to sublimate biological drives designates what Freud sees as "civilized people" ("A Short Account of Psycho-Analysis" 4110).[9] With its fast-talking, anxiety-ridden characters living in a Sidney aquarium, *Finding Nemo* animates this culture in the urban or metropolitan tradition of Woody Allen. As "the capacity for sublimating is limited, and as the intensive suppression of primitive drives without sublimation may lead to neurosis," the urban context of the aquarium speaks particularly to Freud's (and Allen's) notion that "the growth of civilization must inevitably imply a growth of neurosis" (Horney 229). By using animals born and raised in captivity, *Finding Nemo* exemplifies the Freudian notion of neurosis as "the price humanity has to pay for cultural development" (229) and as intimately linked to urban life and "civilization."[10]

Although the film animates its anxious aquarium inhabitants as good-hearted characters and illustrates its psychoanalytical references in a tongue-in-cheek fashion, the portrayal of neurosis also possesses a troublesome undertone. After all, the aquarium inhabitants spend their entire life confined to a fish tank. Furthermore, the fish live in constant fear of becoming a present to the dentist's niece who treats her pets crudely and violently. When the young girl ferociously shakes the plastic bag with a goldfish she received from her uncle and thereby (unintentionally) kills the fish in her excitement, we can wonder as to whether neurosis is merely a consequence of life in a highly technologized environment. While the niece episode functions as an (eco-critical) example of how *Finding Nemo* "casts humans as careless and crude, unable to share space and resources" (Halberstam 80), the death of the goldfish also illustrates the social structure governing the fate of the aquarium inhabitants. Their anxiety does not merely

9 With biological drives, Freud mostly refers to sexual drives. Unsurprisingly, there is hardly any trace of those in *Finding Nemo*. Among the most prominent biological drives that undergo repression in the film, one finds the sharks' natural desire to feed on meat.

10 The fact that *Finding Nemo* uses animal characters to illustrate this Freudian idea further emphasizes its biologistic logic.

arise from an 'unnatural' space but from the continuous threat of death, as neither the dentist nor his niece seem to be entirely concerned with the fish's well-being. Although cheerful in tone, *Finding Nemo* animates the fish as vulnerable to human carelessness. Life in the captivity of an aquarium and the constant danger of violence speak to the social and historical contexts shaping anxiety disorders.

In highlighting the social contingencies shaping the formation of neurosis, Karen Horney questioned the Freudian concept of neurosis as ahistorical in the 1930s. Since "neurosis is due not simply to the quantity of suppression of one or the other instinctual drives, but rather to difficulties caused by the conflicting character of the demands which a culture imposes on its individuals" (230), Horney advocates a socio-cultural approach to neurosis. In her view, what one culture deems neurotic may be completely normal in another: scholars in the 1930s and 1940s often refer to Nazi Germany to assert the cultural and social volatility of neurosis. As George Devereux explains: "No one will deny that a person who, in the current sense of the word, is well adjusted in Nazi Germany is and must be a neurotic, because the Nazi socialcultural environment is an extremely clearcut example of a social neurosis, if not psychosis" (849). Following Horney's and Devereux's argument, anyone who proves able to manage or adjust to the competing demands of a particular culture "shares in the neurosis of his society, although he may not present any additional neurotic symptoms of his own" (Devereux 849). With their interventions, Horney and Devereux advanced and enhanced the Freudian model of neurosis with reference to the social and cultural spheres; through the animation of a trio of vegetarian sharks living in a derelict military submarine, *Finding Nemo* also illustrates an understanding of neurosis as socially contingent. The portrayal of the sharks as decidedly working-class characters further illuminates the ways in which neurosis functions as a form of social structuring.

With their pledge "I am a nice shark, not a mindless eating machine. If I am to change this image, I must first change myself. Fish are friends, not food" (*Finding Nemo*), the three sharks Bruce, Anchor, and Chum aspire to embrace a vegetarian diet. The sharks desire to adjust to the norms of fish society as they hold regular meetings to count the days they have spent without eating fish and renew their support for the vegetarian cause. Because of their frightening appearance and their exuberant grinning, which exhibits endless rows of sharp teeth, however, the sharks' friendliness possesses a pathological quality. Underneath their pleasant demeanor lurk their barely sublimated, biological drives – the skeletons and bones of former "friends" scattered in their submarine home suggest the inadvertent violation of the "friends not food" statute. In Freudian terms, this tension between the sharks' id and the fish society's superego explains their neurotic cordiality. Moreover, when Bruce inhales a drop of blood, his aspiration to adhere to social conventions cannot suppress his drive any longer and the shark goes on a violent rampage in his attempt to eat the horrified Marlin.

Finding Nemo, however, animates the violent hunting scene in a tongue-in-cheek fashion as the sharks resort to psychoanalytical jargon to elicit sympathy for Bruce's behavior. Bruce "really doesn't mean it," they apologetically exclaim, "[h]e never even knew his father" (*Finding Nemo*). The dialogue conveys the humorous tone of the scenes, yet also speaks to the reflexivity of the cinematic text, its psychological premises, and, indeed, to the idea that "[i]n a given culture, those persons are likely to become neurotic who have met these culturally determined difficulties in accentuated form, mostly through the medium of childhood experiences; and who have not been able to solve their difficulties, or have solved them only at great expense to personality" (Horney 230). With its vegetarian sharks, the film animates a culturally contingent notion of neurosis yet also exhibits the ways in which neurosis inscribes and structures social norms.

As their voice acting may already announce, *Finding Nemo* animates Bruce, Anchor, and Chum as decidedly working-class characters whose inability to sublimate their biological drives speaks to the normative portrayal of class in the film. The large and muscular bodies of the sharks along with the physical violence the bulky Bruce exacts as he tears through thick metal doors appropriates stereotypical notions of male working-class characters popular since the 1970s. The trope of the muscular blue-collar body with its "touch of violence, glimpses of brawn, an[d] aura of primitivism" (Biskind and Ehrenreich 214) still aptly describes the sharks.

Even as Hollywood may continue to romanticize the male working-class hero from time to time, the sharks' home in *Finding Nemo* emphasizes their marginal position. Constantly on the brink of giving in to their carnivorous instincts, the sharks reside in a scrapped military submarine located in the middle of a minefield at the periphery of fish society. When his previously sublimated drives erupt, the large, muscular Bruce regresses into an animalistic state, tears metal apart and bursts doors open, and is only brought to his senses after realizing that his violent frenzy led to the detonation of the entire mine field. The dark, gloomy, and menacing-looking mine field as well as the military submarine at its heart foreshadow the eruption of violence, yet, as mechanical devices responsive to physical contact, the hulking machinery of iron and steel also mirrors the physicality of its inhabitants. The deep-sea equivalent of a junkyard comes to symbolize the sharks' psychological state as a volatile equilibrium permanently on the verge of explosion. Bruce's inability to sublimate his biological drives leads to a relapse into an animalistic state of uncontrollable, corporeal violence and thereby illustrates the destructive dimension of neurosis. The disastrous implications of the failed sublimation – the sharks' "violence," "brawn," and "primitivism" – exemplify the working-class clichés and stereotypes informing (not only) *Finding Nemo*.

The grime depiction of the minefield yard and the corporeal illustration of its inhabitants introduce violent counterparts to the urban aquarium inhabitants in their sanitized and technologized environment, with their in-depth debates about dental surgery, and their non-violent forms of neurosis. The illustration of space, the animation of bodies, the dialogues, and the voice acting in *Finding Nemo* portray the sharks as blue-collar figures unable to sublimate their biological drives while the aquarium inhabitants stand in for the urban experiences in a technologized world. Particularly the animated sharks illustrate the inherent carnal brutality of (Freudian) neurosis lurking underneath a thin layer of social order: irrespective of his aspirations to treat "fish as friends," and the psychological tongue-in-cheek explanation for his behavior, the working-class Bruce transforms into a menacing, instinct-driven animal. *Finding Nemo*, thus, uses working-class stereotypes to remind audiences of the instinctual and beastly nature of its blue-collar characters. Eventually, the minefield and the aquarium function as transitional spaces for Marlin and Nemo since the family returns to their suburban anemone and happily concludes its adventure at home.

As a story about male traumatization, *Finding Nemo* animates its narrative of healing as a journey to different sea-communities, all of which are home to diverse casts of figures with anxiety disorders. Despite its moments of othering, the film also breaks out of normative narrative patterns. For one, *Finding Nemo* does not end in a happy, heterosexual romance with a re-united nuclear family. Instead, the concluding shots celebrate a diverse fish community of assured single parents, vegetarian sharks, and fish with disabilities living happily ever after. Jack Halberstam reads this ending as a progressive moment since "the father-son dynamic is dependent upon the queer 'helper' fish, Dory, and can never simply resolve into a patriarchal bond" (79). Due to her short-term memory loss and ensuing neurosis, Dory, voiced by entertainer and LGBTQ activist Ellen DeGeneres, dis-orders the ideal of the heterosexual, nuclear family model, because the surgeonfish embodies "a queer version [of selfhood] that depends upon disconnection from the family and contingent relations to friends and improvised relations to community" (80). In undoing a community organized by paternal structures, as Halberstam suggests, Dory (and to a lesser extent the sharks) exposes the norms informing the discourse of neurosis in the Pixar film, an endeavor that Frantz Fanon had undertaken in the field of psychology at the height of Freudian theory in the mid-twentieth century.

The Social Functions of Neurosis

Writing in the 1950s, Frantz Fanon uses psychoanalysis in *Black Skin, White Masks* (1952) to illuminate the psychological consequences of Western imperialism in the Antilles and the Antillean experience. He questions the narrow assumptions of what qualifies as 'stable' or even 'normal' in Freudian thinking. For Fanon, the psychoanalytical assumption of a semblance between childhood, family, and society (or, indeed, nation) is a quintessential Western notion: "In Europe and in every country characterized as civilized or civilizing, the family is a miniature of the nation" (109). For Black families, however, this connection does not hold true since "[a] normal Negro child, having grown up within a normal family, will become abnormal on the slightest contact with the white world" (111).[11] As a result, psychoanalytical frameworks automatically qualify Black experiences as deviant and eventually neurotic. Whereas for Horney, Devereux and others, Nazi Germany illustrated the ways in which neuroses may not necessarily signal mental or psychological illness but questionable social norms, in Fanon's post-colonial writing the West becomes the neurosis-producing point of reference; not only within national borders but as a global, transnational phenomenon.[12]

---

11 As the white family structures the French nation (and vice versa), Black French people are torn between their individual families and the desire to be part of the nation. Fanon explains: "[T]he Antillean family has for all practical purposes no connection with the national – that is, the French, or European – structure. The Antillean has therefore to choose between his family and European society; in other words, the individual who *climbs up* into society – white and civilized – tends to reject his family – black and savage – on the plane of imagination, in accord with the childhood *Erlebnisse*" (115; emphases in the original). Rather than having to choose to "*turn white or disappear*," Fanon announces that "my objective [...] will be to put him [the Black man] in a position to *choose* action (or passivity) with respect to the real source of the conflict – that is, toward the social structures" (75; emphases in the original).

12 In *Crazy like Us: The Globalization of the American Psyche* (2010) Ethan Watters continues this line of reasoning by looking at the emergence and transformation of different mental illnesses in various cultures around the globe. Watters observes a "flat-

For Fanon, Freudian notions of sublimation, neurosis, pathology, and trauma only begin to offer an understanding of Black experiences in a world shaped by white people. When people of color "come into contact with the white world," this first encounter or *Erlebnis* fosters an "inferiority complex" as they live in a society that "proclaims the superiority of one race" (74). Subsequently, the ubiquitous encounters with and internalization of deprecating notions of Blackness prevalent in white culture, then, "work their way into one's mind and shape one's view of the world of the group to which one belongs" (118), and eventually foster, in Fanon words, "neurosis [...,] abnormal manifestation [...,] affective erethism" (117). What Fanon describes as identification with white culture – and later thinkers would label *interpellation*[13] – leads to "the formation and crystallization of an attitude and a way of thinking and seeing that are essentially white" (114). This form of alienation fosters "an obsessive neurotic type" or positions people of color in "a complete situational neurosis" (42-43).

In contrast to the imperialist Western models of family, society, and individuality Fanon analyzes as particularly destructive for Black communities, exclusion in *Finding Nemo* stays within the framework of an entirely white culture. The absence of ethnic or racial diversity in a cinematic text set in the Southern hemisphere speaks exactly to the hegemony of whiteness Fanon aimed to dispel. Although *Finding Nemo* engages with some forms of neurosis, this inclusion eventually privileges white experiences. Tellingly, all characters are not "marked as anything other than white and Western (based on the voice-over dialects, our knowledge of the actors who perform those voices)" (Brydon 135). Although "the film features a virtual ocean menagerie of cooperative species" (Halberstam 79) and a diverse portrayal of anxiety disorders all of which suggests an inclu-

---

tening [of] the landscape of the human psyche" (1) in the past thirty years as American notions of mental illness and their treatment came to be considered global standards. As his research demonstrates, mental illnesses are culturally and temporally contingent, and their diversity and complexity is disappearing. While "[a] few mental illnesses identified and popularized in the United States – depression, post-traumatic stress disorder, and anorexia among them – now appear to be spreading across cultural boundaries and around the world with the speed of contagious diseases," Watters asserts, "[i]ndigenous forms of mental illness and healing are being bulldozed by disease categories and treatments made in the USA" (3).

13 With its examination of cultural norms perpetuated in "books, newspapers, schools and their texts, advertisements, films, radio" (118), *Black Skin, White Masks* draws attention to questions of representation as an essential feature of fostering Black neurosis.

sive narrative, Fanon reminds us that psycho-analytical phenomena (and their animation) adhere to logics of visibility and invisibility.[14] The heart-warming, tongue-in-cheek, or even uncanny portrayals of fish with neurosis in *Finding Nemo* all revolve around the experiences of white characters.

In demanding fundamental social change, Fanon aimed to disrupt the psychology of imperialism in which the internalization of racist stereotypes and a colonial gaze fosters the formation of an inferiority complex (see Sardar x). His psychoanalytical approach to culture and literature, furthermore, offered novel possibilities to interrogate the perpetuation of normative discourses with the help of Freudian vocabulary. Particularly the 1960s and 1970s emerged as a period in which film theorists from Jean-Louis Baudry to Christian Metz and Laura Mulvey utilized psychoanalytical insights and neo-Marxist political theory to develop an understanding of the viewing experience in the space of the cinema as prescribed by the male gaze (of Hollywood productions) and the technical apparatus of screening film (in the cinema). Although *Black Skin, White Masks* anticipated many ideas prominent in apparatus theory, from examinations of the gaze to questions of alienation, internalization, and inferiority, the psycho-analytical thinking of Jacques Lacan with its exploration of the mirror stage and its focus on misrecognition primarily informed cinematic theory in that period.

In their attempt to demonstrate the totality of the capitalist system and the male gaze, film scholars of the 1960s and 1970s may have looked for stronger clinical taxonomies than anxiety disorders, "obsessive neurosis," or "situational neurosis" could offer. Even as the adaptation of Lacan's work further introduced neurosis to literary and cultural studies, the concept slowly began to lose its analytical and intellectual pertinence. As literary and cultural studies increasingly moved to interest in aesthetic frameworks, phenomenological thinking, or reception theory among others,[15] scholars increasingly considered psychoanalytical approaches reductive in their conceptualization of agency, culture, individualism, and broader economic, political, and social systems. This shift followed a wider transformation in the field of psychology in which practitioners and scholars increasingly considered Freudian psychoanalysis in general and his notion of

14 For a detailed discussion of race and psychoanalysis, see, for example, Christopher Lane *The Psychoanalysis of Race* (1998).

15 See, for example, Dick Hebdidge *Subculture: The Meaning of Style* (1979), Stuart Hall "Encoding / Decoding" (1980), Miriam Hansen *Babel and Babylon: Spectatorship in American Silent Film* (1991), Steven Shaviro *The Cinematic Body* (1993), or Jackie Stacey "Feminine Fascinations: A Question of Identification?" (1994).

neurosis in particular to be inapt and outdated in light of the shift to genetic and neurological research.

"WHERE HAVE ALL THE NEUROTICS GONE" AND WILL THEY BE BACK?

Beyond literary and cultural studies, ideas about anxiety disorders as well as psychology transformed fundamentally in the 1970s and 1980s. As the latter shifted to exploring the biological dimensions shaping mental and psychological conditions, the former lost their analytical and medical value (see Tone 18). Indeed, much of the Freudian vocabulary and the notion of neurosis in particular came to be seen as increasingly vague and old-fashioned; after all, neurosis was deemed ill-suited to properly differentiate between various disorders whether these derived from, for example, social anxiety or obsessive-compulsive behavior. In 1994, the *DSM* dropped neurosis from its medical vocabulary.

Today, a detailed catalogue of anxiety disorders has not only supplanted the notion of neurosis in medical discourse but its study has shifted from a psychological perspective to neuroscience and genetic analysis, and its treatment from talk therapy and the analysis of the unconscious to the extensive use of prescription drugs. With the vanishing of Freudian ideas, neurosis has also lost its validity in psychology and its popular appeal. Some bemoan this disappearance as a loss of "the romance with neurosis" (Carey) when having a neurotic personality "meant being interesting" and signaled cultural or intellectual sophistication as illustrated in the works of Woody Allen or Alfred Hitchcock. While this "romance with neurosis" minimizes the psychological suffering and social exclusion intimately linked with neurosis, its elusiveness may offer a path for a productive retrieval.

In literary and cultural studies, we would be hard-pressed to adapt most of the current medical and genetic insights in psychology for textual interpretations. Few texts allow for a neuroscientific diagnosis or the study of a character's genetic history to interpret their anxiety. We can appropriate panic disorders, post-traumatic stress disorders, or obsessive-compulsive behavior for close-readings and literary analyses. However, while the medical vocabulary offers novel reading opportunities, its evocation of contemporary psychological discourse may not allow for an exact diagnosis at all times. Whether obsessive-compulsive behavior, for example, aptly describes the sharks in *Finding Nemo* or whether post-traumatic stress disorder applies to the aquarium inhabitants is hard to assess with the little information viewers receive. In describing these fish as wrestling with neurosis, however, we can appropriate an elusive vocabulary to situate their behavior in the context of anxiety disorder. While a precise medical vocabulary functions to diagnose the everyday experiences of mental conditions, neurosis can be productively employed to address their various fictional reconfigurations and spectacularizations, which can be found in films, media, TV shows, novels, news coverage, and other texts.

This appropriation offers the possibility to separate neurosis from its psychoanalytical history and entangle it in debates about its cultural implications and meanings. To put this differently: in using a medically elusive concept, we aim to shift attention away from the psychoanalytical context of neurosis to concentrate on its portrayal and function in a text. In doing so, we do not aspire to rehearse Freudian notions of psychoanalysis for understanding either neurosis or culture. Instead, we propose a conceptualization of neurosis as a form of embodiment, intersubjectivity, and temporality.

NEUROSIS AND NARRATIVES OF NORMALCY

In *Finding Nemo*, characters with neurosis challenge narratives of normalcy and indicate the possibility for an inclusive community. In contrast to the preoccupation with closure in trauma narratives, Dory, for example, finds a home in the coral reef community without having to master or transcend her short-term memory loss. Whereas the search for Nemo restores a sense of (masculine) wholeness in Marlin, Dory manifests a "queerness" – to borrow from Jack Halberstam – that seemingly subverts the narrative of male empowerment. The blue surgeonfish "ends up 'knowing' all kinds of things that go against received wisdom but that facilitate Marlin's quest to find his son. So while Dory suffers from short-term memory loss, she also reads human texts, speaks whale, charms sharks, and understands the primacy of friends over family" (79-80), as Halberstam explains. Many of Dory's feats, however, do not merely stem from her knowledge of aquatic life. Instead, as she constantly misreads the awkwardness or even danger of a particular situation, she is able to engage with the most fearsome sea animals: the surgeonfish's forgetfulness allows her to plunge blissfully into conversation with menacing sharks and colossal whales unbiased. Her amnesia-induced open-mindedness enables her to find friends in the most unexpected situations and thereby make the search for Nemo possible.

Her knowledge and competence in combination with her short-term memory loss question the narrative of normalcy and the patriarchal family model Marlin's trauma experience symbolize. With her inclusion in the coral reef community at the end of the film, suburban paradigms of normality come into flux as boundaries of inside and outside, wisdom and ignorance, competence and helplessness begin to dissolve. In disrupting a community organized by patriarchal structures, Dory initiates the formation of an inclusive underwater society. As a consequence, *Finding Nemo* animates neurosis not as a detriment to personal or communal fulfillment but as a contingent experience – and thereby animates neurosis "as a socially constructed category that derives meaning and social (in)significance from the historical, cultural, political, and economic structures that frame social life" (Erevelles and Minear 132). Rather than an individual or social liability, neurosis functions as a source of agency and knowledge beyond suburban spaces and experiences.

Nevertheless, even as Dory possesses autonomy and agency, *Finding Nemo* also animates her amnesia as a source of vulnerability, consigns her to a liminal social space, and weakens her subversive potential. When Dory, for example, tries to convince Marlin that travelling through a seemingly haunting underwater ravine is completely safe, anxious Marlin exploits her forgetfulness and distracts her long enough for her to have no memory of what her initial plan was. Ignoring her warnings, Marlin steers Dory into a swarm of jellyfish eventually poisoning and nearly killing her. Although Dory warned Marlin of the dangers a detour poses, his conscious decision to manipulate her speaks to the vulnerability of her condition. In addition, *Finding Nemo* infantilizes Dory as the film often shows her to be closer to children than adult characters: she blissfully plays hide-and-seek with little ocean turtles and spends her time in the coral reef kindergarten at the end of the film. As Dory, furthermore, contributes decisively to restoring Marlin as the head of the family, her function in the narrative dilutes the subversive potential of her queerness: only because of Dory and her neurosis is Marlin able to physically and emotionally endure the journey, is the father figure eventually re-masculinized, and is a functional patriarchal order restored. Whether we disqualify these gestures as instances in animation in which "the politics of rebellion can be cast as immature, pre-Oedipal, childish, foolish, fantastical, and rooted in a commitment to failure" or read *Finding Nemo* as a "real and compelling possibility of animating revolt" (Halberstam 52) continues to be a broader debate.[16] For our purposes, however, the Pixar film animates neurosis not as a

16 In contrast to the queer reading Halberstam proposes, David Prescott-Steed sees a perpetuation of "the dominant voice of heteronormativity" at work in *Finding Nemo* since the animation omits important "marine-biological information" about clownfish and thereby "obscures a range of gender-minority voices, particularly those pertaining to gender-ambiguous subjectivities" (34). Prescott-Steed especially highlights "the ab-

wound that necessitates closure or an illness that requires curing, but as a quintessential feature of daily life Dory and the coral reef community learn to cope with. Eventually, Dory exemplifies the potential neurosis holds in shaping a diverse and inclusive community.

At the end of *Finding Nemo*, the suburban community welcomes Dory in a gesture of care that is, to appropriate David Russon's formulation, "responsive to the troubles and tensions that animate th[e] neurotic posture" (121). As neither Marlin nor Dory can thrive in the isolation of an anemone or in aimlessly wandering the sea, their care for each other allows for a happy conclusion. Dependent on and responsible for each other, the clown fish and the surgeonfish exhibit a communal sense of life, and animate the notion that "singular existence is never won in isolation but is, rather, won only through participation and absorption in our surroundings" (90). *Finding Nemo*, hence, oscillates between an ethics of care and inclusiveness and the portrayal of its ideal community as white and suburban.

When Bruce, Anchor, and Chum pay a cheerful visit to the suburban reef community at the end of *Finding Nemo*, their appearance not only emphasizes the film's narrative of normalcy but also tests the boundaries of care; regardless of their friendly and sociable appearance, the sharks pose an ever-present menace. Although well meaning, the trio continues to be intimidating as their neurotic facial expressions hint at their failure to sublimate their brutal drives. Their visit, therefore, instills fear in some coral reef inhabitants – most prominently in a kraken who accidentally spills his ink – and functions as a reminder of the violence lurking underneath social pleasantries. Their appearance also evokes an earlier, life-threatening violence Dory and Marlin barely survived. In contrast to Dory and her integration into the coral reef community, Bruce, Anchor, and Chum continue to pose an eerie threat to its sense of order, shelter, and care. Indeed, the fish community can only extend its care to the sharks as long as their drives do not erupt violently and turn play into carnage. The rupture of barely sublimated violence speaks to the threat and destructive potential of neurosis.[17]

---

sence in *Finding Nemo* of any mention of the fact that, being a clownfish, Nemo is a sequential hermaphrodite" (34).

17 *Finding Nemo*, however, does not end with Marlin and Nemo, with Dory and the fish kindergarten, or even with Bruce, Anchor, and Chum hovering about. Instead, the film concludes with shots of the aquarium inhabitants and their attempt to escape. After Gill and his friends manipulate the computerized monitoring system of the fish tank and pollute the water, the dentist places the animals in plastic bags while cleaning the aquarium. The fish launch their elastic entrapments through an open window, survive

As the meaning of neurosis slowly transformed from designating a failed suppression of biological drives to indicating the culturally contingent norms of a society, its taxonomy as an illness also changed. This is not to dispute the psychological and medical treatment people with anxiety disorders require; expressed in narratives and through fictional characters, however, neurosis allows seeing the subversive potential these often liminal figures possess. Particularly in contrast to notions of wholeness and restoration, narratives of neurosis offer glimpses into everyday modes of coping, caring, and accepting. While narrating the neurotic allows us to expose, question, and possibly transform narratives of normalcy, hostile forms of neurosis can also test an ethics of care.

The chapters in this volume address diverse manifestations of the poetics of neurosis across countries and disciplines, with special emphasis on the entanglements between the figure of the neurotic and the specifics of their place and time. In his contribution "The Lure of Space: Psychasthenia as Mnemonic Device in Michael Cunningham's *Specimen Days*," László Munteán introduces psychasthenia not only as a form of neurosis but also as a literary mode of mimicry. Rather than an imitation, Munteán follows Roger Caillois in conceptualizing psychasthenia as a form of assimilation to the environment and subsequent depersonalization. This assimilation is particularly visible in the opening novella of *Specimen Days* (2005), "In the Machine," in which its main character, Lucas, articulates his feelings and makes sense of his surroundings by quoting compulsively from Walt Whitman's *Leaves of Grass*. Although set in the late nineteenth century, Lucas's obsessive recital furthermore invokes mediated images of the attacks on September 11, particularly falling bodies, at the end of the novella. As a literary trope, then, psychasthenia functions as a mnemonic device to summon the traumatic memories of 9/11 without explicitly citing the event.

Elena Furlanetto's "Disintegrated Selves: Dissociative Disorders and Colonial Anxiety in Orhan Pamuk's *The Black Book*" illuminates the intersections of the colonial and the neurotic in Pamuk's 1990 novel, laying particular emphasis

---

the crossing of a nearby street, and drop into the ocean. Filled with pride and joy, the fish quickly realize that they are bound to remain trapped as the plastic bags float neatly on the ocean preventing the fish from swimming away. Although the upbeat musical score frames the scene as a comical conclusion to the film, these characters will stay trapped in a technologized space without the possibility to escape. In its last shots, *Finding Nemo* animates a perspective about neurosis informed neither by an ethics of care nor by the threat of barely sublimated violence. Instead, the escape from the aquarium ends for the urbanites with neurosis in a (technological) limbo of plastic bags floating on the ocean.

on characters who suffer from amnesia, multiple personalities, and depersonalization – which the author of the chapter groups under the umbrella term of "dissociative disorders." Furlanetto shows how, within the economy of the *The Black Book*, these manifestations of psychological discomfort vehicle a critique of Westernization and address the controversial issue of Western cultural imperialism in Turkey. Additionally, Furlanetto indicates that this kind of disorders are poignant metaphors of the colonial condition, as they disturb the individual's sense of self and continuity with the past: the same principles that colonial domination seeks to undo at a collective level.

In "Reading Rap with Fanon and Fanon with Rap: The Potential of Transcultural Recognition," Jarula M. I. Wegner brings the work of Frantz Fanon in conversation with rap music. In particular, the chapter examines the inhibiting consequences of the past expressed in the form of colonial neurosis Fanon theorizes in *Black Skin, White Masks* (1952). Similar to the colonial experiences Fanon draws from to challenge Western presumptions about the Antillean experience, the song "Street Corner" (2006) by Masta Killa (feat. GZA and Inspectah Deck) portrays "the hood" or "the ghetto" as a neurosis-inducing space. However, whereas Fanon urges to transform the future by re-inventing the past, the treatment of neurosis demands extensive engagement with the past – an appreciation of memory "Street Corner" vocalizes when drawing on the history of the trans-Atlantic slave trade. Eventually, in reading rap music with Fanon Wegner demonstrates the continued relevance of colonial neurosis in contemporary popular culture, yet reading Fanon through rap music also indicates the ways in which the demand for re-invention of the past translates into the (continued) facilitation of counter-memories.

In "Neoliberalism, Terror, and the Etiology of Neurotic Citizenship," Ariane de Waal examines the security discourse shaping the experience of public spaces in London. Whether police posters asking citizens to maintain vigilance, apartment advertisements highlighting the security apparatus of a building, or the proliferation of SUVs, de Waal sees in these practices a neurotic notion of citizenship at work. Rather than a paranoid suspicion of public or private surveillance practices, the compliant engagement of white, middle-class Londoners in counter-terrorism culture speaks to their obsessive investment in adopting and perfecting a plethora of security measures. In doing so, de Waal questions the notion of rationality attributed to counter-terrorism policies to highlight the (displacement of) anxiety inherent in their expansion and privatization.

Derya Gür-Şeker's contribution focalizes on a German right-wing movement born in Dresden in 2014, known as an alliance of "Patriotische Europäer gegen die Islamisierung des Abendlandes" (patriotic Europeans against the Islamization of the Occident), or "Pegida." Through her linguistic analysis in "Pegida as *Angstneurotiker*: A Linguistic Analysis of Concepts of Fear in Right-wing Populist Discourses in German Online Media," Gür-Şeker shows that Pegida's rhetoric is marked by frequent references to fear (*Angst*), so much so that an anonymous internet user perceived this insistence as neurotic and ironically 'diagnosed' Pegida members as *Angstneurotiker*. Examining the statements by and about Pegida in media articles, social media posts, and speeches by key public figures, Gür-Şeker shows that Pegida strategically mobilizes a vocabulary of fear to establish itself as a political actor.

In "Ain't It Funny? Danny Brown, Black Subjectivity, and the Performance of Neurosis," ethnomusicologist Alex Blue V presents a reading of the video and lyrics to Danny Brown's song "Ain't it Funny" (2016), exposing the objectification of African American suffering. In the music video, directed by Jonah Hill, "Uncle Danny" (played by Danny Brown himself) is the only black member of an all-white family, within which he lives a marginalized existence. The sarcasm embedded in the song title becomes ever more palpable as "Uncle Danny" emerges a tragic figure suffering from substance abuse, ignored by his own family, and laughed at by a fictional studio audience, composed solely of white people, who consume his body and pain as entertainment. Blue reads "Ain't it Funny" through the lens of neurosis, voyeurism, and the "doubleness" that marks the everyday experience of African Americans in the United States.

Angelo Monaco's "Neurosis as Resilience in Jhumpa Lahiri's Diasporic Short Fictions" examines the portrayal of Indian American characters in "Mrs. Sen's" from *Interpreter of Maladies* (1999) and "A Choice of Accommodation" from *Unaccustomed Earth* (2008). In the two short stories he sees a neurotic tension at work between the pressure to conform to social expectations and individual experiences of diaspora as the Indian American protagonists wrestle with (adjusting to) life in the United States. "Mrs. Sen" captures a nostalgic longing the protagonist expresses through her routinized preparation of Indian dishes. Monaco reads the metonymies that describe her repetition-compulsion as the continual presence of the past, which eventually figures as an expression of vulnerability. "A Choice of Accommodation" aligns melancholia, not nostalgia, with the pains of growing up in the United States for protagonist Amit Sarkar, while metaphor and prosopopoeia figure as the main literary tropes. Both short stories, however, also describe moments of resilience thereby drawing attention to an aesthetics of neurosis that resist socio-economic pressures.

In "Allegories of Pathology: Post-War Colonial Expatriate and Imperial Neurosis in F. Scott Fitzgerald's *Tender is the Night* and Derek Walcott's *Omeros*," Sneharika Roy examines the white experience of postcolonial expatriation in fiction. In *Tender is the Night* (1934) as well as *Omeros* (1990), Roy sees the familiar postcolonial literary strategy of portraying personal experience as national allegory. Both texts furthermore describe their protagonist as neurotics wrestling with psychological wounds: Nicole Warren, the protagonist of Fitzgerald's novel, responds to symbolic and visual reminders of the violence she experienced at the hands of her incestuous father with erratic behavior; Major Plunkett, a character in Walcott's poem who lives in the former British colony (and now independent island-state) of Saint Lucia, obsessively searches for past British military glory in historical archives to compensate for the physical damages he suffered in World War I. Their neurotic responses to physical and psychological wounds not only capture the white expatriates' experience of spatial and temporal dislocation, but also prefigure the first albeit ambiguous steps towards the possibility of healing. Indeed, as Roy carefully indicates, a continued exposure to their suffering may enable the white expatriate figures to come to terms with their neurotic behavior.

LIST OF WORKS CITED

Biskind, Peter and Barbara Ehrenreich. "Machismo and Hollywood's Working Class." *American Media and Mass Culture. Left Perspectives*, edited by Donald Lazere, University of California Press, 1987, pp. 201-215.

Bogacz, Ted. "War Neurosis and Cultural Change in England, 1914-22: The Work of the War Office Committee of Enquiry into 'Shell-Shock'." *Journal of Contemporary History*, vol. 24, no. 2, 1989, pp. 227-256.

Breithaupt, Fritz. "Rituals of Trauma: How the Media Fabricated September 11." *Media Representations of September 11*, edited by Steven Chermak, Frankie Y. Bailey, and Michelle Brown, Praeger, 2003, pp. 67-82.

Breuer, Josef and Sigmund Freud. *The Standard Edition of the Complete Work Psychological Works of Sigmund Freud: Studies on Hysteria.* Edited by James Strachey and Anna Freud, vol. 2, The Hogarth Press, 1955.

Campbell, Brad. "The Making of 'American': Race and Nation in Neurasthenic Discourse." *History of Psychiatry*, vol. 18, no. 2, 2007, pp. 157-178.

Campbell, J. Bradford. "The Schizophrenic Solution: Dialectics of Neurosis and Anti-psychiatric Animus in Ralph Ellison's *Invisible Man.*" *Novel: A Forum on Fiction*, vol. 43, no. 3, 2010, pp. 443-465.

Carey, Benedict. "Where Have all the Neurotics Gone?" *The New York Times*, 31 March 2012, SR1.

Däwes, Birgit. *Ground Zero Fiction: History, Memory, and Representation in the American 9/11 Novel*. Universitätsverlag Winter, 2011.

Devereux, George. "Maladjustment and Social Neurosis." *American Sociological Review*, vol. 4, no. 6, 1939, pp. 844-851.

Diagnostic and Statistical Manual of Mental Disorder. American Psychiatric Association, 1952.

Diagnostic and Statistical Manual of Mental Disorder. 4th ed., American Psychiatric Association, 1994.

Erevelles, Nirmala and Andrea Minear. "Unspeakable Offenses: Untangling Race and Disability in Discourses of Intersectionality." *Journal of Literary & Cultural Disability Studies*, vol. 4, no. 2, 2010, pp. 127-146.

Faludi, Susan. *The Terror Dream: Fear and Fantasy in Post-9/11 America*. Henry Holt and Company, 2007.

Fanon, Frantz. *Black Skin. With Masks*. 1952. Pluto Press, 2008.

Fassin, Didier, and Richard Recthman. *The Empire of Trauma: An Inquiry into the Condition of Victimhood*. Princeton University Press, 2007.

Finding Nemo. Directed by Andrew Stanton, Pixar Animation Studios, 2003.

Freud, Sigmund. "A Short Account of Psycho-Analysis." *Freud: Complete Works*, edited by Ivan Smith, 2000, pp. 4099-4118.

---. "Neurosis and Psychosis." *Freud: Complete Works*, edited by Ivan Smith, 2000, pp. 4063-4068.

---. "On the Grounds for Detaching a Particular Syndrome from Neurasthenia under the Description 'Anxiety Neurosis'." *Early Psycho-Analytic Publications*, edited and translated by James Strachey, The Hogarth Press, 1955, pp. 87-117.

Gilroy, Paul. *After Empire: Melancholia or Convivial Culture?* Routledge, 2004.

Greenberg, Judith: *Trauma at Home: After 9/11*. University of Nebraska Press, 2003.

Halberstam, Jack. *The Queer Art of Failure*. Duke University Press, 2011.

Hall, Stuart (1980). "Encoding / Decoding." *Culture, Media, Language: Working Papers in Cultural Studies, 1972-79*, edited by Stuart Hall, Dorothy Hobson, Andrew Lowe, and Paul Willis, Routledge, 1980, pp. 117-127.

Hansen, Miriam. *Babel and Babylon: Spectatorship in American Silent Film*. Harvard University Press, 1991.

Hebdidge, Dick. *Subculture: The Meaning of Style*. Routledge, 1979.

Horney, Karen. "Culture and Neurosis." *American Sociological Review*, vol. 1, no. 2, 1936, pp. 221-230.

---. *Neurosis and Human Growth: The Struggle Toward Self-Realization*. W.W. Norton and Company, 1952.

---. "What Is a Neurosis?" *American Journal of Sociology*, vol. 45, no. 3, 1939, pp. 426-432.

Kaplan, E. Ann. *Trauma Culture: The Politics of Terror and Loss in Media and Literature*. Rutgers University Press, 2005.

Killen, Andreas. "From Shock to Schreck: Psychiatrists, Telephone Operators and Traumatic Neurosis in Germany, 1900-26." *Journal of Contemporary History*, vol. 38, no. 2, 2003, pp. 201-220.

Lacan, Jacques. *The Seminar of Jacques Lacan: Book III: The Psychoses 1955-1956*. Edited by Jacques-Alain Miller, W.W. Norton & Company, 1993.

Lane, Christopher. *The Psychoanalysis of Race*. Columbia University Press, 1998.

Leys, Ruth. *Trauma: A Genealogy*. University of Chicago Press, 2000.

Pinero, Jose M. Lopez. *Historical Origins of the Concept of Neurosis*. 1983. Cambridge University Press, 2009.

Russon, John. *Human Experience: Philosophy, Neurosis, and the Elements of Everyday Life*. State University of New York Press, 2003.

Sardar, Ziauddin. Foreword to the 2008 Edition. *Black Skin, White Masks*, by Frantz Fanon, 1952, Pluto Press, 2008, vi-xx.

Shaviro, Steven. *The Cinematic Body*. University of Minnesota Press, 1993.

Spivak, Gayatri Chakravorty. "Who Claims Alterity?" *Remaking History*, edited by Barbary Kruger and Phil Mariani, Bay Press, 1989, pp. 269-292.

Stacey, Jackie. "Feminine Fascinations: A Question of Identification?" *Star Gazing: Hollywood Cinema and Female Spectatorship*, Routledge, 1994, pp. 126-175.

Tone, Andrea. *The Age of Anxiety: A History of America's Turbulent Affair with Tranquilizers*. Basic Books, 2009.

Watters, Ethan. *Crazy Like Us: The Globalization of the American Psyche*. Free Press, 2010.

Young, Alan. *The Harmony of Illusions: Inventing Post-Traumatic Stress Disorder*. Princeton University Press, 1995.

The Lure of Space

Psychasthenia as Mnemonic Device in Michael Cunningham's *Specimen Days*

László Munteán

In a puzzling essay written in 1935, French critic Roger Caillois problematizes the notion of mimicry as a solely defensive device in the animal world. He suggests, instead, that mimicry is governed by a "veritable *lure of space*" (99; emphasis in the original), as a result of which particular species morph into their environment regardless of the need to camouflage themselves. Caillois claims that a similar drive to assimilate into one's spatial surroundings can also be traced in humans. What functions as mimicry in certain animal species he identifies as a "disorder of spatial perception" (99) in humans, which manifests itself as "*depersonalization through assimilation into space*" (100; emphasis in the original). A significant inspiration behind Jacques Lacan's conceptualization of the mirror stage, Caillois's essay, written in a Surrealist vein, syncretizes biology and psychology with magic and, similarly to many of the precepts of psychoanalysis, holds little relevance to psychological practice today. Still, his conceptualization of psychasthenia as a disorder fueled by the lure of space, rather than the urge to hide, has granted it a long afterlife in the humanities.

Finding its etymological roots in the Greek *psykhe* (soul or spirit) and *astheneia* (weakness), the term psychasthenia had been introduced to psychological discourse by Pierre Janet's pioneering and hitherto untranslated works *Lés Obsessions et la Psychasthénie* (1903) and *Les Névroses* (1909), where he describes psychasthenia as a neurotic condition that entails anxiety and obsessional disorders on the one hand, and the subject's loss of a sense of reality on the other (see Gossop 9). Following Janet, Karl Jaspers describes the psychasthenic syndrome as a "diminution of psychic energy" often connected to "some somatic and physiological weakness though they may also occur without this. […] The psyche generally lacks an ability to integrate its life or to work through and manage its various experiences; it fails to build up its personality and make any steady development" (442).

Although the term is no longer used as a diagnostic category in psychological practice, Caillois's application of psychasthenia in relation to mimicry has unmoored it from the realm of medical discourse and gave it a new life as a cultural trope denoting the desire to become one with the environment. Towards the end of his essay, he refers to Flaubert's *The Temptation of Saint Anthony* (1874) as a literary example of psychasthenia. In the novel Saint Anthony "falls prey to the lure of material space: he wants to disperse himself everywhere, to be within everything, 'to penetrate each atom, to descend into the heart of matter – *to be* matter'" (101; emphasis in the original). In Caillois's interpretation, Flaubert's aesthetization of Anthony's descent into hell "appears as a form of that process whereby *space is generalized* to the detriment of the individual" (102; emphasis in the original).

In Michael Cunningham's 2005 novel *Specimen Days* a similar "generalization" of space is at work, though here it is Walt Whitman's *Leaves of Grass* (1855) that functions as an intermediary force that instigates a mimetic identification with space. *Specimen Days* is made up of three interlocking stories set in New York and playing out in different time frames. The first one, "In the Machine," takes place at the end of the nineteenth century, featuring a twelve-year-old boy with a disability, Lucas, as the main character. A son of Irish immigrants living in abject poverty in a Lower Manhattan working class neighborhood, Lucas loses his brother Simon to an industrial accident and needs to take Simon's place at the factory to fend for his ill parents. Haunted by what he recognizes as his dead brother's voice coming from the machinery, Lucas tries to warn Simon's fiancée, Catherine, who works as a seamstress, of the lethal danger that awaits her. Lucas's conversations with Catherine, however, are often unproductive; whenever overexcited and unable to express himself, he uncontrollably recites seemingly random lines from Whitman's *Leaves of Grass.* The second story, "The Children's Crusade," is set in the immediate aftermath of 9/11 and focalized through an African American police psychologist, Cat, who investigates the case of underage suicide bombers using *Leaves of Grass* to justify their actions. Unable to prevent the bombings, Cat seeks solace in her boyfriend Simon and ultimately bonds with a twelve-year old suicide bomber who reminds her of her dead son, Luke. The third story takes the reader to a post-apocalyptic future when deserted Manhattan has already been transformed into a theme park. Simon appears in this story as an android that quotes Whitman whenever close to feeling human emotions. With his lover Catareen, a lizard-like alien, and the twelve year-old kid Luke, they are on route to escape to a new planet that promises the chance for a new beginning.

The term 'novella,' which Cunningham himself also uses in interviews to refer to these stories, is particularly significant in light of the formal structure of the novel. As a form-within-a-form, each novella is built up of recurring images that intersect through multiple intratextual relations in the novel as a whole. Following in the vein of Cunningham's previous bestseller *The Hours* (1998), the three novellas are interlocked by Lucas/Luke, Catherine/Cat/Catareen, and Simon, three characters that appear and reappear in different disguises, with *Leaves of Grass* weaving them together. Likewise, a bowl and a music box recur in all three novellas as artifacts that outlive humans and connect temporalities.

This chapter focuses on Cunningham's novel through the lens of psychasthenia as a "disorder of spatial perception" in Caillois's sense (99). Going beyond the understanding of psychasthenia as a form of neurosis in the medical sense, I follow Caillois's surrealist reinterpretation of the term as a form of mimicry the goal of which is not so much to hide as to assimilate into the environment at the cost of depersonalization. For instance, the ways in which characters in the novel speak and relate to the environment through Whitman's *Leaves of Grass* constitute instances of psychasthenia that, as I will argue, operate in Cunningham's hands as an *aide-mémoire* that compels readers to recall particular aspects of 9/11. Although 9/11 appears as a temporal reference point only in "The Children's Crusade," I will demonstrate how psychasthenia as a literary trope in the novel functions as a mnemonic device that activates mediatized memories of bodies falling from the World Trade Center, as well as the mixing of victims' bodies with those of the terrorists and architectural debris. In his comprehensive study of the 9/11 novel, Kristiaan Versluys focuses on "The Children's Crusade" and regards it as a "9/11 parable" that "goes a long way toward recognizing the Other, even in the terrorist" (166). Instead of limiting my discussion to the scope of "The Children's Crusade," I will extend my focus to the first novella, "In the Machine," to explore how Lucas's psychasthenic compulsion to perceive the world through a Whitmanesque lens conjures up traumatic memories of 9/11 without explicitly mentioning the event.

SPEAKING IN FITS

Lucas's compulsion to recite lines from *Leaves of Grass* goes beyond mere fascination with Whitman's poetry. "He hadn't meant to speak as the book. He never did, but when he was excited he couldn't help himself" (Cunningham 4). The overwhelming excitement that prevents him from speaking his own words allows Whitman's poem to flow into his speech in an undifferentiated fashion. Whenever in the company of Catherine, his brother's fiancé, he feels the urge to say

> something he felt but could not describe: porous and spiky, shifting with flecks of thought, with urge and memory; salted with brightness, flickerings of white and green and pale gold, like stars; something that loved stars because it was made for the same substance. He needed to tell her it was impossible, it was unbearable, to be so continually mistaken for a misshapen boy with a walleye and a pumpkin head and a habit of speaking in fits.
>
> He said, "I celebrate myself, and what I assume you shall assume." It was not what he'd hoped to tell her. (4-5)

Here, we cannot read Lucas's sentence as a *sentence* but must hear Whitman's *line* underneath. At the same time, we also hear Lucas 'saying' Whitman as part of his own speech act, attesting to the Bakhtinian notion of *heteroglossia* and, more pertinently, to Julia Kristeva and later Linda Hutcheon's reworking of this notion into theories of intertextuality. It is in this sense that we can register in Lucas's *sentence* a "permutation of texts" that "intersect and neutralize one another" (Kristeva 36). The line from "the book," as *Leaves of Grass* is referenced throughout the novel, is thus an intertext which Lucas unwittingly transforms into a speech act. It is the book, in other words, that not only allows but also compels him to assume a Whitmanian voice, where the lure of space instigates depersonalization insofar as it is not so much Lucas that quotes Whitman as it is the book that speaks through him.

The book for Lucas is what space is for the psychasthenic. In Caillois's description of the psychasthenic syndrome,

> space seems to constitute a will to devour. [...] The body and mind thereupon become dissociated; the subject crosses the boundary of his own skin and stands outside of his own senses. [...] He feels that he is turning into space himself – *dark space into which things cannot be put.* He is similar; not similar to anything in particular, but simply *similar*. And he dreams up spaces that "spasmodically possess" him. (100; emphasis in the original)

For Lucas, it is the book that constitutes a will to devour; he literally embodies the book. As much as his "misshapen" body is in*formed* by the corpus of the book, the voice of the narration is similarly focalized through Lucas as a viewpoint character. He perceives the city as myriads of constellations he yearns to absorb all at once, not unlike Saint Anthony in Flaubert. "What he wanted was the raucousness of the city, where people hauled their loads of corn or coal, where they danced to fiddles, wept or laughed, sold and begged and bartered, not always happily but always with a vigor that was what he meant, privately, by soul" (Cunningham 13). Here, the pronoun "he" delineates a site of ambiguity: we are made to see through Lucas's eyes and yet we hear Whitman "cataloging" what Lucas sees.

However, what manifests itself as an incongruence of voices at one level may turn into an uncanny congruence once Lucas unwittingly translates Whitman into speech acts. Uttered as a sentence, the Whitman-line "Every atom belonging to me as good belongs to you" (5) fits well to express what remains unspeakable to him: his adoration for Catherine. Likewise, when he receives his payment by the end of his shift in the works, he happily shakes his supervisor's hand and says, "Prodigal, […] you have given me love – therefore I to you give love" (21). His speaking in fits, therefore, has a double meaning. On the one hand, the word "fit" refers to his inability to control 'his Whitman,' while on the other hand, it also denotes his ability to apply Whitman fittingly, albeit unwittingly.

The event in Lucas's recent past which complements as well as exacerbates his psychasthenia is the death of his brother Simon. This traumatic loss affects his compulsion to speaking in fits in the sense that his psychasthenic assimilation into *Leaves of Grass* becomes a means to assimilate the traumatic experience. Consequently, his neurotic speaking fits constitute conjunctions of psychasthenia and traumatic reenactment. Lucas has no facility to mourn (see Cunningham 13), which indicates his loss as an experience "withdrawn from consciousness" (Freud 205), a loss that does not allow for mourning as a path towards closure. Obliged to replace Simon in the works to provide for his incapacitated parents, Lucas is made to perform the same movements at the exact same machine that caused Simon's death. His work thus amounts to both a physical and a psychic reenactment in which the machine gains central stage. First, by operating the machine Lucas is made to produce "housings" (Cunningham 19), the function of which remains a mystery to him even after he inquires into it. Read metaphorically, he produces forms that will "fit" a content of which he has no knowledge or, because of its traumatic nature, cannot comprehend.

However, the machine as a physical catalyst of his movements reveals that the content of his trauma has to do less with his brother's death *per se* and more with the very method of his 'death by the machine.' It is therefore the *how,* rather than the *what,* that is traumatic for Lucas. This aspect of his brother's loss is revealed when Lucas's sleeve accidentally gets caught in the machine's clamp, pushing him to the very edge of death: "Lucas looked with mute wonder at the end of his sleeve. This was how. You allowed your attention to wander, you thought of other things, and the clamp took whatever was offered it. That was the clamp's nature" (20). As he succeeds in removing his sleeve from the grip of the clamp, he realizes that "[t]he cloth still bore the imprint of the clamp's tiny toothmarks" (20). This imprint, which Lucas's shirt preserves as though a negative of a photograph (resonating with Freud's use of the photographic imprint as a metaphor for trauma [see Meek 50]), amounts to a transmission of the wound, inflicted on his brother by the machine that "stamped" and "expelled" (Cunningham 47) him, onto Lucas's body.

While the free indirect speech of the narration ascribes anthropomorphic and zoomorphic dimensions to the machine, Simon, in turn, is mechanized. This juxtaposition of the body and the machine as a site of (both physical and psychic) trauma is illustrated by the voice Lucas hears emanating from the machine: "It might have been the squeak of an unoiled bearing, but it sounded more like a voice, a tiny voice, though its words were indistinguishable. The song wasn't sung in a language, not in a language Lucas recognized, but gradually, over time, the song began making itself clear, even though its words remained obscure" (47). Similarly to his lack of knowledge as to what the housings that he produces will contain, the song is a 'product' of his traumatic reenactment – a form indicating content as an absence. For him, the song is vaguely familiar, recalling a "time and place that hovered on the outer edge of memory" (47). The site that these words denote, of course, is the site of trauma which asserts itself in the form of the song as the "voice of the other" (Caruth 8), which returns to haunt the traumatized subject precisely because it cannot be remembered. The "other" in Cathy Caruth's phrase refers to the content of trauma itself, which has been "othered" by way of repression. The song signifies what Freud describes as the contemporariness of trauma and establishes a nexus between Simon's physical and Lucas's psychic wound. What pulsates at the vortex of this nexus is the hum of the machine, the melody of the technological sublime,[1] into which Lucas projects the traumatic loss of his brother: "This seemed, in fact, to be Simon's voice, rendered mechanical" (Cunningham 47). Undecipherable and cryptic, the song attests to the unspeakability of Simon's physical body, "stamped and expelled" (47) by the machine as an industrial product which amplifies the method of Simon's death that Lucas assimilates into his Whitman-corpus, which simultaneously assimilates him. Psychasthenia and trauma thus feed into each other with

1 I am using this term in the sense that David Nye uses it in his book *American Technological Sublime* (1994).

the former serving as a symptom of the latter. Lucas's uncontrollable mimicry of the book is at once the language through which his trauma manifests itself.

Although the machine is not at all a "counterforce" to nature in Whitman's oeuvre (222), it is nature that he identifies as the place of rebirth, the ultimate site for the reincarnation of the dead. For Lucas, what Whitman perceives as "the beautiful uncut hair of graves" in "Song of Myself" (101) makes the absence of grass on Simon's grave a marker of difference unaccounted for in Whitman's metaphysics. However, the personification of the grass in "Song of Myself," which Desirée Henderson regards as a sacrilegious move towards "unmasking the ground, peeling off the surface and revealing the bodies underneath" (102), does not offer the form necessary for Lucas to justify his brother's reincarnation in machinery. For him, the machine is a site of traumatic deferral, at once heterochronic (in terms of the cyclical return of Simon's voice) and heterotopic (marking a juxtaposition of corporeality and machinery as a site of trauma).

This discrepancy between Whitman's system and the method of Simon's death indicates how the traumatic experience that takes hold of Lucas affects his psychasthenic relationship to the book. He needs to expand the scope of *Leaves of Grass* so as to fabricate an explanatory frame for Simon's song: "It seemed, as he loaded the plates onto the belt, that the machines were not inanimate; not quite inanimate. They were part of a continuum: machines, then grass and trees, then horses and dogs, then human beings" (Cunningham 20). Extending Whitman's definition of the grass in section 6 of "Song of Myself" to the machine as a narrative frame, Lucas produces a "housing" for the inassimilable contiguity of body and machine convoluting in Simon's death. Personification is one such housing device: "He wondered if the machine had loved Simon, in its serene and unthinking way. He wondered if all the machines at the works, all the furnaces and hooks and belts, mutely admired their men, as horses admired their masters" (20-21). Incorporating machines into the continuum, Lucas creates a lens through which to perceive them as animate things that kill out of affection – a motif which recurs in the second novella, "The Children's Crusade," in the form of teenage suicide terrorists blowing up their victims by embracing them. Essentially catalyzed by the phenomenology of detail, Whitman's poetics of space assimilates Lucas as an instance of psychasthenia and is simultaneously reconfigured by Lucas to serve as a *model* of traumatic epistemology, a *tabula* that accommodates death by machine – markedly absent from the catalogs of the *Leaves of Grass* – into a transcendentalist dynamics of life and death, welding the technological into the Whitmanesque image of grass as a "uniform hieroglyphic" (Whitman 96).

Fitting Words

We have seen that the song Lucas hears emanating from the machinery is one whose words he does not understand yet recognizes as vaguely familiar from "elsewhere." This "elsewhere," hovering on the "outer edge of memory" (Cunningham 47), points to the very content of trauma as a site uncharted and unremembered, yet constantly revisited. In his psychological account of phantoms, secreted traumas passed on within families from generation to generation, Nicolas Abraham talks about verbal traces that indicate the phantom's incessant presence in the psyche of the traumatized person. "What haunts," Abraham argues, "are not the dead, but the gaps left within us by the secrets of others" (287), secrets that have not been verbalized. Thus the phantom embodies secreted traumas and is sustained by what Abraham calls "phantomogenic words [that] become travesties and can be acted out or expressed in phobias of all kinds (such as impulse phobia), obsessions, restricted phantasmagorias" (292). In Abraham's terms, Simon's death by machine constitutes a foreign body "lodged within the subject" (290), addressing Lucas through the phantomogenic words of the song. In what follows, I will apply Abraham's notion of the phantom to Lucas's conversations with Catherine, his dead brother's fiancée, to further nuance the connection between psychasthenia and trauma. I will demonstrate that Catherine's recognition of her own trauma being 'spoken' by Lucas during one of his speaking fits should be addressed as a mode of listening which, in turn, teaches us, readers, to not only read but 'listen' to Cunningham's text as a repository of phantomogenic words that speak to 9/11's tabooed traumas.

On the occasion of presenting Catherine with a bowl to express his naïve adoration, Lucas utters two Whitman-lines in which the girl 'recognizes' Simon's voice addressing her:

> He said, "The spinning-girl retreats and advances to the hum of the big wheel."
> […]
> "The prostitute draggles her shawl, her bonnet bobs on her tipsy and pimpled neck. The nine months' gone is in the parturition chamber, her faintness and pains are advancing."
> Catherine paused. She looked at him with a new recognition.
> "What did you say?"
> He didn't know. She had never before seemed to hear him when he spoke as the book.
> "Lucas, please repeat what you just said."
> "I've forgotten."
> "You spoke of a spinning-girl. You spoke of a bride, and … a prostitute. And a woman about to give birth."

"It was the book."
"But why did you say it?"
"The words come through me. I never know."
She leaned closer, gazing into his face as if words were written there, faint but discernible, difficult to read. (Cunningham 54, 55)

The "new recognition" that Lucas's utterance elicits is in fact the uncanny recognition of the self in the other. By unknowingly speaking in a fit, Lucas performs a text that "fits" Catherine's own trauma. His utterance, in this sense, is doubly performative insofar as he unwittingly produces his Whitman-lines as fits that Catherine simultaneously produces as a reader reenacting and thereby confronting her repressed secret in them. Lucas's psychasthenia consequently becomes an interface for Catherine to confront her own trauma. To adopt Abraham's term, Lucas acts like a "ventriloquist" (290), a voice 'saying' not only Whitman but Catherine as well. Suspecting that Simon had confided a secret in him, Catherine collapses and discloses to Lucas what she perceives as her complicity in Simon's death: "'I told your brother he must marry me. I don't know if the child is his. It probably isn't. But Simon was willing.' […] 'I suspect. He had his accident because he was unhappy. He may have been so distracted by the thought of our wedding that he allowed it to happen'" (Cunningham 69). This silenced trauma is thus not merely the wound that the loss of her fiancé inflicts on her but rather the haunting suspicion of her own agency in Simon's death – made "discernible" for her by Lucas's psychasthenia.

Catherine's reading of Lucas, however, also gives us a model as to how to read Cunningham's work as a voice emanating from the outer edge of *our* memories, but without giving us a way to translate it into a narrative of cause and effect. I would like to suggest that in the same way that the words "spinning girl," "prostitute," "nine months," and "bride" are (mis)read by Catherine as reverberations of her trauma, Cunningham's work provides us with a psychasthenic text that exposes the phantomogenic contours of 9/11's tabooed traumas. In order to identify these contours let me focus on the scene that concludes "In the Machine." Sensing the danger that machines pose to Catherine at her workplace, Lucas tries to divert her from going to work. To do so, he self-mutilates himself by allowing his hand to be devoured by the machine so that Catherine would take him to the hospital instead of going to the factory. Waiting for treatment with Catherine at his side, Lucas suddenly succumbs to the pull of an irresistible drive and, with his mangled hand soaking in blood, dashes out of the hospital and runs to the site where Catherine's workplace, the Mannahatta Company, is already on fire. The "house in the sea of grass" (98), where he imagines himself running to, ultimately materializes in its dialectical opposite: a factory on fire, a "building blazing" (100). More than speaking in fits, his psychasthenic assimilation into *Leaves of Grass* thus serves him as an epistemological lens through which he experiences the world.

This calamitous fire, taking place at the fictitious Mannahatta Company, acquires new meanings once read in the light of the second novella. Set in the immediate aftermath of 9/11, "The Children's Crusade" recycles imagery familiar from "In the Machine," which instantiates a retroactive reading of the first novella. If, in the wake of the terrorist attacks, as we read in "The Children's Crusade," "it was impossible not to be struck by the emptiness where the towers had stood" (113), it is just as impossible for the reader not to re-visualize Lucas's apocalyptic vision of the "unspeakable beauty" (101) of the catastrophe at the Mannahatta Company in terms of the spectacular events of 9/11. Using "The Children's Crusade" as a retrospective vantage point, Lucas's perception of the fire that left onlookers "horrified and excited" (99) reads uncannily germane to the aftermath of the collapse of the Twin Towers: "[t]he dead had entered the atmosphere. [...] With every breath Lucas took the dead inside him. This was their bitter taste; this was how they lay – ashen and hot – on the tongue. [...] The dead filled Lucas's mouth and lungs" (100). Similarly to Catherine's reading of her own trauma in Lucas's Whitman-words, we recognize the uncanny content of the dust of 9/11 emerging in the form of phantomogenic words embedded in Cunningham's text. The burning building of the Mannahatta Company is construed by Lucas's gaze as part of the continuum, a building-machine, metonymic of the machinery it houses. Because the sight phantomogenically recalls 9/11, we find ourselves looking at Ground Zero through Lucas's psychasthenia.

All these instances attest to the dynamics of repetitions that catalyzes the reading of "The Children's Crusade" as a narrative layer 'deposited' on "In the Machine," whereby a palimpsest of inter- and intratextual relations is formed. Although the ruins of the World Trade Center anchor "The Children's Crusade" in a historical setting outside the text, its spatiotemporal framework seeps into fiction once the teenage terrorists appear on the scene. This apparent *difference* between historical fact and fiction wraps the former into the latter and allows Cunningham's text to articulate the 'unbelievable' through phantomogenic words installed into a historiographic scaffolding. Catherine's reading of Lucas/Whitman thus gives us a model for reading Cunningham's work as an *aide mémoire*. As such, insofar as Lucas's psychasthenic assimilation into *Leaves of Grass* provides him with an epistemological apparatus to process the scale of calamity that unfolds in front of his eyes, so does Cunningham's *Specimen Days* invite us, readers, to engage with the novel psychasthenically, as an apparatus through which to process the trauma of 9/11.

FOUR BUILDINGS

In order to examine how Cunningham's novel lends itself to a psychasthenic reading and serves as a mnemonic device, let me return to the industrial catastrophe at Catherine's workplace, which concludes "In the Machine." Cunningham's description of the fire at the fictitious Mannahatta Company seems uncannily congruent with the historical event of the Triangle Shirtwaist Factory fire of March 25, 1911, which took the lives of 146 garment workers, many of whom jumped to their deaths from the top floors of the building (see von Drehle 152-156). "In the Machine," however, is set in a New York of some 20 years before the fire, when an accidental (if not magical) meeting between Lucas and Walt Whitman on Broadway was still possible.[2] In a self-referential manner, Cunningham accounts for this temporal discrepancy in his authorial note to the novel. This note is a disclaimer in which he politely refers the reader to yet another text as a source of truth: "Anyone interested in the absolute truth about New York in the mid to late nineteenth century would be well advised to consult *Gotham* by Edwin G. Burrows and Mike Wallace, which was the primary source from which I spun my own variations" (xiv). But if this "absolute truth" is located in another text, Cunningham's ironical remark confers historical truth on the very text that produces it. Cunningham's reference to *Gotham* as "absolute truth" wherefrom he spins his own variations is not without an intratextual reference. His words echo Lucas's own way of spinning his variations from "the book" whose constructed nature is echoed by Cunningham's own book, as well as the ultimate source he pins down as "truth." Through these multiple layers of textual fractals Cunningham dramatizes the cyclical structure of traumatic reenactment and allows the voice of 9/11's "phantom," in Abraham's sense, to echo within the interstice between "In the Machine" and "The Children's Crusade." The textual formation of the phantom as an absence is most conspicuous in Cunning-

2 In a serendipitous instance, as Lucas is looking for coins on Broadway he bumps into Walt Whitman's "gray-white cascade of beard" (Cunningham 72). Their dream-like conversation is crucial for Lucas because Whitman confirms him in his belief that the dead can return in machinery as well: "They are in machinery too. They are everywhere," answers Whitman. "Lucas had been right, then. If he'd harbored any doubts, here was the answer" (73-74).

ham's treatment of architectural spaces which I will demonstrate through the interrelations formed among four buildings: the NYU building, the Triangle Shirtwaist Factory, the Mannahatta Company, and the ruins of the World Trade Center.

As "The Children's Crusade" gestures back to "In the Machine," an intratextual relation is formed between the Mannahatta Company and the Triangle Shirtwaist Factory. The nexus between the two buildings is established by the police psychologist Cat's visit to New York University – the present-day owner of what used to be the Triangle Shirtwaist Factory – in order to meet a Whitman-specialist and seek an explanation as to why the teenage suicide bombers use *Leaves of Grass* as their "language" (Cunningham 153) when Cat talks to them on the phone. Upon her entering the building, the narration gestures toward a historical reality outside the text (the NYU building is indeed identical to the old Triangle Factory)[3] through the textual coordinates of the horrific fire at the Mannahatta Company:

> One of these buildings, Cat had never been quite sure which, had been that sweatshop, where the fire was. She knew the story only vaguely – the exits had been blocked to keep the workers from sneaking out early. Something like that. There'd been a fire, and all those women were trapped inside. Some of them had jumped. From one of these buildings – was it the one she was entering? – women with their dresses on fire had fallen, had hit this pavement right here or the pavement just down the street. Now it was all NYU. (156)

The historical event reiterated here functions both as an intertextual reference to a historical event as well as an intratext retroactively superimposed on the Mannahatta Company. Cat's rumination on the story, which she "only vaguely" remembers, inserts the historical link between NYU and the Triangle Shirtwaist Factory Fire of 1911 as an intertext, while her entering the NYU building offers us, readers, an intratextual gateway to read the text psychasthenically, that is, to 'recognize' Cat as Catherine and 're-read' the fire of the Mannahatta Company in terms of the disaster of the Triangle catastrophe (and vice versa) and, by extension, hear the echo of 9/11 behind 1911.

By the same token, the ominous presence of the ruins of the World Trade Center in "The Children's Crusade" as yet another historical intertext interacts with both the Triangle Shirtwaist Factory and the Mannahatta Company at an intratextual level. The dynamic interaction of these textual traces is imbued with

3 The building is indeed NYU property (see von Drehle 327) and there is a plaque on its façade commemorating the fire of 1911 (see Foote 295-297).

the presence of *genius loci,* which, paradoxically, gains its aura by being detached from and at once intimately tied to Lower Manhattan as a metafictional palimpsest. In this sense, Cat's ruminations on the fire, which she presumes had happened "right here" (156), certainly does more than identify the NYU Building as the Triangle Shirtwaist Factory inserted as a historical intertext. Being "right here" constitutes a nexus of textualized traces, in which the Mannahatta Company and Ground Zero are "entered" as part of the same act of entering the NYU building and the Triangle Shirtwaist Factory.

If reading Cunningham's work demands the recognition of these architectural and historical interrelations, it also requires something more. For the industrial catastrophe described in "In the Machine" does not merely interact with the Ground Zero evoked in "The Children's Crusade" as nodes in a nexus of intertextual relations, but also creates a virtual site in which the uncanny constellation of body and building, the animate and the inanimate explode in an emphatic absence. Cat's vague recollection of "women with their dresses on fire [who] had fallen, had hit this pavement right here or the pavement just down the street" (156), gives textual form, a textual *genius loci,* to the people that jumped/fell from the towers on 9/11.

As we have already seen, Lucas's psychasthenic recital of Whitman stages a reenactment of Catherine's own trauma which she recognizes as a text "faint but discernible, difficult to read" (55). I have also suggested that Cunningham's work replicates Lucas's "book" in that it invites psychasthenic reading as a narrative to absorb the trauma of 9/11. More specifically, I will argue that *Specimen Days* works as a mnemonic device for the recollection of 9/11's falling bodies. As the Mannahatta Company is burning, Lucas looks up at one of the workers:

> The woman stood in the window, holding to its frame. Her blue skirt billowed. The square of brilliant orange made of her a blue silhouette, fragile and precise. She was like a goddess of the fire, come to her platform to tell those gathered below what the fire meant, what it wanted of them. From so far away, her face was indistinct. She turned her head to look back into the room, as if someone had called to her. She was radiant and terrifying. She listened to something the fire told her.
>
> She jumped.
>
> [...]
>
> The woman's skirt rose around her as she fell. She lifted her arms, as if to take hold of invisible hands that reached for her.
>
> When she struck the pavement, she disappeared. She'd been a woman in midair, she'd been the flowering of her skirt, and then in an instant she was only the dress, puddle on the cobblestones, still lifting slightly at its edges as if it lived on. (98)

Lucas's perception of the jumper bespeaks a transcendentalist geometry into which death by machine is inscribed. In much the same way that his brother was "stamped and expelled" by the machine, it is now the tall building that devours and expels the workers. For Lucas, the industrial catastrophe unfolds as a transition from life to death, experienced through the lens of *Leaves of Grass*. Perceived in her fall as "the flowering of her skirt" and then becoming "the dress, puddle on the cobblestones," the falling woman's death is inscribed into what Lucas conceptualizes as "a huge and mesmerizing wholeness" (100), a continuum that brings the machine (metonymically represented by the factory building and the cobblestones of the city) and the garden (the flowering of her skirt) to an equilibrium in the moment of death.[4] At this time, psychasthenia allows Lucas to transcend his pain: "The pain was there still, but it was not in him any more" (93).

In much the same way that he assimilates into *Leaves of Grass* throughout his life, his death constitutes an enactment of the poem. At the novel's end Catherine cannot withhold him from leaving the hospital and running to the site of the fire. The lure of space that depersonalizes the psychasthenic manifests itself in the lure that drives Lucas to witness the building consumed by fire. Once there, Lucas dies in much the same way that he lived his life. He dissolves into the book and, through the book, into the materiality of space. Filtered through Whitman's poem, the horror of death that engulfs Lucas is framed as a source of beauty: "He knew that his heart stopped. He wanted to say, I am large, I contain multitudes. I am in the grass under your feet. He made as if to speak but did not speak. In the sky, the great celestial horse turned its enormous head. An unspeakable beauty announced itself" (101). The beauty of his death is coterminous with what he perceives as the "flowering" of the falling woman's skirt in midair. By extension, reading the text psychasthenically, this image operates as a mnemonic device insofar as it reminds us of the iconic image of a woman holding down her skirt before jumping from one of the WTC towers on 9/11.

Another passage that describes the fire at the Mannahatta Company yields an even more distressing configuration, which translates impending death into freedom. As Lucas catches sight of another woman just about to jump out of the building, he translates the fall into flying:

4 In his book *The Machine in the Garden* (1964) Leo Marx discusses the pastoral and the industrial ideals as deeply entrenched imaginaries in American cultural history. These antagonistic binaries are reconciled in Lucas's imagination.

She looked down. She looked at Lucas.
[...]
He returned her gaze. He could do nothing else. His heart raged and burned, full of its own fire. [...] She said (though she did not speak in words), We are this now. We were weary and put-upon, we lived in tiny rooms, we ate candy in secret, but now we are radiant and glorious. We are no longer anyone. We are part of something vaster and more marvelous than the living can imagine.
[...]
The fire woman spread her wings and flew.
[...] He saw the woman cross the sky. [...] He knew that his heart had stopped. He wanted to say, I am large, I contain multitudes. I am in the grass under your feet. (100-101)

Similarly to the passages cited earlier, Whitman's "Song of Myself" pulsates behind Lucas's 'reading' of the catastrophe. The aesthetic turn, however, which transforms falling into flying bears echoes of the composed posture of Richard Drew's famous photograph known as "The Falling Man" (2001). Depicting a man falling headfirst with one leg bent at the knee in perfect harmony with the girders of the towers behind him, the photograph was first published in the *New York Times* on September 12, 2001, only to be denounced by readers as irreverent and disrespectful to the man depicted. In his article "The Falling Man," published in *Esquire Magazine* in 2003, journalist Tom Junod urges readers to bear witness to Drew's photograph as an ethical imperative. "Although he has not chosen his fate," Junod writes, "he appears to have, in his last instants of life, embraced it. If he were not falling, he might very well be flying. [...] Some people who look at the picture see stoicism, willpower, a portrait of resignation; others see something else – something discordant and terrible: freedom" ("The Falling Man"). The "unspeakable beauty" (Cunningham 101) that envelops Lucas in the closing scene of the story resounds the "terrible freedom" that suffuses Drew's photo, but while Junod talks about a "discordant" aesthetics, a freedom tainted by suicide as the unsettling connotation of death by jumping, Lucas perceives the fall in terms of becoming part of "something vaster."

Lucas's death also echoes the unvoiceable nature of 9/11: his function as projecting screen for his environment (the city, the inhabitants, Catherine, and her trauma) fails at the end, as he is overburdened by having to reflect the Mannahatta Company fire. Indeed, Lucas gives in to the lure of space and dissolves into the sight of the burning building. The exchange of glances between the "fire woman" and Lucas brings about meaning as a fulfillment of the script provided by *Leaves of Grass*. By the same token, the traumatizing image of "The Falling Man," and the inevitability of death that it denotes, are simultaneously recalled and filtered through Cunningham's novel as a mnemonic device. In the same way that Lucas perceives the fire at the Mannahatta Company through the filter of *Leaves of Grass,* we are reminded of Drew's unsettling photograph but in the same breath assimilated into *Specimen Days* as a narrative. As a form of neurosis that transcends its medical understanding in Caillois's reconceptualization, Cunningham employs psychasthenia as both a literary trope and a model of engaging with the trauma of 9/11.

CONCLUSION

If Cunningham's palimpsest operates by the logic of fractal geometry centered on the dialectics of listening to the voice of the other and the construction of a narrative to rationalize that voice, the reader of *Specimen Days* is positioned as a reader of phantomogenic words, mimicking Lucas's listening to Simon and Catherine's listening to Lucas. The same pattern can be traced in the four buildings that dovetail within a complex web of intra- and intertextual nexuses. The core formation that defines this pattern is, of course, the machine that devoured Simon, his "death by machine" that echoes in the dust of the World Trade Center and the 9/11 jumpers – both recalled as particular instances of the trauma of 9/11. As we recognize 9/11 *in terms* of the fire at the Mannahatta Company/Triangle Shirtwaist Factory, the Whitmanesque continuum that helps Lucas absorb what exceeds his comprehension looks back at us, echoing Junod's call to confront the photograph of the Falling Man.

We have seen how Caillois's association of psychasthenia with mimicry gives a new life to this neurotic condition. Rather than conceiving it as an inability to demarcate the boundaries of the self, he reconceptualizes this form of neurosis along the lines of desire that drives the neurotic subject to give in to the lure of space. The subject assimilates into the environment not so much in order to seek shelter but for the sake of assimilation itself. While the phenomenological tone of Cunningham's text convincingly highlights this aspect of Lucas's neurosis, we also learn that his psychastenia is inextricably tied to his trauma. His assimilation into *Leaves of Grass* thus foregrounds the function of mimicry from which Caillois diverges in his essay: defense. Cunningham reframes psychasthenia as a form of neurosis that is obsessive and at once defensive. In much the same way that Whitman's *Leaves of Grass* resonates through Cunningham's text, so does Lucas's psychasthenic assimilation into the poem map Whitman's poetics on 9/11 as a transcendentalist compass that ultimately leads him to dissolve into the continuum of the animate and the inanimate as a structuring principle of his cognitive map. If Whitman serves him as a navigational tool in the world, Cunningham deploys Lucas's psychasthenia as a vehicle to confront the raw materiality of 9/11 without directly referencing it in his novel.

LIST OF WORKS CITED

Abraham, Nicolas. "Notes on the Phantom: A Complement to Freud's Metapsychology." *Critical Inquiry*, vol. 13, 1987, pp. 287-292.

Caillois, Roger. "Mimicry and Legendary Psychasthenia." *The Edge of Surrealism: A Roger Caillois Reader*, edited by Claudine Frank, translated by Claudine Frank and Camille Naish, Duke University Press, 2003, pp. 89-103.

Caruth, Cathy. *Unclaimed Experience: Trauma, Narrative, and History.* The Johns Hopkins University Press, 1996.

Cunningham, Michael. *Specimen Days.* Picador, 2005.

Drehle, David von. *Triangle: The Fire that Changed America.* Grove Press, 2003.

Foote, Kenneth. *Shadowed Ground: America's Landscapes of Violence and Tragedy.* University of Texas Press, 2003.

Freud, Sigmund. *On Murder, Mourning and Melancholia.* Translated by Shaun Whiteside, Penguin, 2005.

Goldberger, Paul. *Up from Zero: Politics, Architecture, and the Rebuilding of New York.* Random House, 2005.

Gossop, Michael. *Theories of Neurosis.* Springer, 1981.

Henderson, Desirée. "'What is the Grass?': The Roots of Walt Whitman's Cemetery Meditation." *Walt Whitman Quarterly Review*, vol. 25, no. 3, 2008, pp. 89-107.

Jaspers, Karl. *General Psychopathology.* Translated by J. Hoenig and Marian W. Hamilton, The University of Chicago Press, 1963.

Junod, Tom. "The Falling Man." *Esquire*, September 2003, esquire.com/features/ESQ0903-SEP_FALLINGMAN. Accessed 14 July 2011.

Kristeva, Julia. *Desire in Language: A Semiotic Approach to Literature and Art.* Translated by Thomas Gora, Alice Jardine, and Leon S. Roudiez, Columbia University Press, 1980.

Marx, Leo. *The Machine in the Garden: Technology and the Pastoral Ideal in America.* Oxford University Press, 2000.

Meek, Allen. *Trauma and Media: Theories, Histories, and Images.* Routledge, 2010.

Nye, David N. *American Technological Sublime.* MIT Press, 1994.

Sturken, Marita. *Tourists of History: Memory, Kitsch, and Consumerism from Oklahoma City to Ground Zero.* Duke University Press, 2007.

Versluys, Kristiaan. *Out of the Blue: September 11 and the Novel.* Columbia University Press, 2009.

Whitman, Walt. *Leaves of Grass.* Penguin, 1986.

Yaeger, Patricia. "Rubble as Archive, or 9/11 as Dust, Debris, and Bodily Vanishing." *Trauma at Home: After 9/11*, edited by Judith Greenberg, University of Nebraska Press, 2003, pp.187-94.

Disintegrated Selves

Dissociative Disorders and Colonial Anxiety in Orhan Pamuk's *The Black Book*

ELENA FURLANETTO

Tim Arango, of *The New York Times*, claims that "conspiracy theories about Western plots to undermine Turkey run so deep in the nation's collective psyche that only the language of psychology is suitable to understanding them." Arango locates the origins of Turkey's anxiety about Western intervention in the Sèvres Treaty of 1920, according to which former Ottoman territories were to be dissected and parceled out to the powers of the Entente. Even though the treaty was never put into practice, it left a mark on the country's collective consciousness. "Analysts have used the terms 'phobia,' 'trauma' and 'syndrome' to describe the country's mindset," Arango continues, "ever since Sèvres […] Turkey as a nation has been suffering from posttraumatic stress disorder." What emerges from Arango's analysis is that, in the Turkish context, the neurotic goes hand in hand with the shadow of Western interference. I agree with Lerna Yanık that "though neither Turkey nor its precursor Ottoman Empire was ever colonized, both entities have had an uneasy relationship with the 'West' and displayed the reflexes of a post-colonial country" (83). In his 2006 assessment of Turkey's postcoloniality, Erdağ Göknar explains that Turkey has been affected by forms of "semi-colonial" occupation:

> As the late Ottoman state fell into the position of being semi-colonized, the legacy of this semi-colonization, or colonial encounter with Europe, informed the breadth, scope, and legacy of severity of the Kemalist cultural revolution that gave shape to the Republic of Turkey. And though it is a commonplace to hear modern Turks boast that Turkey – meaning the Ottoman state and the Republic – was never colonized, history presents us with a quite different account. (37)

Here Göknar refers to the Ottoman Empire's nineteenth-century cultural and financial dependency on Europe, but the occupation of the empire's territory by the Allied powers after World War I and during the Turkish War of Independence qualifies as a "colonial encounter" as well.

This study applies Arango's hypothesis to the realm of literature and focuses on the interconnections between the colonial and the neurotic in Orhan Pamuk's novel *The Black Book* (1990), which articulates a critique of Western imperialism and imperial nostalgia through the language of psychological discomfort. Pamuk published *The Black Book* (*Kara Kitap*) in Turkish in 1990.[1] The story is set in Istanbul in the 1980s and develops around the sudden disappearance of Rüya, a mysterious woman who sleeps by day and reads by night. Rüya's husband, Galip, expects to find her in the company of his brother in law Celâl – a charismatic journalist whom he has always revered and envied – only to discover that Celâl, too, has vanished. Hoping to learn about Rüya's whereabouts, Galip delves deeper and deeper into Celâl's life and writings, to the point that he begins to impersonate his brother in law. The chapters that follow Galip's adventures alternate with excerpts from Celâl's columns for the Turkish newspaper *Milliyet*. Galip's search for Rüya –Turkish for 'dream' – can be read as a metaphysical journey through the individual's and the country's Self, as many of the places Galip visits in the course of his frantic peregrinations, many of the stories he is told by men and women he encounters, "bear upon the central question whether it is possible for a man to be himself" and are "metaphor[s] for the collective unconscious of Istanbul" (Wright 149, 150).

Both Arango and Pamuk verbalize the aftermath of Western interference with Turkey's political or cultural sovereignty through the language of neurosis: if the former casts the Treaty of Sèvres as the moment that threw the country into "posttraumatic stress disorder" (Arango), the latter locates the originative trauma in the Kemalist reforms of the early twentieth century, suggesting it may be at the roots of the characters' neurotic behaviors. The Kemalist model established itself in 1923, with the birth of the Republic of Turkey under the leadership of Mustafa Kemal Atatürk. Kemalism remained Turkey's leading ideology until the 1980s, when Neo-Ottomanism, a political doctrine endorsing a revival of Ottoman culture, proposed a shift from Kemalism's Westward trajectory. Kemalism lay strong emphasis on secularism, the separation of state and religion, radical Westernization, and an idea of Turkish identity primarily based on ethnicity. Kemalist reforms, determined to eradicate the Ottoman heritage from the coun-

1 The first English translation by Turkish American novelist Güneli Gün came out in 1994, followed by a new translation by Maureen Freely in 2006.

try's collective self, included the banishing of Islam from school curricula, the closing of Sufi schools and religious centers, the introduction of the Latin alphabet, the expulsion of Arab and Persian terms from the Turkish language, and the forced assimilation of non-Turkish ethnicities as 'Turks' (see Çandar 89). *The Black Book* narrates the experiences of Istanbulites who, decades after this profound disruption of their cultural system, display the symptomatology of dissociative disorders. Dissociative disorders, Spiegel and Cardeña explain, may develop as a consequence of traumatic events, "involv[e] alterations in the relationship to the self [...], to the world [...], and to memory processes," and include amnesia, multiple personalities, and depersonalization or derealization (367-368).[2]

As Dietmar Meinel writes in his introduction to this volume, "fiction [...] shows very little concern for diagnostic exactness, as mental disorders are routinely romanticized or vilified, bent to suit aesthetic and narrative choices" (14). Accordingly, Pamuk does not delve into diagnostics nor does he name his characters' psychopathologies, which unfold at the level of language, metaphor, and imaginary. Moreover, these nameless conditions – which I loosely identify as dissociative disorders – are of intensely literary quality: characters drift off into fictional worlds of Western cinema and literature. Germane to the sphere of literary and cinematic imagination rather than that of clinical rigor, these psychopathologies constitute the bedrock of a "poetics of neurosis" that pervades the novel. The term neurosis, expunged from medical discourse when deemed "too elusive for a proper diagnosis of psychological disorders" (Meinel 9) proves useful to tackle the poetics and politics of Pamuk's literary, loosely described psychopathologies. The aim of this study, therefore, is not to diagnose Pamuk's subjects, but to investigate the complexity of the neurotic imaginary in *The Black Book,* which Pamuk 'bends' to articulate a critique of cultural imperialism.

In *The Black Book*, dissociative disorders such as those mentioned above are a means to tackle the contended specter of the colonial in Turkey, alternately exposed and dismissed in public and scholarly discourses. According to Kader Konuk, for example, Turkey appropriated Western culture on its own terms (see *Mimesis* 87). The modernization and Westernization policies adopted by the Ottoman Empire starting in the nineteenth century were, Konuk notes, the product

2 This article employs psychology studies from the 1990s contemporary practitioners of the field would probably dismiss as dated. Yet, this article is not preoccupied with achieving state-of-the art clinical accuracy. In order to show the interrelatedness of *The Black Book*'s literary language and the language of psychological analysis, it is imperative to refer to studies that are contemporary to the novel.

of "an autonomous decision" and seeing late Ottoman and early republican Turkey as subjected to Western cultural hegemony would therefore be "too narrow, if not misleading" (10). Thus, Konuk prefers to consider Ottomans and Turks as "agents, not victims, of Westernization" (10). The narrator of *The Black Book* presents the reader with a view on Western cultural interference in Turkey that echoes Göknar's specter of the semi-colonial.

In a chapter called "We Lost our Memories at the Movies," *The Black Book*'s third person narrator conspiratorially describes a scenario in which Istanbulites are deprived of agency and appear as acquiescent victims of European and North American cultural imperialism.

> The first step would be to establish a new state along the Bosphorus and the Dardanelles. But instead of bringing in new settlers to populate this new state, as their predecessors had done a thousand years ago, they would turn the old inhabitants into "new people" tailored to serve their purposes. [...] Those charged with this task would quickly guess that the only way forward was to rip away our memories, our past, our history. It was known that Turkish children attending the shadowy missionary schools in the back streets of Beyoğlu and the hills overlooking the Bosphorus had once been made to drink a certain lilac-colored liquid [...]. But later on, the Western block's "humanitarian wing" had declared this reckless initiative too dangerous on chemical grounds and switched to a gentler approach that promised longer-lasting results: the new plan was to erode our collective memory with movie music. (126-127)

The passage continues by mentioning a variety of cultural products that, by invading the Turkish market, contribute to the erasure of the country's collective memory: "church organs, pounding out chords of fearful symmetry, women as beautiful as icons, the hymnlike repetition of images, and those arresting scenes sparkling with drinks, weapons, airplanes, designer clothes" (127). The new wave of colonization affecting Turkey does not rely on the establishment of settlements nor does it happen through relocation. The implantation of a "new state" depends instead on an induced amnesia, resulting in the complete erasure and renewal of the local inhabitants' consciousness. The Istanbulites, who give in to the idea that their survival depends on their willingness to "rip away [their] memories, [their] past, [their] history," are awarded very little agency in the process of Westernization of their country, described later as a "terrible plot being perpetrated on them" (127).

By employing the language of neurosis to narrate the uneasy relationship between post-Empire Turkey[3] and the West, *The Black Book* brings the connection between the colonial and the neurotic to the foreground in the tradition of Frantz Fanon's postcolonial landmark study *Black Skin, White Masks* (1952). To construct the neurotic Istanbulite of *The Black Book*, Pamuk resorts to three, loosely described dissociative disorders. First of all, amnesia, which entails a limited or extended loss of memory and personal identity; second, multiple personality, in which the subject presents "two or more different personalities"; third, depersonalization (or derealization), which alters the perception of the self and the world as "unreal or otherwise fundamentally changed" (Kihlstrom, Glisky, and Angiulo 117).

CITY OF AMNESIA

Definitions of amnesia position the phenomenon in the field of medicine and psychopathology, generally describing it as a loss of memory caused by brain injury, psychological traumas, shock, or illness.[4] Amnesia presents itself in a variety of forms, including, among others, the inability to remember events up to a particular moment, often the disruptive episode that originated this condition (retrograde amnesia), and the inability to record events that followed it (anterograde amnesia). In an interview with Pamuk, Eleanor Wachtel interrogates the author on his choice to define Turkey as a land affected by amnesia.[5] Pamuk answers that his use of the word refers to

---

3 For an accurate theorization of "post-Empire imaginaries" refer to Barbara Buchenau and Virginia Richter, *Post-empire Imaginaries? Anglophone Literature, History, and the Demise of Empires* (2015). I resort to this term as it can be argued that Turkey is both postimperial and postcolonial. In the Turkish case, as Donna Landry puts it, "the postimperial is not a rival to the postcolonial but its comrade" (127).

4 See entries in the *Merriam-Webster* and *Oxford* English Dictionaries. For clinical definitions of amnesia see also "A Neuropsychological Study of Fact Memory and Source Amnesia" (1987) by Arthur P. Shimamura and Larry R. Squire; and "Episodic Memory, Semantic Memory, and Amnesia" (1998) by Larry R. Squire and Stuart M. Zola.

5 References to amnesia as a collective problem affecting Turkey as a consequence of Atatürk's reforms recur frequently in the press and in the work of another internationally renowned Turkish author, Elif Shafak. Her article "Memory-less Turkey/Amnesiac Turkey" (2017) is one prominent example.

> the attempts of the Turkish Republic to Westernize. They thought – and I think this was the major mistake of the founders of the Turkish Republic – that they could Westernize this country if they forgot the past. [...]. So in the country there was a huge sense of *amnesia*, but nothing new to fill the void. This is what I am critical of. (Pamuk in Wachtel 63; emphasis added)

In this excerpt, Pamuk blames the condition of national amnesia on the "founders of the new republic," Mustafa Kemal Atatürk and the ideologues of Kemalism. Although Kemalism implemented a Westernization from within, to put it with Konuk, that happened on Turkey's own terms (see *Mimesis* 87), characters in *The Black Book* juxtapose the Kemalists' Westernizing efforts with the specter of Western colonial interference. Spiegel and Cardeña describe amnesia as the basic component of all dissociative disorders, in so far as personal memory is the key to a unified sense of self (see 372). In a similar way, the novel suggests that continuity with the past is essential to a nation's cultural identity, and the rupture with the imperial legacy causes the fictional population of the city of Istanbul – once the capital of a vast empire – to wonder who and where they are. All Istanbulites who present dissociative disorders in *The Black Book* – Galip, a film extra, and a journalist who thinks he is Marcel Proust – are first and foremost amnesiacs. The state of permanent or temporary alienation they find themselves in is due to the rupture between their present lives in a systematically Westernized Turkey and their cultural heritage.

In *The Black Book*, Istanbul appears as a 'double city.' While the surface succumbs to the succession of new names and empires – the Achaemenid, the Roman, the Eastern Roman, the Ottoman – the remnants of the defeated civilizations tumble into Istanbul's subterranean passages and canals and are consigned to oblivion. Yet, these "old, discarded objects that make us who we are" (Pamuk 188) gradually accumulate and compose a hybrid 'museum' underground. *The Black Book* suggests that yet another colonizing power has taken over the surface, one without settlers, whose goal has been "to establish a new state along the Bosphorus and the Dardanelles" by turning "the old inhabitants into 'new people'" (126). This new colonizing agent is not political, but cultural, as European and American literature, films, and commodities are forcing Turks into alienation and imitation of foreign cultural practices. The city on the surface plays a crucial role in *The Black Book*'s critique of Kemalist policies of Westernization, whose influence extends until the time of the narration, the 1980s.

In Pamuk's novel, the Westernized city on the surface appears as a space of meaninglessness and dispossession where cultural identity has been compromised by policies that encouraged the individual to adopt different aesthetics and sets of values, thus creating a sense of rupture between Istanbul's rapid urbanization and the city's history, between monumental buildings and their lost relevance, between citizens and the spaces the inhabit. One character, for example, drives through a deserted Istanbul at night and feels a hiatus between urban elements and their function, as if they had forgotten it or they were unable to perform it.

> We travelled […] up hard narrow lanes whose sallow streetlamps cast more shadows on the ground than light. We passed […] crumbling wall, broken chimneys, fountains that had gone dry, sleepy mosques that suddenly looked more like sleeping giants and left me trembling with fear […], we passed through our great public squares with their empty pools, forgotten statues, and broken clocks. (314-315)

This rupture triggers neurotic responses in Galip as well, who contemplates the city from the top of a minaret and hallucinates about an underworld – frightening but luminous – within the shapeless surface city.

> It seemed to him that the mosque and the concrete hovels below him and even the smoke rising from their chimneys were illuminated from within. He could almost believe that he was looking at the surface of a planet that had yet to find its final shape. The domes of the city and these vast stretches of concrete, stone, tile, wood, and Plexiglas were coming apart, and in the cracks you could just see the underworld's molten glow. (198-199)

Rita Sakr underscores the neurotic relationship between Pamuk's Istanbulites and their lived spaces as she interprets Galip's *flanerie* across Istanbul as driven by a "paranoid search for hidden meaning" (170). His inability to connect landmarks of Istanbul's cityscape to their geopolitical function is, for Sakr, the result of "compulsive-obsessive reading practices as he walks and reads the signs of Istanbul" (170).

The predominant psychotic condition affecting the surface city is, undoubtedly, amnesia, to be understood as a condition affecting the entire Turkish culture and not merely individual citizens. As he roams through the city, Galip stops "to read faces" (Pamuk 223). A small crowd stationing in front of a movie theatre informs him that

> on Sunday afternoons people in this country escaped boredom by watching dreams imported from abroad […] their sad dreams and sadder memories were fast fading from their minds; the line of dark bare trees running down the center of the avenue told him that they would grow darker still as evening fell, to signify the sorrow of an entire nation. (223)

The small crowd becomes metonymic of "people in this country" who are losing their memory as a result of their weekly consumption of Western films ("dreams imported from abroad"); in the same way, the trees lining a street downtown become barer and darker in response to "the sorrow of an entire nation." The breaking of the multiple connections between a people and its history causes not only an individual memory loss but a collective one: a national amnesia. As Ian Almond remarks in his article on *The Black Book*: "this loss of identity is [...] not just the death of the self, but of the collectivity to which it belongs" (82). Almond also points out that national identity has been lost "to something else," namely "to the cultural and economic centers of North America and Europe" (82).

In the novel, the problem of imitation goes hand in hand with the narrative of amnesia as if in a vicious circle: Turks imitate Western habits, clothing, and gestures because they conform to new identitarian narratives that erased their Ottoman culture, and vice versa, they have taken on imitating "the European models to which [they] were meant to aspire" so passionately that they cannot remember their original identity any longer (Pamuk 61). Amnesia and erasure, in fact, feature prominently in the construction of Turkey's modern self: "ideas of what it means to be Turkish," Amy Mills explains, "are [...] created through actions to remember and to forget particular histories" (386). On overground Istanbul, everything is "a copy of something else," people are "at once themselves and their own imitation" (Pamuk 165). The surface city, which a character in the book calls "ghost city" (249), is populated by "amnesiac" citizens "long resigned to the certainty that their memories would never return to them," irremediably detached from what Celâl calls "inner essence," "innocence," and "true identity" (61).

THE EMPTYING OF THE SELF

The use of a vocabulary of psychopathology to outline and critique the semi-colonial quality of Westernization in Turkey is not limited to amnesia. While the previous section has introduced the rupture between Istanbulites and the architectural elements in the city on the surface, it is important to remark that a similar process of disconnection also affects the Istanbulite's physical body.

A first example for this kind of bodily dissociation can be found in chapter six of *The Black Book*, titled "Bedii Usta's Children," in which Celâl tells the story of the legendary Bedii Usta, the "first undisputed master, the patron saint" (59) of Turkey's mannequins. Already forced to move his business to the underground as, according to the Islamic authorities, the perfection of his creations offended the Creator himself, Bedii Usta saw in the Westernization of the country an opportunity for success, hoping that the Kemalist cultural revolution could revive the forgotten art of mannequin-making.

> In the great westernizing wave of the early years of the Republic, when gentlemen threw aside their fez to don panama hats and ladies discarded their scarves in favor of low-slung high heels, mannequins began to appear in the display windows of the finest clothing stores along Beyoğlu Avenue. These however, were brought in from abroad, and when he first set eyes on these foreign mannequins, Bedii Usta was sure that the day he'd awaited for so long was upon him. (60)

Unfortunately, the diffusion of mannequins "brought in from abroad" – replicating Eurocentric canons of beauty – create a fracture between Turkish bodies and the gallery of desirable bodies exhibited in department stores. Once again, Turkish shopkeepers prove uninterested in Bedii Usta's work due to the excessive resemblance between his mannequins and the "real Turks," as "they did not look like the European models to which we were meant to aspire," Celâl explains in his column, "they looked like us" (61).

What can be observed in Pamuk's characters is, to put it with Homi Bhabha, "a process of identification in the analytics of desire" (xxxi). In this situation, the desire for the Other becomes the primary locus of identification for the Self, who empties of its former characteristics, of its "person and place" (xxxi), to exist exclusively in the articulation of desire. Identification is accompanied in both cases by an "evacuation and emptying of the I" (xxxii) and, as the following passages illustrate, by a rejection of one's own corporeal schema.

> [The customer] is not going to want a coat he sees worn by someone who looks like the swarthy, bow-legged, mustachioed countrymen he sees ten thousand times a day in our city streets. He wants a coat worn by a beautiful creature from a distant unknown land, so he can convince himself that he, too, can change, become someone new, just by putting on this coat. (Pamuk 61)

In *The Black Book*, the Istanbulites prefer not to be reminded of the familiar corporeality of their fellow nationals, whose ethnic markers such as body hair are exaggerated and presented as undesirable: they prefer to evacuate their Self and their corporeal schema to fill it with the desire for the Other.

It is the desire for identification with the Other that drives the evacuation of the Istanbulite's self, who is invested in the effort of 'becoming' someone else, or, as Bhabha notes, "in the elusive assignation of myself with a one-self," which inevitably causes "the elision of person and place" (xxxi). Celâl echoes this point very closely: "Turks no longer wanted to be Turks, they wanted to be something else altogether. This was why they'd gone along with the 'dress revolution,' shaved their beards, reformed their language and their alphabet" (Pamuk 61).[6] This process of self-evacuation and the extraction ("elision") of the subject's consciousness from "person and place" (Bhabha xxxi), lends itself to a psychoanalytical reading. It is in fact reminiscent of the symptomatology of the depersonalization or derealization disorder, which Sedeño et al. describe as a "syndrome characterized by a disruption of bodily self-awareness" (14) and by a "sense of detachment and disconnection from the body" (1); in other words, "an experience of feeling estranged or alienated from the surroundings" (1). The desire to reject one's corporeal schema to assimilate to the white, Eurocentric models introduced by the ideologues of the country's Westernization conjoins depersonalization within a critique of European interference.

According to Fanon, the process of "whitening" – which I deem comparable to Turkey's Westernization as the model is, in both cases, Eurocentric – throws the subject in a neurotic condition and puts his/her psychological well-being in danger of disintegration. For this reason, Fanon speaks of "hallucinatory whitening" (74), namely, the person of color's obsessive desire to "*turn white or disappear*"; a desire so pervasive – Fanon explains – to put their "psychic structure [...] in danger of disintegration" (75; emphasis in the original). The *Oxford English Dictionary* defines hallucination firstly as "the mental condition of being deceived or mistaken, or of entertaining unfounded notions [...], an idea or belief to which nothing real corresponds" and, secondly, as "the apparent perception (usually by sight or hearing) of an external object when no such object is actually present." Spiegel and Cardeña list hallucinatory phenomena as part of dissociative symptomatology (see 367), which allows them to be integrated in the discussion of Pamuk's poetics of neurosis.

The Black Book includes a compelling example of hallucinatory whitening in conjunction with what appears as multiple personality disorder: in chapter fifteen ("Love Stories on a Snowy Evening"), an old journalist who believes he is Proust embodies the process of cultural whitening with particular emphasis on its neurotic quality. He reminisces about the plot of Proust's masterpiece *À la Re-*

6 Here, Celâl implies that a general cultural hollowness in the aftermath of the fall of the Ottoman Empire has laid the basis for a cultural revolution that drove the Turks towards Euro-conformity. Nevertheless, the adoption of Western aesthetics exacerbates the process of "evacuation and emptying of the I" (Bhabha xxxii).

cherche du Temps Perdu as if it were part of his own memories, "until his face stream[s] with tears of pain and joy" (372), and he imagines the characters of the novels to be physically present in his apartment: "He'd turn to his imaginary maid and say, 'No, Françoise,' – loud enough for his tabby cat to hear him – 'Albertine did not forget to take this ring with her, and there is no point in sending it on, as she's going to be coming back to this house very soon'" (372). In light of these two quotations, however, the Proustian journalist's behavior is best explained through the lens of the multiple personality disorder. Among the criteria for a diagnosis of this affliction, in fact, Spiegel and Cardeña list "the existence within the person of two or more distinct personalities" and "an inability to recall important personal information that is too extensive to be explained by ordinary forgetfulness" (372). Moreover, the journalist's alter ego, Proust, and the characters he hallucinates are French: the Europeanization that the journalist neurotically pursues is reminiscent of Fanon's "whitening," as both Fanon's subjects and Pamuk's journalist desire to emulate European culture, ways, even skin color (see Sardar xiii).

The old journalist's neurotic identification with the characters of *À la Recherche du Temps Perdu* or with Proust himself corresponds to an emptying of the I, which is then filled by Proustian fiction. The figure of the journalist is reminiscent of Fanon's black subject as s/he makes contact with the white society of the metropolis: "if his psychic structure is weak, one observes a collapse of the ego [...]. The goal of his behavior will be The Other (in the guise of the white man), for The Other alone can give him worth" (Fanon 119). Emptied of his everyday-life Turkish Self, Pamuk's journalist relies heavily on his Proustian alter-egos for self-esteem and self-legitimization: "whenever something upset him, whenever he had to deal with rudeness or cruelty from coarse, insensitive, greedy, uncultured philistines, he'd console himself by thinking, 'Who cares? I'm not really here anyway, I'm at home, in my bed, reading of Albertine asleep in the next room'" (Pamuk 371).

Not only does the journalist supplant his personal experience and memories with those of the characters of a European novel, he wishes they would take over the entire country. Pamuk's journalist feels nauseated by his compatriots who display the corporeal and behavioral markers he has evacuated from his Self.

> It was because no one here knew who Albertine was, or even knew who Proust was, that this country was in such a wretched state [...] but one day, if this country ever produced people capable of understanding Albertine and Proust, yes, maybe then these poor mustachioed men he saw roaming the streets would begin to enjoy a better life; [...] it was because they didn't read Proust [...] that they were so evil and thickheaded. (373)

In doing so, the journalist also demonstrates an incapability of feeling empathy and a fundamental estrangement from the world surrounding him, both of which are markers of a dissociated personality (see Sedeño et al. 1). Incidentally, his complete identification with Western narratives make him an instrument of government propaganda: he promotes the agenda of the Kemalist Westernization process, its "over-obsession" (Taspinar 14) with a Western trajectory, and its aspiration to change "the whole fabric of Turkish society" (Kili 385) by encouraging the population to consume (and, in this case, be consumed by) Western cultural products.

In both Fanon and Pamuk, corporeal and cultural whitening – understood as the overpowering desire to become the white Other – brings about the collapse and emptying of the individual's self. Pamuk explicitly depicts what Fanon calls "hallucinatory whitening" as pandemic in Turkish society from the 1920s until the time of the narration. The Turks, Celâl explains, "were discarding their old ways, [...] each and every thing they did was an imitation," which caused a collective "loss of innocence" (63).

CINEMA AND DEPERSONALIZATION

Bedii Usta's son notices a widespread change not only in his compatriots' fashion inclinations but also in their way of moving. The Istanbulites gradually replace "their stock of everyday little gestures" with "fake, new, ultimately meaningless ways of moving" (63). Initially the two struggle to identify "whom these people were imitating, whom they had as their models for change," until Bedii Usta's son cries out: "It's because of those damn films!" (63).

The Proustian journalist is not the only character in *The Black Book* who longs for dissolution within the forms and contents of Western imagination. The novel includes the story of a waiter who takes on a job as an extra in a film production.[7] When for the first time he watches the film in which he starred, the man does not recognize his body as his own – "his back, shoulders, and neck were not, in fact, his own" (365). Even his voice felt as if "it belonged to some-

7 Even if the film is a Turkish production starring Türkan Şoray, characters in the novel generally refer to the cinematic form as a Western import. In the passage mentioned previously, for example, films are "dreams imported from abroad" (223); in "Bedii Usta's Children," Celâl writes that films were "brought in from the West canister by canister" (63).

one else" (365). When describing a patient affected by depersonalization, Sedeño et al. note that the subject reported "anomalous body experiences. Additionally, his voice sounded distant and unfamiliar to him and the experiential component of agency was lacking" (2). Spiegel and Cardeña explain that the so-called depersonalization or derealization disorder includes a variety of phenomena including "a mild sense of detachment from one's experience to drastic alterations of mind-body perception, such as out-of-body experiences" (373). The way the two authors further define depersonalization is particularly suited to the "dreamlike" (Pamuk 366) cinematic experience of the film extra, as the subject of depersonalization feels s/he is "an *outside observer* of [his/her] body or as if in a dream" (Spiegel and Cardeña 373; emphasis added). The waiter welcomes the experience with "a most delicious fright" (Pamuk 366) and with the hope that his alter-ego on the screen may grant him to "embark in a new life" (366). Like the Proust aficionado, who read and re-read *À la Recherche du Temps Perdu* "for the rest of his life," and "reaching the end of the book, [...] went straight to the beginning to read through to the end again" (370), the waiter spends many years "in the vain hope that he may catch another glimpse of himself" (366). *The Black Book* does not clarify what exactly happens when the waiter sees himself on the screen: is the waiter the man in the film? Has his appearance been modified through "trick photography" (366)? Yet, the experience of seeing himself projected into a medium that is connected, as the cinematographic art is, to the West and the U.S., of being cast into a different universe of values, is a thrilling experience. So much so that he will devote the rest of his life to the hallucinated search of his cinematic double – a completely delusive and yet flattering version of himself.

In *The Black Book*, Western literary classics notwithstanding, cinema has a more relevant function in the process of Westernization. Edibe Sözen suggests that "American cinema has been allowed to dominate the [Turkish] market" (Sözen in Raw 81) and *The Black Book* seems to voice this concern. "Yes it was because of those damn films – brought in from the West canister by canister," Celâl explains, echoing Bedii Usta's son, "that the gestures of our people used in the streets began to lose their innocence" (63). Western movies and their impact on Turkish culture are discussed again in chapter eleven, evocatively titled "We Lost our Memories at the Movies." Here, films are presented as the primary means of erasure of Turkish cultural memory and (a debatable notion of) precolonial authenticity. Movie music is addressed as part of "the new plan [...] to erode [Turkish] collective memory" (127) and movie theaters are represented as dystopian spaces where Turks are metaphorically "blinded by the proliferation of new images" (127) or robbed of their knowledge. The book especially mentions "a peasant boy from Malatya who'd fallen into the habit of going to the movies once a week, and who realized, on the way home, that he'd lost his memory, along with everything he'd ever learned" (127).

Pamuk stresses the role of cinema in bringing to the surface neurotic behaviors produced by the imposition of Western cultural forms in a non-Western context. The irreconcilability of the local's self-perception and cultural memory with the imposed European schemata, fantasies, and worldview produces, in the local's consciousness, phenomena that recall "an ambiguity that is extraordinarily neurotic" and the perception of "living in an error" that Fanon discusses in *Black Skin, White Masks* (148). *The Black Book* showcases how this "error" – a flawed mimetic process oriented towards the repression and stigmatization of the colonial subject's corporeal schema – is encouraged by Westernization and colonial projects worldwide. Like the Proust fanatic, the film extra also unwittingly acts as a facilitator for the Westernization of the country: "as for those who identified with the stars they saw on the screen – our new masters refused to see them as 'sick' or '*in the wrong*,' enlisting them instead as partners in the project" (128; emphasis added). Although the novel remains ambivalent with regards to the identity of these "new masters," it is legitimate to consider this a reference to Western interference in Turkey. In the logic of the text, by willingly replacing their own personalities with those of "stars they saw on the screen" or European literary figures, Turks would become the "new people" (126) these new imperial masters aspire to produce.

In *The Black Book* the uncritical absorption and reproduction of Hollywood beauty paradigms causes alienation on multiple levels: in other words, the characters become unreadable to each other. When Galip meets Belkıs, a long-lost female acquaintance, he resorts to cinematic references to describe her appearance: "She had combed her hair back in the style of Ava Gardner in *55 Days at Peking* and painted her lips with the same Supertechnirama Red" (444). Most importantly, the cinematic details Galip notices in Belkıs's appearance confuse him, as he is unable to 'read' his friend: "it seemed as if she was wearing a mask. If he took that mask by its Supertechnirama lips and pulled it off, he'd have no trouble reading the face underneath, but he still had no idea what it would mean" (448). The issue on unreadability in *The Black Book* does not merely concern the impossibility to access the 'Turkish face' under Belkıs's 'white mask,' but expands into the realm of language, addressing the rupture between signifier and signified.

To conclude this analysis, it is worth touching upon the issue of estrangement and alienation, which feature as symptoms of dissociative disorders along with lack of empathy: Sedeño and his co-authors, for example, mention a patient who felt he was "walking in a world [he] recognize[d] but [didn't] feel" (1). For Fanon, the emigrants who return from the metropolis to their homeland are highly exposed to the risk of experiencing alienation from their culture of origin due to their thorough assimilation of Western/white cultural paradigms and their capacity to navigate them. Fanon explains that the educated colonial subject "feels at a given stage that his race no longer understands him. Or that he no longer understands it. Then he congratulates himself on this, and enlarging the difference, the incomprehension, the disharmony, he finds in them the meaning of his real humanity" (7). By the same token, the film extra and the Proustian journalist feel abandoned, rejected, or repelled by their fellow citizens who do not demonstrate a comparable (i.e. neurotic) level of absorption in Western culture. The journalist found no one "with whom to share his excitement" for Proust, and, when confronted with the "rudeness or cruelty" of his fellow Istanbulites, would "console himself" (371) by self-contentedly taking shelter in a fictional Proustian universe. The waiter who thought he had caught a glimpse of his real self in a film also lived his delusion in complete isolation, as "none of his friends and relatives seemed too interested in these confusing, spine-tingling, dreamlike substitutions" (366). Both the waiter and the journalist doubtlessly felt that "[their] race no longer underst[ood] them" (Fanon 7). When analyzing the figure of the "returnee" (7), the 'whitened' Antillean who returns home after a long stay in the metropolis, Fanon stresses that the returnee "assumes a critical attitude towards his fellow islanders" (7), which can be said for some of Pamuk's Westernized Istanbulites, including the hypothetical customer who is "not going to want a coat he sees worn by someone who looks like the swarthy, bow-legged, mustachioed countrymen he sees ten thousand times a day" (61).

The Black Book's portrait of Westernized Turkey as ridden with neurosis and of Kemalism as generative of collective amnesia begs the question whether the novel may be read as a site of Ottoman nostalgia. The notion of cultural authenticity and an idealized precolonial unity is in fact ubiquitous in *The Black Book*, as a number of characters (e.g. Bedii Usta and his son, Galip and Celâl) embrace notions of cultural authenticity at some stage. Yet, the novel consistently undermines them: not only does it expose the quasi-colonial neurosis produced by Kemalism but also dismisses the return to the Ottoman past as a fantasy. An indication of the novel's ultimate skepticism about cultural authenticity rests in the fact that formulations such as "the special thing that makes us who we are" (62), "loss of innocence" (63), or "the thing [...] that came 'from us'" (63), often appear in inverted commas or reflect the personal views of a specific character such as, for example, Bedii Usta's son, whose frenzied manners invite questioning.

But perhaps the most illustrative example is to be found in "The Mystery of the Letters and the Loss of Mystery," where Galip chances upon a seventeenth-century poem about a mystical past of cultural wholeness and an idyllic village where an undisturbed harmony existed among speakers, signifiers, and signified.

> In the poem's distant Golden Age, action and meaning were one and the same. Heaven was on earth, and the things we kept in our houses were one with our dreams. Those were the happy, happy days when everything we held in our hands – our tools, our cups, our daggers, our pens – was but an extension of our souls. A poet would say tree and everyone who heard him would conjure the same perfect tree [...]. For words were so close to the things they described that [...] poetry mixed with life and words with the objects they signified. (626-627)

The smooth continuity in the Golden Age described in the passage above seems antithetical to the unreadability of faces and objects in twentieth-century Turkey, and to the amnesia affecting citizens as well as objects, making them oblivious of their identity and function. This mythical past is reminiscent of the words of Stuart Hall, who points out that identity in postcolonial or diasporic contexts may be regarded either as a layered compound of native and imported features, or, alternatively, "as a sort of collective 'one true self,' hiding inside the many other, more superficial or artificially imposed 'selves' [...]. This 'oneness,' underlying all the other, more superficial differences, is the truth, the essence" (223). But the exaggerations and hyperboles that punctuate Pamuk's passage – "heaven was on earth," "those [...] happy, happy days," "everyone," "the same perfect tree," and later, "those happy, distant, timeless days" (627) – suggest that this projection of a wholesome Ottoman past is located outside history, in the realm of folklore and the imagination.

A Poetics of Dissociation

Interconnections between literature and dissociative disorders are hardly coincidental. First of all, the latter possess an exquisitely literary nature, as they "raise fundamental questions about the nature of self and identity and the role of consciousness and autobiographical memory in the continuity of personality" (Kihlstrom et al. 117). Secondly, John F. Kihlstrom, Martha Glisky, and Michael Angiulo identify two conditions that, among others, may favor the development of dissociative disorders: these are "fantasy proneness" and "absorption" (117). To the authors, a fantasy-prone personality is characterized by a "deep, profound, and long-lasting involvement in fantasy and imagination" and "live much of the time in a world of their own making," in which they are likely to be fully absorbed, ultimately letting it transform and restructure their "phenomenal self and world" (120). As Rita Felski suggests in *Uses of Literature*, similar practices appear to be involved in the very act of engaging with a cultural text, as reading is about "intoxication rather than detachment, rapture rather than disinterestedness," it is "a yielding that is not abject or humiliating, but ecstatic and erotically charged" (51). The idea of "fantasy-prone" personalities as a breeding ground for dissociation due to their proclivity to permanently dwell on "reminiscences, images, and imaginings" (Felski 51) explains how the domains of literature and neurosis may seem adjacent or overlapping.

It also comes as no surprise that dissociative disorders appear compatible with the articulation of an imperialist critique in Turkey. When shifted from the level of the individual to the level of the collectivity, categories such as "autobiographical memory" and "the continuity of personality" (Kihlstrom et al. 117) lead to vaster questions about collective memory and historical continuity that were central to Turkish culture in the passage from empire to republic and have catalyzed the interest of much Turkish literature in the twentieth century and beyond. In *The Black Book*, the dissociated psyche of the individual becomes a synecdoche for a dissociated culture. Most importantly, dissociative disorders lend themselves to metaphorical usage within a critique of imperialism. Amnesia, multiple personalities, and depersonalization disrupt an individual's identity, memory, and sense of self – the very three categories colonial domination seeks to undo. The productive intersection of literature, dissociation, and Turkish history in *The Black Book* suggests that the novel articulates meaning through a poetics of neurosis. The novel employs the vocabulary of neurosis to imagine, in a strictly fictional universe that demands to offer neither historical nor medical lessons, the effects of Westernization on Turkey's collective self.

LIST OF WORKS CITED

"Amnesia." *The Merriam Webster Dictionary*, www.merriam-webster.com/dictionary/amnesia. Accessed 18 June 2017.

"Amnesia." *OED Online.* Oxford University Press, June 2017, www.oed.com/view/Entry/6483?redirectedFrom=amnesia#eid. Accessed 18 June 2017.

Arango, Tim. "Turkey's Suspicious Mind-Set Has Been a Century in the Making." *The New York Times*, 12 September 2016. www.nytimes.com/2016/09/13/world/what-in-the-world/turkey-conspiracies-sevres-syndrome.html. Accessed 18 June 2017.

Bhabha, Homi. "Foreword to the 1986 Edition." *Black Skin, White Masks*. Frantz Fanon. 1952. Pluto, 2008. Xxi-xxxvii.

Buchenau, Barbara and Virginia Richter, editors. *Post-empire Imaginaries? Anglophone Literature, History, and the Demise of Empires*. Brill, 2015.

Çandar, Cengiz. "Atatürk's Ambiguous Legacy." *The Wilson Quarterly*, vol. 24, no. 4, Fall 2000, pp. 88-96.

Fanon, Frantz. *Black Skin, White Masks*. Translated by Charles Lam Markmann. 1952. Pluto, 2008.

Felski, Rita. *Uses of Literature*. Blackwell, 2008.

Göknar, Erdağ. "Orhan Pamuk and the 'Ottoman' Theme." *World Literature Today*, vol. 80, no. 6, 2006, pp. 34-38.

Hall, Stuart. "Cultural Identity and Diaspora." *Identity, Community, Culture, Difference*, edited by John Rutherford, Lawrence and Wishart, 1990, pp. 222-37.

"Hallucination." *OED Online.* Oxford University Press, June 2017, www.oed.com/view/Entry/83613?redirectedFrom=hallucination#eid. Accessed 18 June 2017.

Kihlstrom, John F., Martha L. Glisky, and Michael J. Angiulo. "Dissociative Tendencies and Dissociative Disorders." *Journal of Abnormal Psychology*, vol. 103, no. 1, 1994, pp. 117-124.

Kili, Suna. "Kemalism in Contemporary Turkey." *International Political Science Review*, vol. 1, no. 3, 1980, pp. 381-404.

Konuk, Kader. *East West Mimesis: Auerbach in Turkey*. Stanford University Press, 2010.

Landry, Donna. "The Ottoman Imaginary of Evliya Çelebi: From Postcolonial to Postimperial Rifts in Time." *Post-Empire Imaginaries? Anglophone Literature, History, and the Demise of Empires*, edited by Barbara Buchenau and Virginia Richter with Mareijke Denger, Brill, 2015, pp. 127-158.

Mills, Amy. "Narratives in City Landscapes: Cultural Identity in Istanbul." *Geographical Review*, vol. 95, no. 3, July 2005, pp. 441-462.

Pamuk, Orhan. *The Black Book*. Translated by Maureen Freely. 1990. Faber and Faber, 2011.

Raw, Laurence. "Communicating America, Validating Turkey." *Journal of American Studies of Turkey*, vol. 10, 1999, pp. 81-89.

Sakr, Rita. *Monumental Space in the Post-imperial Novel: An Interdisciplinary Study*. Bloomsbury, 2011.

Sedeño, Lucas, et al. "How Do You Feel when You Can't Feel Your Body." *PLoS*, vol. 9, no. 6, 2014. www.ncbi.nlm.nih.gov/pmc/articles/PMC4072534. Accessed 18 June 2017.

Shafak, Elif. "Memory-Less Turkey/Amnesiac Turkey." *Turkish Daily News*, May 2006, www.elifsafak.us/yazilar.asp?islem=yazi&id=392. Accessed 18 June 2017.

Shimamura, Arthur P., and Larry R. Squire. "A Neuropsychological Study of Fact Memory and Source Amnesia." *Journal of Experimental Psychology: Learning, Memory, and Cognition*, vol. 13, no. 3, 1987, pp. 464-473.

Spiegel, David, and Etzel Cardeña. "Disintegrated Experience: The Dissociative Disorders Revisited." *Journal of Abnormal Psychology*, vol. 100, no. 3, 1991, pp. 366-378.

Squire, Larry R., and Stuart M. Zola. "Episodic Memory, Semantic Memory, and Amnesia." *Hippocampus*, vol. 8, no. 3, 1998, pp. 205-211.

Taspinar, Omer. "Turkey's Middle East Policies: Between Neo-Ottomanism and Kemalism." *Carnegie Endowment for International Peace*, vol. 10, 2008, pp. 1-29, carnegieendowment.org/files/cmec10_taspinar_final.pdf. Accessed 18 June 2017.

Wachtel, Eleanor. *The Best of Writers and Company: Interviews with Fifteen of the World's Greatest Authors*. Biblioasis, 2016.

Wright, Neil. "The Underworld of the Lost Turkmen in Orhan Pamuk's *The Black Book*." *Journal of Kentucky Studies*, vol. 30, 2013, pp. 148-154.

Yanık, Lerna K. "Constructing Turkish 'Exceptionalism': Discourses of Liminality and Hybridity in Post-Cold War Turkish Foreign Policy." *Political Geography*, vol. 30, no. 2, 2011, pp. 80-89.

Reading Rap with Fanon and Fanon with Rap

The Potential of Transcultural Recognition

JARULA M.I. WEGNER

Already in the early twentieth century, Frantz Fanon advanced the decolonisation of psychiatric praxis (see Vergès and Razanajao et al) and his writings have been receiving renewed and intensifying attention in recent years. Evidence of an increasing engagement can be found in, for instance, the re-publication of his best-known texts *Black Skin, White Masks* (2008 and 2017) and *The Wretched of the Earth* (2004) in new translations and with new introductions,[1] while publications considering his life, writings and ideas have contributed to a body of Fanonian thought. Homi Bhabha (1993; 2004), Paul Gilroy (2000; 2005; 2010) and Achille Mbembe (2011; 2013), to mention only a few, have contributed decisively to this reconstruction, elaboration and dissemination of Fanon's ideas.[2] In his W.E.B. Du Bois lectures, Gilroy gives an explanation for the renewed interest. He argues that Fanon's "insights reveal him, perhaps unexpectedly, to be our contemporary. Whatever resonance his writing may have had in the past, it speaks powerfully to the political circumstances of this era" (*Darker than Blue* 155). Gilroy specifically highlights Fanon's relevance in relation to the USA in the twenty-first century. Russell A. Potter, for instance, discusses Fanon in relation to rap music's response to detrimental urban environments in the USA. In

---

1 In the French language, Achille Mbembe edited and prefaced Fanon's newly released *Œuvres* in 2011. In 2013, after the book was out of print for several decades, the publishing house Turia + Kant reissued the German edition of *Black Skin, White Masks*.

2 The body of texts on Fanonian thought is vast, widespread and continues to grow. As it is impossible to do justice to this thriving field by mentioning all of these here, I only refer to scholars of Fanonian thought that are quoted in the present essay.

this context, Potter argues that "Fanon's revolutionary program has taken on a sudden new relevance" (87).

At the same time Gilroy argues in reference to rap music that "[t]he countercultural voice of black Atlantic popular music has faded out" (*Darker than Blue* 121 and 124; see also *Against Race* 179-182). More specifically, he analyses popular music's critical potential in "[m]aking the past audible in the present" (*Darker than Blue* 127) and laments that this kind of "historic system now also appears to be in retreat" (127). Gilroy's argument contradicts earlier critics who highlight rap music's remarkable quality as a medium of (music-) historical citation. Potter, for instance, highlights "[h]ip-hop's continual citation of the sonic and verbal archives" (26).[3] Rap music thus establishes and enables a continued, complex sonic engagement with the past.

The relation to the past is an important yet conflicted aspect in Frantz Fanon's reflections on one of the central concerns of his writings, colonial neurosis. In *Black Skin, White Masks*, Fanon writes that "there is a determined *Erlebnis*[4] at the origin of every neurosis" (123). The *Erlebnis* he refers to is colonization. In *The Wretched of the Earth*, he explains that "[t]he colonized world is a world divided in two" (3). This world produces alienated Blacks on the one side and alienated Whites on the other (see Fanon, *Black Skin, White Masks* 12) so that both exist "along neurotic lines" (42). In the opening of *Black Skin, White Masks*, Fanon argues that "the juxtaposition of the black and white races has resulted in a massive psycho-existential complex. By analysing it we aim to destroy it" (xvi). As the reference to "complex" indicates and the subsequent psychoanalytical analyses demonstrate, he seeks explanation for the pathological state in past events. Searching for a possible remedy to this state, he nonetheless writes: "Whether you like it or not, the past can in no way be my guide in the actual

---

3 Potter furthermore explains that "rap DJs have continued their raids not only on African-American musical traditions, but on every form of discourse, ranging from newscasts, talk-shows, movie dialogue, sound effects, television themes and answering messages" (42). See also Richard Shusterman (passim esp. 623), Tricia Rose (*Black Noise* 79) and Cheryl Keyes (25 and 147).

4 Early twentieth-century German philosophy saw an extensive debate over the distinction between *Erlebnis* and *Erfahrung*. This discussion involved, among others, Wilhelm Dilthey, Walter Benjamin and Hans-Georg Gadamer. Fanon describes colonization as an *Erlebnis* instead of an *Erfahrung*, because the traumatising events do not add up to an understanding but rather dismember experience and fracture everyday life. The problem with transferring *Erlebnis* and *Erfahrung* into English is that both translate as 'experience' and thus blur the distinction.

state of things" (200). He demands to stop being "a slave to the past" as "the real *leap* consists of introducing invention into life" (200, 204, emphasis in the original). According to Fanon therefore the solution is not remembering but inventing. With this claim he runs into an apparent paradox as he demands to focus solely on the future, while the treatment of neuroses, as with psychiatric praxis in general, is grounded in the past (see Kruks 132).

On a general level, this essay highlights the actuality of Fanon and the political relevance of rap music by pointing out a possible dialogue between Fanon's reflections on colonial neurosis and discussions in contemporary rap lyrics. More specifically, it seeks to solve the apparent contradiction – between focusing on the past and leaping into the future – by reading Fanon in conjunction with the rap song "Street Corner" released in 2006 by Masta Killa featuring Inspectah Deck and the GZA. Firstly, I will argue that the genre of reality rap is particularly revealing in reference to what Fanon calls colonial neurosis. Secondly, rap music will be shown to potentially point beyond a state of neurosis: analysing Masta Killa's "Street Corner," I will exemplarily demonstrate how this process functions in form and in content. The discussion will show that in twenty-first-century rap music colonial neurosis in the Fanonian tradition continues to play an important role as both relate to the past and demand recognition in the present.

REPRESENTING A STATE OF NEUROSIS THROUGH RAP MUSIC

One fundamental argument Fanon introduces in *Black Skin, White Masks* is the conjunction of the psychic with the social environment in the constitution of the subject. As Fanon puts it: "Alongside phylogeny and ontogeny, there is also sociogeny" (xv). This means that additionally to the evolutionary development of humans and the development of an individual subject, the social environment needs to be considered in order to understand pathological formations. The consequence is crucial as it historicizes theories and methods of psychoanalysis (see Lebeau 120): Pathologies have to be understood in their time and place, in their social and political environment. When Fanon analyses the source of colonial neurosis, therefore, he turns to its social and spatial organization. He writes: "The colonial world is a compartmentalized world" (*The Wretched* 3). If for Fanon the notion of colonial neurosis is related to geographical separation and social segregation and if (a certain genre of) rap music is able to represent such structures, it can be hypothesized that such a genre harbours the potential to present a state of colonial neurosis.

To begin with, rap music emerged in a time and place of increased segregation. In *Black Noise* (1994), Tricia Rose describes the emergence of rap music as one aspect of the hip hop movement in the 1970s and '80s in New York City. In this period, New York and other urban centres across the USA transformed into post-industrial spaces. Summarising the living conditions, Rose writes that "[s]ince this period, low-income housing has continued to disappear and blacks and Hispanics are still much more likely to live in overcrowded, dilapidated, and seriously undermaintained spaces" (28). In these areas, economic, political and social factors "exacerbated the already widening gap between classes and races" (27). Furthermore, "[e]ven though urban America has always been socially and economically divided," Rose argues, "these divisions have taken on a new dimension" (28).

Aggravated segregation created the "shantytown" (Potter 86), or ghetto, as a specifically circumscribed space, which is shunned by those outside and stigmatises those inside.[5] It is important to recognise that outside forces crucially produced detrimental conditions inside the ghetto: white flight to the suburbs, municipal financial cutbacks and reduction of social services.[6] The ghetto is excluded from the surrounding environment, yet simultaneously governed by it. In this way, the ghetto exemplifies what Giorgio Agamben calls the camp. He writes that "*[t]he camp is the space that is opened when the state of exception begins to become the rule*" (168-169, emphasis in the original). He argues that the spatial arrangement of the camp derives from the temporal state of exception. In this state of exception, a hegemonic power decides to exclude a population from the rule of law and, nevertheless, rules it, that is dominates it, outside the law. According to Agamben, a population thus specified becomes *homo sacer*, or bare life, which can be killed but cannot be mourned; it is left to die without compassion. In "Necropolitics," Achille Mbembe agrees with Agamben yet adds that the

5 This social and cultural segregation nonetheless also attracts outsiders to venture inside, just as insiders travel outside. The history of rap music contributes significant evidences of these dynamics (see Chang, *Can't Stop, Won't Stop* 145).

6 Douglas S. Massey and Nancy A. Denton argue that these developments did not take place unintentionally and anonymously through abstract market forces, but were deliberately created through federal policy (see 2). Michelle Alexander goes a step further in arguing that ghetto citizens are also kept from positively transforming the ghettos by being "trapped in a closed circuit of perpetual marginality, circulating between ghetto and prison" (196).

colony and the apartheid regime constitute a "concentration of biopower, the state of exception, and the state of siege" (22). This leads Mbembe to understand "the efficacy of the colony as a formation of terror" (23). Mbembe calls this colonial strategy necropolitics. Potter highlights parallels between the colony and the ghetto:

> Just as in any colonial city, urban African-Americans have found themselves in a virtual shantytown, only this time near the center rather than on the periphery of the postmodern city. Again, just as in colonized nations, black Americans have been subject to aerial flybys, frequent and arbitrary police raids, lengthy imprisonments, and at times of open revolt (such as the Los Angeles rebellion) occupying troops. In this context, Fanon's revolutionary program has taken on a sudden new relevance. (86-87)

Rap music emerged in this environment and struggle. Comparable social relations and material conditions in the colonial world and the post-industrial ghetto – as both emerge as geographically separate, socially segregated and racially hierarchical spaces – may produce comparable pathologies.

Fanon autobiographically explores the aetiology of what he calls colonial neurosis. In his two main texts, *Black Skin, White Masks* and *The Wretched of the Earth*, Fanon describes a process of objectification leading to a mental state of alienation. He recalls an encounter with a small boy who exclaims to his mother: "Look! A Negro!" (*Black Skin, White Masks* 91). Fanon describes his immediate response: "Disoriented, incapable of confronting the Other, the white man, who had no scruples about imprisoning me, I transported myself on that particular day far, very far, from my self, and gave myself up as an object" (92). This *Erlebnis* enforces the dissociation of "himself," separating "him" from "self" to alienate the mind from the body, turning what was his self into an Other. "The result," writes Ronald A. T. Judy, "is the dissolution of the ego, the split, or double consciousness of the *nègre*" (68, emphasis in the original; see also Lebeau 115). The documentation and discussion suggests that this *Erlebnis* continues to influence Fanon's thoughts, experiences and actions. Fanon is haunted by the memory of the White man as another Other.[7] This recollection

7 While colonised and coloniser may be affected differently, the process of othering also imprisons the boy; the coloniser is haunted (see Bhabha, "Remembering Fanon" 120). Following Fanon's reflections on the Manichean structure suggests that the split Judy mentions repeats itself in varying ways and degrees: in Fanon, between Fanon and the small boy, in the small boy and possibly beyond. One may wonder how the event affected future actions of Fanon, the child or the child's mother, possibly by im-

indicates why Fanon defines colonisation as an *Erlebnis* and not an *Erfahrung*. Severed *Erlebnisse* fail to create *Erfahrung*; a succession of events that do not add up to (constructively informing) experience. Against his gesture of relinquishing the past, in this case Fanon recalls the past to understand his present condition. This potential of remembering the past to transform the present also constitutes a central feature of some rap songs.

The musicologist Adam Krims identifies what he labels "reality rap" as a sub-genre of rap music which is concerned with "an epistemological/ontological project to map the realities of (usually black) inner-city life" (70; see also Keyes 90). Krims' definition focuses on concrete living environments and their philosophical implications. The preceding discussion of Fanon, Agamben and Mbembe highlights that concrete environments give expression to more abstract economic, political and social factors. Krims' definition can thus be revised in the sense that reality rap not necessarily describes inner-city life or the ghetto, but more generally processes of stigmatization, objectification and alienation.[8] Instances of this genre can be found in record releases as early as 1979 (only one year after the first rap record's release) in Brother D with Collective Effort's "How We Gonna Make the Black Nation Rise?", Grandmaster Flash's critically acclaimed "The Message" in 1982 and Wu-Tang Clan's "C.R.E.A.M." in 1993. While reality rap is economically speaking not the most successful rap genre, it bears the potential of revealing and transcending processes causing colonial neurosis.[9]

TOWARD TRANSCENDING COLONIAL NEUROSIS

To understand how pathologising circumstances can be transcended, it is helpful to analyse their aetiology. According to Fanon, traces of neurosis can be found in the compartmentalization of "[t]he colonial world" which, he writes, "is a Mani-

aging and creating further 'Others.' (For a useful and critical discussion of the Other, see Young 36-39.)

8 If rap music presents a state of colonial neurosis, this does not necessarily mean that this state is mimetically reproducing a rapper's experience, but rather that the rap song's features enable the audience to reflect on the emergence, present and possible future of colonial neurosis.

9 The following discussion focuses on the genre of reality rap. It goes without saying that the long history and diverse genres of rap music produced many more varieties than the specific project of reality rap.

chaean world" (*The Wretched* 6). The sectors of the coloniser on the one hand and the colonised on the other "follow the dictates of mutual exclusion" (4). Fanon claims that "[b]y penetrating its geographical configuration and classification we shall be able to delineate the backbone on which the *decolonized* society is reorganized" (3, emphasis added). He not only regards the social and geographical structure as fundamental to the colonial world, but also anticipates that unsettling this order challenges the colonial structure. At the same time, Fanon claims that "[w]e cannot go resolutely forward unless we first realize our alienation" (163). His strategy of decolonisation thus combines an analysis of objective circumstances and subjective experiences. Consequently, segregation of the colonial world can be analysed in relation to environments and subjects. Put into relation, alienation on the individual level can be understood as objectification on the social level. To end individual alienation, objectification on the social level has to be overcome (and vice versa). Transcending social and geographical borders sonically, that is, through sound such as rap music, may enable identification and alliances across borders.

The emergence of rap music in the late 1970s and early 1980s caused considerable irritations. Rap was (and still is) scandalised for displaying racism, violence, misogyny, homophobia, anti-Semitism etc.[10] In response to public outcry, the 'parental advisory' notification was introduced in 1985 and henceforth displayed on CD covers, on posters and in video clips. Adam Bradley and Andrew DuBois point out that ironically "this renegade attitude contributed to rap's commercial success" (xxxviii). In other words, the irritations furthered circulation, which in turn increased irritations and so on. In 1989, against the backdrop of these scandalising indictments, Nelson George argues that the controversial content simply displays rap music's "ultra-urban, unromantic, hyperrealistic, neo-nationalist, antiassimilationist, aggressive Afrocentric impulse" (40). According to George, rap music does not paper over social cracks but rather airs them in public. While averse discourse uses rap music as a scapegoat, blaming it for instigating moral and legal transgressions, sympathisers of rap music, like George and Rose (*Black Noise* and *Hip Hop Wars*), argue that it enables the fundamentally necessary representation of critical issues.[11] Public discourse evi-

---

10 See, for instance, concerning racism (Chang "Race, Class, Conflict and Empowerment"), violence (Rose, *Black Noise* 1), misogyny (150), homophobia (151), anti-Semitism (Chang, *Can't Stop* 284).

11 Tricia Rose furthermore argues that accusations against rap music take place in an "uneven and sometimes racist way in which sexist [and other] offences are prosecuted, stigmatized, and reported" (*Black Noise* 150). Most importantly, specific instances

dences that not only moral and legal but also geographical boundaries are being crossed. Irrespective of positive or negative judgements, the ongoing political, juridical and cultural negotiations of rap music highlight that rap music has transcended and continues to transcend political, social and cultural borders.[12]

Rap music's transgressive potential has historically been a significant feature. Reality rap is often created in communities that are abandoned by national and municipal policy and is employed by community members as well as spokespersons to address national and even international audiences (see Keyes 157-185, see Chang *Can't Stop* 224-229). This publicity enables discussion as well as critique of segregation, discrimination and so forth. Rose argues that rap music coincidentally "produced internal and external dialogues that affirmed the experiences and identities of the participants and at the same time offered critiques of larger society that were directed to both the hip hop community and society in general" (*Black Noise* 60). Alongside engagements within the community and majority culture, other marginalised communities are also addressed for potential transcultural alliances. As rap music "invites identification across forbidden lines," Potter ascribes to it a "liberatory potential" (10). Rap music's commercial success surpasses geographical, ethnic, or cultural settings. Its success thrives on its transcultural dissemination and communication as it functions as a globally circulating medium enabling dialogue, identification and alliances.[13] In a parallel manner, Mbembe elaborates Fanon and argues that even if decolonisation "mobilized local actors in a circumscribed country or a national territory, each time they forged from the beginning a solidarity on a planetary and transnational scale" (*Critique* 248).[14] In the process of rap music's creation, dissemination and reception, connections are made possible with other marginalised

---

of offensive lyrics cannot account for the whole genre of music (see 150). Therefore, it is necessary to analyse performances of rap music individually and evaluate them accordingly. This necessity, furthermore, exists in both ways, for the accusations as well as the vindications by George and Rose. For the present case of Masta Killa's "Street Corner," see also footnote 27.

12 See, for instance, Sujatha Fernandes's recollection of feeling addressed by Grandmaster Flash and the Furious Five's "The Message" in a working-class beachside neighbourhood of Sydney, Australia (xi).

13 See, for instance, also Fernandes as well as Porfilio and Viola.

14 Translation by the author. In the original Mbembe writes: "Même lorsqu'elles mobilisaient des acteurs locaux, dans un pays ou sur un territoire national bien circonscrit, elles étaient chaque fois au point de départ de solidarités forgées sur une échelle planétaire et transnationale" (*Critique* 248).

communities as well as with majority communities. These connections bear the potential to destabilise the assumed Manichaean structures identified and criticised by Fanon – of us versus them, for instance, – as they transcend artificially erected boundaries.

Fanon theorises the encounter and engagement of the coloniser and the colonised through G.W.F. Hegel's concept of recognition. On the final pages of *Black Skin, White Masks*, Fanon explains how objectification and consequently alienation can be overcome. The state of "thingness" (170) can only be left behind in the discovery of humanity. He claims: "I am fighting for the birth of a human world, in other words, a world of reciprocal recognition" (193). Fanon suggests that the conflict between coloniser and colonised, between master and slave, can be overcome through reciprocal recognition, as a move beyond othering and the colony's Manichaean structures.[15] It is exactly at this point that ontogenesis and sociogenesis converge. The subject strives for recognition in society, which in turn is constituted by individual subjects. The act of recognition is not only a symbolic process, but it entails individual, legal and social aspects.[16] Importantly, Fanon moves beyond Hegel by extending his reflections to transracial,

15 At the same time, rap music itself inhabits a position of power that possibly functions as a means to marginalise, exclude or oppress (see, for instance, Chang, *Can't Stop Won't Stop* 348-349). While the songs exhibit dialogic encounters in terms of musical, dubbed and lyrical patterns, the commodification of these dialogic instances not only enables, but also stifles the endeavour of reciprocal recognition. It reintroduces reification – the audience pays for its sonic experience while rappers are remunerated for their performances – and money potentially takes centre stage as the means of exchange instead of rap music. The problem, then, is less the communication through money, than that money may become the central thing exchanged; stifling in turn communication. Here it is of course important to differentiate between different forms of musical exchanges, such as record sales, online circulation and live performances.

16 Corresponding to Fanon's argument of subjective and objective conditions, Axel Honneth productively discusses recognition in its individual *and* institutional realisations (see *Reification* 60) and thus invalidates critiques that only focus on the symbolic level (see García Düttmann 32). Furthermore, Fanon's analysis of the *Ereignis* of being recognised through the exclamation "Look! A Negro!" (*Black Skin, White Masks* 91) highlights that recognition is not always necessarily positive (see Foucault 246). This ambiguity necessitates an analysis of what it means to recognise someone's humanity. Unfortunately this task exceeds the scope of the present analysis. For further investigations of the concept of recognition, see, for instance, Honneth (*The Struggle for Recognition*; *Die Idee des Sozialismus*) as well as Fraser and Honneth.

transnational and transcultural engagements.[17] While the medium of rap music may initially enable symbolic recognition, its contents harbour the potential to include more far-reaching implications. Some instances of reality rap perform and demand recognition for rappers, marginalised communities and aggravating social conditions.

DECOLONISING IN FORM AND CONTENT – MASTA KILLA'S "STREET CORNER"

Masta Killa is the ninth member of the Wu-Tang Clan from Staten Island, New York City (see Bradley and DuBois 532-533). The song "Street Corner" also features two of the Wu-Tang Clan's senior artists, Inspectah Deck and GZA the Genius. The following analysis attempts to answer three questions: Firstly, do the lyrics indicate colonial neurosis?[18] Secondly, does the song point toward a possibility to transcend colonial neurosis? Thirdly, does it enable us to reread Fanon?

When Inspectah Deck describes daily life in "Street Corner" as an "every day war," he gestures towards the neurotic conditions of surviving in a metaphorical combat zone.[19] Parallel to Fanon's reflections, the lyrics describe this combat zone through objective circumstances and subjective experiences. The objective circumstances are indicated metaphorically, when Inspectah Deck says: "The 'hoods are prisons inside / the only difference is the doors don't

17 Since Fanon extensively reflects on the conditions, implications, and potentials of a transcultural encounter from the "small boy" (*Black Skin, White Masks* 91) to "humanity" (78 and 204), his writings contradict Henry Louis Gates Jr's important but finally reductive analysis (see Gates 470).

18 A more detailed analysis could also treat the subject of colonial neurosis in reference to musical patterns. Poetic significations of objectification can also be found on this level (see Wegner "Kompetitiv Multidirektionale Erinnerung im Medium der Rap Musik"), yet unfortunately exceed the current analysis.

19 The song's official lyrics have not been published, online lyrics are often faulty and therefore all lyrics were transcribed by the author.
With the names Masta Killa, Inspectah Deck and GZA the rappers employ pseudonyms for their rap performances. It can be assumed that these pseudonyms refer less to their private identities than to these public rap performances. Consequently in this text the pseudonyms are related directly to the artistic personas in their respective lyrics, rather than to their private selves.

slide." The word 'hood' is derived from 'neighbourhood' in African-American Vernacular English (AAVE), where it signifies "one's own neighbourhood" (*Oxford Dictionaries*), often "a poor neighbourhood" (*Cambridge Dictionary Online*), or more explicitly "the ghetto" (*urbandictionary.com*). The fact that the term 'hood' emerged in AAVE in the 1970s furthermore highlights the community, time and place in which such an abode gained relevance. Inspectah Deck highlights a crucial conflict: The poor, dilapidated place he calls his own is created and controlled from the outside. Yet it seems questionable to call a prison one's own if one lives inside of it, while one is dominated, regulated and incarcerated from outside. The "hoods are prisons inside," because there is no possibility to make a satisfactory living or escape the environment due to "the ghetto's invisible walls" (Alexander 124).

Inspectah Deck also explores subjective experiences facilitating colonial neurosis. He indicates the hoods' basic tension when he says that he tried "to stay civilized," signalling good intentions, while he received the obverse from outside, as "my whole life, they told me I was good for nothing." Social setting and individual experience reveal a detrimental and dominant violence. The experience of psychological suffering is indicated by his remark that "I blame the struggle nearly drove me insane." In this psychological struggle, Inspectah Deck finds preliminary relief by building a community of likeminded people: "Thought I lost my head, till my brethren told me the same." The lyrics move beyond individual experience, undermine the idea that the pathology is ontogenetic and suggest that the basic tension is sociogenically founded. Fanon argues that "colonialism has not simply depersonalized the colonized. The very structure of society has been depersonalized on a collective level" (*The Wretched* 219). Due to these circumstances, a community's mutual assistance offers only limited relief. The solution is not permanent as detrimental violence continues to impose itself from outside the community.

The lyrics signify outside force with distancing markers, such as indefinite third-person plural pronouns and the demonstrative pronoun "those." Contrary to the prevalent use of pronouns marking the in-group such as 'I,' 'you,' 'we,' and 'these,' 'they' or 'those' signify an outside. Such markers appear three times throughout the song, once by each rapper. This outside is simultaneously signified and screened off; it makes itself felt in the community, while remaining oblique, detached and removed.[20] The opposite forces are signified, for instance,

20 The last rapper to speak, GZA, particularly underscores this tension. The contrast between an inside and outside territory are further highlighted by television programmes that cross the ghetto borders and thereby make these felt more insistently. Narrating

by the indefinite third-person plural pronoun 'they.'[21] This force remains unfathomable, unrestrained and unpredictable. GZA says: "It's a known fact, they will attack, 'cause it's like that, / and, depending on the kind of impact, the strike back." According to GZA, it is a fact that an attack against the community will happen, that it does happen but when and how is unknown. The ghetto community sees to it that the attack will be encountered, matched and fended off. The only knowns are the occurrence of the event itself and the response to the event as such. The state of permanent insecurity and impending violence creates an immeasurable, indelible psychic and physical challenge reminiscent of the situation of the Black subject who, as Fanon writes, "is constantly tense, on hold, between life and death" (*The Wretched* 219), in a state of colonial neurosis.

"Street Corner" opens with an audio sample that signifies the song's position in music history and suggests a commentary on African-American life in the USA. The opening features sections of Gil Scott-Heron's song "Brother," released in 1970 on *Small Talk at 125th and Lennox*. Scott-Heron was a central figure of the Black Arts Movement, which is regarded as an important trailblazer for rap music in terms of minimisation of musical patterns and lyrical performances "using breath cadences, alliteration, repetition and expletives for emphasis" (Keyes 34). The sample quotes Scott-Heron and, thus, establishes his (music-) historical importance. Scott-Heron's songs, poems and commentaries furthermore express a turning point for African Americans in the USA. Following the assassinations of Malcolm X and Martin Luther King Jr. as well as the waning ties with Jewish intellectuals, the orientation of Black communities shifted recognisably from hope for individual, legal and social recognition to pessimism and Afrocentrism (see Salzman; Greenberg). Gil Scott-Heron was an important

---

life in the hood, he states: "In a broke neighbourhood, where the kids often dream / about a lavish life that is mostly seen on the screen." The children show affection towards and involvement in a way of life they only receive through televised images. Cultural values are transmitted, but their actual fulfilment is not admitted. This screen reproduces the hood's inside as the lived but unseen and the hood's outside as the seen but unlived. It nurtures desires and fears.

21 The opposite forces remain unspecified in the lyrics, while one may speculate that these forces include police violence, racial killings and other oppressive measures and the attack may happen in form of racial profiling, lack of social services etc., both ultimately remain unfathomable. This strategic openness possibly also indicates the circumstance that the opposition is not determined (by race, class, or gender, for instance) apart from individual and social engagement. In other words, certain actions, such as political, social, or economic decisions, define the opposition.

mouthpiece of the movement and the song "Brother" represents a landmark statement in this reorientation. Yet, Scott-Heron's introductory statement is not quoted in total. While Masta Killa's "Street Corner," like the original source "Brother," refers to "alleged brother[s]" standing at street corners "dressed in blue, or green, red and black," it omits several relevant elements. Firstly, the discussion "who's blacker than you are and who's blacker than she is"[22] is omitted, possibly because Scott-Heron dismisses it immediately following the introduction when he says: "We deal in too many externals, brother!" Secondly, the street corner's location "Harlem" is omitted, transposing the song from a local setting to a more general appeal. Thirdly and most importantly, "Street Corner" mutes the Afrocentric movement of the 70s and 80s by occluding references to dashikis in the original line "dressed in blue and black dashikis or green, red and black dashikis."[23] The song thereby recalls past and present-day conflicts while downplaying earlier demands for repatriation. In other words, the omission of references to the Afrocentric movement expresses irrevocable entanglement with a globalised world. Rapping from and to street corners, the song is located paradigmatically in what Homi K. Bhabha describes as the "liminality of the Western nation" (*Location of Culture* 241), where subjects "speak betwixt and between times and places" (227) as carriers and agents of what the song calls the coming revolution.

Eventually the song aims to transcend the betwixt experience of the ghetto suggesting to break through the conditions of colonial neurosis, indicated by the proclamation of a coming revolution. The song sets out from a state of arrested development, which Inspectah Deck voices when he finishes his contribution with "[f]rom the slave ships to today's bricks, same shit." This line refers to the beginning of colonisation, abduction and enslavement from the African continent, and relates it to present material conditions in the United States: brown brick houses. These houses once stood for the ideal of upward movement, but have turned into the congealed evidence of failed progress.[24] The chorus portrays a central conflict as Masta Killa describes the community's life: "It's me and you

22 Lyrics transcribed by the author.

23 Dashikis are clothes inspired by African fashion worn by Afrocentric US Americans, Caribbeans and beyond in this period and until today. These were also likely to sport the colours black, green and red as in the Kenyan and partly the Ghanaian as well as the Ethiopian national flags.

24 For a detailed depiction of shattered dreams of progress represented in the brown brick buildings of Harlem and Brooklyn, NYC, see, for instance, Paule Marshall's *Brown Girl, Brownstones* (2006).

son forever in the struggle" and demands fellow rappers, those at the street corners and, importantly, also the audience, to "take care, take a stance for a better tomorrow!"[25] This appears paradoxical since, if the struggle were "forever," how could there be "a better tomorrow," and what reason would there be to take a stance, if progress were impossible? The song demands collective agency, while the direct audience address – "me and you" – further expands and strengthens the collective. The song "Street Corner" acknowledges the danger that progress will never come, but it indicates the possibility to bring about change through collective effort. In requiring the audience to "take care [and] take a stance," it invites identification and alliances across borders.

For building collectives, the past becomes a source of significant memories. The third instance in which a distancing marker, this time the demonstrative pronoun 'those,' is employed, is when Masta Killa explains: "We took words that were nourishing, encouraging / A nation to awaken those who are sleeping." This nation is also built out of those who still have to awaken to the fact that the *status quo* is indelible but intolerable. In order to overcome this state, Masta Killa remembers the past as a contingent event – the enslavement of Black people – in its historical complexity:

Transatlantic import:
Slaves been bought. Secret relations between Blacks and Jews
might set a fuse off in the head. Many dead,
lynch hung, swung from trees.
Brothers in the struggle together, eat from one pot,
hold each other down to the sneaker. Nothing come between us!

By referring to "[s]ecret relations between Blacks and Jews," Masta Killa recalls the involvement of Jewish traders in the transatlantic slave trade *and* the productive cooperation of African Americans and Jewish Americans in the Civil Rights Movement in the USA, including the joint denouncement of lynching.[26] This relationship's complexity and ambiguity is substituted by the comment on "[b]rothers in struggle." It argues that a fraternal alliance reaches from basic is-

---

25 Since the phrase is uttered in an imperative clause without a subject, the listener is likely to identify as the command's addressee.

26 For a more detailed discussion of the song's reference to the long and complex history of Black-Jewish interaction, with its simultaneous evocation and revocation of the Nation of Islam's 1991 publication *The Secret Relationship Between Blacks and Jews*, see Wegner "Kompetitiv Multidirektionale Erinnerung im Medium der Rap Musik."

sues, like eating, to more demanding ones of supporting each other to the very end of the struggle for liberation.[27] Furthermore, the description is phrased as an imperative; solidarity is enabled through joint action. In the words of Paul Gilroy, then, solidarity is not predetermined by blood or land but "has to be won" (*Darker than Blue* 92).

The song connects the recollection of the distant past with an analysis of present challenges. Masta Killa's "Street Corner" recalls failed and successful past alliances between marginalised communities to outline the fundamentals of solidarity. Accordingly the song recalls the disruptive *Erlebnis* of the transatlantic slave trade and suggests that this originary event has solidified into permanent social and spatial structures, such as the ghetto. The state of colonial neurosis is traced beyond everyday experiences to events in the past. Revealing this genealogy enables insights for the present: The past reveals failed and successful alliances, indicating a potential for changes in the present. The song's lyrics thus reconstruct a diachronic history and a synchronic community, both of which reveal an open futurity. The song thereby parallels Fanon's formal movement, but it also differs in several respects: Firstly, the song focuses on the community rather than an individual. Secondly, it recalls the distant past of the slave trade rather than the near past of individual experiences. Thirdly, it centres on African-American communities in the US rather than a Martinican exile or the 'Third World.' Like Fanon, the song demands a revolution: Anticolonial revolutions have changed numerous communities, countries and continents, yet the song suggests that the structures which Fanon described as the "Manichaean world" (*The Wretched* 6) still exist. The rapper's reflections enable the identification of failed and successful transcultural alliances and thereby reveal future potentials that "might set a fuse off in the head."

27 Masta Killa ends his section with the statement that money and women are often the causes for "cliques" to end, which he finds "sickenin.'" Therefore, not only money, but also women are referred to as sources of collective failure. The misogynous statement inevitably weakens the song's critical potential. While its complex system of remembrance and recognition invites alliances of mutual support, the selection, marginalisation and exclusion of women necessarily weakens and inhibits the song's transformative potential. This slip is particularly astonishing and frustrating considering the fact that GZA in the same song emphasises the increased exposure and suffering of women in the daily struggle of the ghettoes.

RECOGNISING A POTENTIAL IN THE PAST

Fanon and Masta Killa bear witness to and point beyond colonial neurosis. Fanon remembers an encounter with a small boy as an *Erlebnis* of subjective fragmentation indicative of the complex structures of colonisation. Inspectah Deck, Masta Killa and GZA remember the transatlantic slave trade and civil rights struggles as crucial encounters that challenge the structures of social fragmentation and, especially in a US context, the lingering politics of segregation embodied by the hood. Fanon remembers past violence to think through individual psychological effects in the present, while the rappers remember past hopes to resist and point beyond present systemic violence. Each instance demonstrates that the present is historically contingent. All four of them point toward a potentially different future by envisioning "culture[s] of freedom sourced from deep within the experience of objecthood" (Gilroy, *Darker than Blue* 72).

Reading rap with Fanon suggests that colonial neurosis exceeds the commonly acknowledged spheres of colonisation.[28] Furthermore, it enables to analyse a dialectic of objectification and alienation in (Western) urban centres. Lastly, my reading demonstrates the medium's potential to communicate across geographies, ethnicities and cultures to envision alliances, resistance and, importantly, change. Reading Fanon with rap, conversely, highlights the potential of continuing, extending and extrapolating Fanonian thought. It suggests that the moment after, or outside, colonisation is not necessarily immune to colonial neurosis. Fanon recognises this when he writes that "the new man is not an a posteriori creation of this [postcolonial] nation, but coexists with it, matures with it, and triumphs with it" (*The Wretched* 233). It gives further evidence that mass media which, as Fanon demonstrated, represent, extend and maintain colonial structures (see *Black Skin* 17), can also be used for critical communication across borders. Lastly, reading Fanon with rap suggests that alienation and objectification may be overcome by remembering and establishing transcultural alliances. While not every song of reality rap may be as explicit on these topics, "Street Corner" evokes transcultural recognition to open a perspective beyond the *status quo*.

Remembering the past is crucial to question the present. As much as Fanon remembers the past in his analysis, "Street Corner" utilizes memories: Due to its musical and lyrical features it enables "a process of musical and cultural archeology" (Rose 79). In *Critique de la raison nègre*, Achille Mbembe argues that

---

28 An argument that is also put forward by Kruks (see 127) and Gilroy (see *Darker than Blue* 161).

memories are permanently endangered by colonial violence. This violence, he writes, "attacks time, one of the most important frameworks of subjectivity, it threatens the colonised to lose all their use of all memory traces" (237).[29] The loss of memory is, thus, a means of colonial control. "This repression," Judy writes, "is a constitutive function of the colonial economy; it is the primary violence that makes the colonial scene determine its psychopathologies. Accordingly, the colonized's neuroses stem from unremembered reminiscences of the experience of events" (69). Remembering, then, means to rescue an idea of the past that allows to interrogate the present (see Benjamin 391). Facing this challenge, Gilroy argues that "[t]he pursuit of an alternative future necessitates the cultivation of counter-memory" (*Darker than Blue* 139).[30] It is in this vein that rap recalls, continues and extends Fanonian thought.

LIST OF WORKS CITED

Agamben, Giorgio. *Homo Sacer: Sovereign Power and Bare Life*. Translated by Daniel Heller-Roazen. Stanford University Press, 1998.

Alexander, Michelle. *The New Jim Crow: Mass Incarceration in the Age of Colorblindness*. Revised edition. With a New Foreword by Cornel West. The New Press, 2012.

Benjamin, Walter. "On the Concept of History." *Selected Writings, 1938-1940*, edited by Marcus Bullock and Michael Jennings, vol. 4, Belknap Press, 2003, pp. 389-411.

Bhabha, Homi K. "Between Identities: Homi Bhabha interviewed by Paul Thompson." *International Yearbook of Oral History and Life Stories*, edited by Rina Benmayer and Andor Skotnes, vol. 3, Oxford University Press, 1994, pp. 183-199.

---. *The Location of Culture*. 1994. Routledge, 2004.

---. "Remembering Fanon: Self, Psyche and the Colonial Condition." *Colonial Discourse and Post-Colonial Theory: A Reader*, edited by Patrick Williams and Laura Chrisman, Harvester Wheatsheaf, 1993, pp. 112-123.

29 Translation by the author. In the original, Mbembe writes that colonial violence "s'attaquant au temps, l'un des cadres mentaux privilégiés de toute subjectivité, elle faisait courir aux colonisés le risqué de perdre l'usage de toutes traces mnésiques" (237).

30 For a detailed discussion of the concept of countermemory, see Wegner "Rethinking Countermemory: Black-Jewish Negotiations in Rap Music."

Bradley, Adam and Andrew DuBois. Introduction. *The Anthology of Rap*, by Bradley and DuBois, Yale University Press, 2010, pp. xxix-xlvii.

Chang, Jeff. *Can't Stop Won't Stop: A History of the Hip-Hop Generation*. St. Martin's, 2005.

---. "Race, Class, Conflict and Empowerment: On Ice Cube's 'Black Korea'" *Amerasia Journal*, vol. 19, no. 2, 1993, pp. 87-107.

Fanon, Frantz. *Black Skin, White Masks*. 1952. Translated by Richard Philcox, Grove Press, 2008.

---. *Œuvres*. Editions la Découverte, 2011.

---. *The Wretched of the Earth*. 1961. Translated by Richard Philcox, Grove Press, 2004.

Fernandes, Sujatha. *Close to the Edge: In Search of the Global Hip Hop Generation*. Verso, 2011.

Foucault, Michel. "How Much Does It Cost for Reason to Tell the Truth?" *Foucault Live: Interviews, 1966-84*, edited by Sylvère Lotringer, Semiotext(e), 1989, pp. 233-256.

Fraser, Nancy and Axel Honneth. *Redistribution or Recognition? A Political-Philosophical Exchange*. Translated by Joel Golb, James Ingram, and Christiane Wilke. Verso, 2003.

García Düttmann, Alexander. *Zwischen den Kulturen*. Suhrkamp, 1997.

Gates, Henry Louis Jr. "Critical Fanonism." *Critical Inquiry*, vol. 17, no. 3, 1991, pp. 457-470.

George, Nelson. "Rap's Tenth Birthday." *The Village Voice*, 24 Oct. 1989, p 40.

Gilroy, Paul. *Against Race: Imagining Political Culture Beyond the Color Line*. Harvard University Press, 2000.

---. *The Black Atlantic: Modernity and Double Consciousness*. Harvard University Press, 1993.

---. *Darker than Blue: On the Moral Economies of Black Atlantic Culture*. Harvard University Press, 2010.

---. *Postcolonial Melancholia*. Columbia University Press, 2005.

Greenberg, Cheryl. "Negotiating Coalition: Black and Jewish Civil Rights Agencies in the Twentieth Century." *Struggles in the Promised Land: Toward a History of Black-Jewish Relations in the United States*, edited by Jack Salzman and Cornel West, Oxford University Press, 1997, pp. 153-175.

Honneth, Axel. *Die Idee des Sozialismus: Versuch einer Aktualisierung*. Suhrkamp, 2015.

---. *Reification: A New Look at an Old Idea*, edited by Martin Jay, Oxford University Press, 2008.

---. *The Struggle for Recognition: The Moral Grammar of Social Conflicts*. Translated by Joel Anderson, MIT Press, 1995.

Judy, Ronald A. T. "Fanon's Body of Black Experience." *Fanon: A Critical Reader*, edited by Lewis R. Gordon, T. Denean Sharpley-Whiting, and Renée T. White, Blackwell Publishing, 1996, pp. 53-73.

Keyes, Cheryl L. *Rap Music and Street Consciousness*. University of Illinois Press, 2002.

Krims, Adam. *Rap Music and the Poetics of Identity*. Cambridge University Press, 2000.

Kruks, Sonia. "Fanon, Sartre, and Identity Politics." *Fanon: A Critical Reader*, edited by Lewis R. Gordon, T. Denean Sharpley-Whiting, and Renée T. White, Blackwell Publishing, 1996, pp. 122-133.

Lebeau, Vicky. "Psycho-politics: Frantz Fanon's *Black Skin, White Masks*." *Psycho-politics and Cultural Desires*, edited by Jan Campbell and Janet Harbord University College London Press, 1998, pp. 113-123.

Marshall, Paule. *Brown Girl, Brownstones*. The Feminist Press, 2006.

Massey, Douglas S. and Nancy A. Denton. *American Apartheid: Segregation and the Making of the Underclass*. Harvard University Press, 1993.

Mbembe, Achille. *Critique de la Raison Nègre*. Éditions La Découverte, 2013.

---. "Necropolitics." Translated by Libby Meintjes. *Public Culture*, vol. 15, no. 1, 2003, pp. 11-40.

Portfilio, Brad J. and Michael J. Viola, editors. *Hip-Hop(e): The Cultural Practice and Critical Pedagogy of International Hip-Hop*. Lang, 2012.

Potter, Russell A. *Spectacular Vernaculars: Hip-Hop and the Politics of Postmodernism*. State University of New York Press, 1995.

Razanajao, CL., J. Postel and D. F. Allen. "The Life and Psychiatric Work of Frantz Fanon." *History of Psychiatry*, vol. 7, 1996, pp. 499-524.

Rose, Tricia. *Black Noise: Rap Music and Black Culture in Contemporary America*. Wesleyan University Press, 1994.

---. *The Hip Hop Wars*. Basic Civitas. 2008.

Salzman, Jack. "Struggles in the Promised Land." *Struggles in the Promised Land: Toward a History of Black-Jewish Relations in the United States*, edited by Jack Salzman and Cornel West, Oxford University Press, 1997, pp. 1-19.

Shusterman, Richard. "The Fine Art of Rap." *New Literary History*, vol. 22, no. 3, 1991, pp. 613-632.

The Historical Research Department of The Nation of Islam. *The Secret Relationship between Blacks and Jews*. Vol. 1, Latimer Associates, 1991.

Vergès, Françoise. "To Cure and to Free: The Fanonian Project of 'Decolonized Psychiatry.'" *Fanon: A Critical Reader*, edited by Lewis R. Gordon, T. Denean Sharpley-Whiting, and Renée T. White, Blackwell Publishing, 1996, pp. 83-99.

Wegner, Jarula. "Kompetitiv Multidirektionale Erinnerung im Medium der Rap Musik." *Musik als Medium der Erinnerung: Gedächtnis – Geschichte – Gegenwart*, edited by Lena Nieper and Julian Schmitz, Bielefeld: transcript, 2016, pp. 191-203.

---. "Rethinking Countermemory: Black-Jewish Negotiations in Rap Music." *Memory Studies*. Forthcoming.

Young, Robert J.C. "Postcolonial Remains." *New Literary History*, vol. 43, no. 1, 2012, pp. 19-42.

Neoliberalism, Terror, and the Etiology of Neurotic Citizenship

ARIANE DE WAAL

On 12 September 2015, the day that Jeremy Corbyn was elected leader of the British Labour Party, Conservative Defense Secretary Michael Fallon approached the cameras with a stern look and an even sterner warning: "This is a very serious moment for our country. This election shows that Labour is now a serious risk to our national security, to our economic security, and to the security of your family" (BBC News). In an unlikely echo of Tony Blair's chorus of the previous decade that played on the theme of Saddam Hussein posing a "risk to our security" (Blair 380), Fallon's statement parades Corbyn as the new public enemy. The reason why this rhetoric of vilification fails to register as an extraordinary speech act lies in the consensus surrounding the term *security*, which largely goes uncontested in contemporary Western societies. Where the security of the nation-state, the market, or the family appears at stake, any type of pre-emptive action tends to receive wide approval. The trend towards securitization permeates global, national, urban, neighborhood, and domestic domains in equal measure. Strategies of surveillance and the (mis)use of police powers have long been the subject of cultural analyses; since 9/11 and the inauguration of the global 'war on terror,' scholarship has paid particular attention to the spread of security culture and the concomitant curtailing of civic rights (see, for instance, Bhattacharyya 74-76). Many of these analyses foreground the extension of state authority and disciplinary power, framing civilians as targets of unchecked intervention and violence. Yet, even though it is important to point out how current security regimes are imposed on populations, one should not overlook the extent to which citizens willingly invest and participate in the project of securitization, especially those who are classified as 'low risk' and deemed worthy of protecting their privileged white middle-class identities (see Rygiel 146). By reporting abandoned items of luggage, avoiding peak-time travel and crowded locations, submitting to searches, packing toiletries into travel-sized plastic containers, or reacting to 'anything suspicious' by reporting it to a member of staff, we all, as performance scholar Diana Taylor puts it, "perform terror every day; we incorporate it" (1893).

This chapter analyzes the (pro)active participation of British citizens in the political project of attaining, increasing, and defending security through the frame of neurosis. While the notion of trauma, which is often applied in this context, highlights the incommensurability of shattering experiences, the structure of neurosis in fact guarantees the social functioning of the subject. The traumatized subject undergoes recurrent, involuntary returns to the repressed traumatic content in the form of flashbacks and nightmares; the neurotic subject, in contrast, holds its repressed unconscious material in check by carrying out a specific action or routine. It is not surprising that scholars have repeatedly drawn on trauma in order to make sense of the psychological impact of the seemingly unassimilable shock of terrorism, not least because the work pursued by Cathy Caruth, Roger Luckhurst, and others in trauma studies offers a terminology that is particularly appealing to those invested in poststructuralist modes of interpretation. Yet the radical rupture connoted by trauma cannot serve to account for the astonishing adaptability of (most) civilians in the face of terror. In British political discourse, this perseverance is frequently commended along the lines of Prince Charles's praise, expressed in relation to the 2005 London bombings, for "the incredible resilience of the British people who have set us all a fantastic example of how to react to these tragedies" (qtd. in Hopkins). Rather than grief and trauma, the normative ideals of stoicism and resilience have dominated public responses to terrorism in the UK. This is partly explicable by tracing the persistent appeal of the so-called Blitz spirit in current reactions to adversity, but this historical perspective does little to disclose the underlying psychosocial mechanism that is both nourished by and sustains contemporary counter-terrorism culture.

This essay draws on the psychoanalytical category of neurosis in order to illuminate the dense network of relations between citizenship, neoliberalism, and (counter-)terrorism discourses. It reworks the Freudian etiology of neurosis through a cultural studies focus on neoliberal governmentality in a critical attempt to amend the ahistorical and universalizing tendencies of psychoanalysis. At first sight, Freud's reductive reading of neurosis as a manifestation of sexual frustration might seem ill-equipped to illuminate the current political predicament. Yet, as will be shown, his explication of obsessional actions nevertheless helps to make sense of the behavior patterns, routines, and anxieties of citizens in view of the terror threat. My aim is to disclose the neurotic tendencies at work in citizens' incessant efforts to secure themselves, their homes, and their urban environments against any number of real or imagined dangers by means of CCTV, SUVs, gated communities, and by reporting their fellow urbanites' suspicious behavior and unattended items of luggage. The prototypical neurotic citizen that this chapter seeks to evoke occupies a privileged socioeconomic and racial position within the cultural mainstream. This citizen is a member of the Christian (or secularized) white middle class and has access to a number of symbolic and financial resources that enable him or her to take an active part in the project of securitization. As my case study of urban discourses and practices in the 'neurotic metropolis' London evinces, the neurotic subject participates in the fortification of the home, the militarization of urban space, and in counter-terrorist surveillance. Due to the neurotic structure that governs such seemingly innocuous (if sometimes costly) everyday activities as advertising a room, buying an SUV, or commuting on the Tube, this citizen is always already predisposed to interpellation into the ideology of securitization to which such statements as Fallon's or Blair's seek to bind them. This chapter aims to elucidate how, on the one hand, the neurotic citizen's subjectivity is 'terrorized' not so much by international terrorist networks or attacks; instead, I join Rustom Bharucha in asking how "terror actually gets implemented through the speech-acts of the state" (20). On the other hand, the reflections offered here try to go beyond linear, top-down accounts of state power by drawing on a psychoanalytically informed mode of cultural enquiry that traces shared affective atmospheres and collective investments in security culture.

The present moment that I am writing about can be productively theorized by drawing on Lauren Berlant's concept of the "situation," which she defines as "a genre of living" that exceeds the subject's control and understanding, yet requires perseverance and adjustment (195). For Berlant, the present presents itself as an impasse, a moment of extended, systemic crisis, or "crisis ordinariness" (10). The subject becomes caught in this impasse, as conventional genres of living – in particular, the fantasy of the 'good life' – have lost their validity, even though they retain their appeal. The impasse is a particularly suggestive trope to capture the neoliberal consensus that determines that citizens must live by the rules of the free market (competition, flexibility, short-term contracts), even if they are clearly not prospering in an era of austerity measures and pervasive precarity. Since neoliberalism effectively lacks "mainstream political opposition" (Tyler 7), there are, however, neither concrete political programs nor symbolic resources that enable the subject to visualize or realize a 'way out' of the impasse. This conception of the neoliberal present as an inscrutable "situation" in which the subject is stuck and pressed for adjustment has pertinent points of contact with the psychoanalytical account of neurosis. Before turning to the psychoanalytical definition, one further qualification may be necessary.

Invoking neurosis to make sense of the psychic life of citizens in the 'war on terror' might seem surprising insofar as exacerbated responses to terror alerts recall the notion of paranoia, rather than neurosis. As Slavoj Žižek writes in his essay collection published in the wake of September 2001, Western societies' awareness of living in a digitalized, hyper-technological, "artificial universe" has engendered "the notion that some ominous agent is threatening us all the time with total destruction" (33). Žižek diagnoses "a new era of paranoiac warfare in which the greatest task will be to identify the enemy and his weapons" (37). The image of a spectral phantom enemy, whose elusiveness necessitates secretive state measures and pre-emptive warfare, can easily be seen to fuel paranoid suspicion. One essential element of paranoia, however, seems far less applicable in the 'war on terror' context, namely, the "delusions of grandeur" that typically accompany "delusions of persecution" (Laplanche and Pontalis 296). The paranoiac fantasy of omnipotence, in combination with a "pathological distrust of rulers" (Freud, "Mourning" 240), appears unhelpful when one seeks to theorize the local, everyday articulations of post-9/11 citizenship, which involve an open, 'trustful' responsiveness to terror alerts, rather than pathological suspicion of the government or the security services – leaving conspiracy theories aside. What the paranoid relation fails to account for, in my view, is the cooperative, compliant aspect of citizens' participation in counter-terrorism culture. Even if there is ground for paranoid suspicions in Blair's warning about Hussein or Fallon's warning about Corbyn, the protective and paternalistic relation these political figures seek to establish with the electorate invokes acquiescence regarding a shared notion of security. More often than not, there is nothing spectacular or grand about the measures undertaken by citizens in the joint project of securitization. Hence, rather than seeing 'terrorized' citizens in terms of a paranoid oscillation between moments of grandeur and despair, I would like to make the case for analyzing their subjectivity as quietly yet obsessively resigned to a security regime that requires perpetual adaptation, effort, and investment – which is where the notion of neurosis comes in.

FROM FREUD VIA JUNG TO "NEUROLIBERALISM"

In his *Introductory Lectures on Psychoanalysis* (first held in 1915-1917), Freud provides an etiology and symptomatology of neurosis. For the contemporary reader, it is particularly his definition of obsessional neurosis that resonates most strongly with colloquial usage of the term: "Obsessional neurosis is shown in the patient's being [...] aware of impulses in himself which appear very strange to him and in his being led to actions the performance of which give[s] him no enjoyment, but [...] is quite impossible for him to omit" (*Introductory Lectures* 297). Tics such as compulsive hand washing or checking repeatedly if the front door is locked come to mind here. This kind of repetitive behavior is nowadays classified as obsessive-compulsive disorder (OCD), which is evidently a pet theme in popular culture and television in the tradition of the American hit comedy *As Good as It Gets* (1997). According to Freud, the first step in the formation of neurosis is a sexual wish that cannot be satisfied because the ego either refuses the impulse or prohibits the desired object: "First there is the most general precondition – frustration" (*Introductory Lectures* 397). What happens next is that the libido becomes fixated, it loses its mobility, as the subject's satisfaction becomes dependent upon the attainment of this particular object or wish. Third, this results in "the tendency to conflict, arising from the development of the ego, which rejects these libidinal impulses" (397). This is why neurosis can most simply be explained as "a conflict between the ego and sexuality" (398), or – as Freud was later to specify in terms of the second topographical model – between the ego and the id. The formation of symptoms is the outcome of this conflict; it is the result of a compromise which is found as the ego forces the libido to find an outlet for the instinctual impulse. Importantly, this outlet reflects both the ego's opposition/defense and the original wish/desire; the symptom thus represents a distortion of and substitute for the unconscious sexual wish. Due to the reappearance of the repressed material in the form of a coded disguise, the symptom can resemble the original impulse quite closely, unless one is dealing with a case of reaction formation where an instinct is turned into its opposite. Moreover, as the outcome of a negotiation between the ego and the id, the neurotic mechanism is relatively stable and powerful, because it is, eventually, supported by both parts. These two aspects of substitutive representation and the stability of symptoms make the concept of neurosis particularly relevant to the present cultural moment.

Translating this model into the terms of contemporary critiques of neoliberalism and counter-terrorism culture would appear like a big conceptual leap, if it were not for C.G. Jung's proposed corrective to Freud's account. Jung's critique is essential insofar as he points out that a sexual etiology is too limited. Instead of considering the neurotic symptom purely as an expression of sexual fantasies – which, in Freud's examples, usually constitute infantile fixations – Jung suggests that the question of when and why the symptom occurs points us to the "aetiological secret of the neurosis" ("Psychoanalysis" 245). As Jung writes, "the moment of the outbreak of neurosis is [...] most critical. It is usually *the moment when a new psychological adjustment, that is, a new adaptation, is demanded*" (246; emphasis in the original). It is for this terminology of *adjustment* and *adaptation* that we need to turn to Jung's critique of Freud in order to be able to apply the psychoanalytical model to the impasse of the neoliberal present. Jung allows us to see the formation of the neurotic symptom as the outcome of a failed adaptation to the present, rather than the failure of repressing a sexual wish. There is something highly suggestive about his definition of neurotic mechanisms as "symptoms of maladjustment" ("Philosophical Tree" 345) when it comes to the neoliberal conditions under which the contemporary neurotic subject finds itself.

Engin Isin is among those scholars who still see validity in the original psychoanalytical account of neurosis. He sketches an update of the psychoanalytical model with a view to the current neoliberal context, arguing that the neurotic subject is integral to neoliberal modes of governmentality. Revising and complementing the rational, self-possessed subject implied by theories of the risk society, Isin proposes the figure of the "neurotic citizen who governs itself through responses to anxieties and uncertainties" (223). He goes so far as to "suggest a new concept, neuroliberalism – a rationality of government that takes its subject as the neurotic citizen" (223). For Isin, neoliberal discourses surrounding the security of the economy, the environment, or the border do not simply construct a neurotic subject, but speak to a subject that is always already constituted as neurotic. This subject calibrates its conduct on the basis of anxieties, rather than cognition; it is "anxious, under stress and increasingly insecure and is asked to manage its neurosis" (225). In acting on the wish to "seek freedom from anxiety" (227), however, the neurotic citizen only engages in a "displacement of one affect from one domain to another" (230). In other words, the neurotic subject thinks, as Sara Ahmed has characterized the cultural politics of anxiety, "of more and more 'things' to be anxious about"; in consequence, its "anxiety [...] accumulate[s] through gathering more and more objects, until it overwhelms other possible affective relations to the world" (66). Ahmed's theorization of anxiety as the subject's predominant "mode of attachment to objects" (66) returns us to Freud, who identified in the neurotic "a kind of freely floating anxiety which is ready to attach itself to any idea that is in any way suitable" (*Introductory Lectures* 446). It bears reiterating here that, although potentially overwhelming, this pervasive anxiety is not to be confused with a paranoid relation to the external world. What characterizes current expressions of neurotic anxiety is the apparent existence of a state-citizen consensus surrounding the need to attain and defend security in all areas of social and political life. Rather than responding with a fundamental distrust and a suspicious detection of malevolence in the address from the 'big other' who interpellates the subject into the ideology of security, the neurotic citizen actively and optimistically cooperates in the neoliberal project.

In the chain of displacement of anxious affects, the terrorist threat can be posited as the prime object, or master signifier. To rephrase this with the terms proposed by Ahmed, terrorism is a sign to which anxious affects 'stick' easily.[1] Even more so than the areas glossed by Isin (the economy, the environment, the border), counter-terrorism discourse addresses a subject whose anxieties are extremely heightened and disproportionate. While widespread disbelief in human-caused climate change might obstruct the environmental discourse's appeal to anxiety, anti-terror campaigns speak to a subject that is already on high alert. Counter-terrorism discourses and practices are therefore ideally suited to an analysis that wishes to move, as has been indicated, beyond top-down models of the state-citizen relationship and focus on the ways in which the neurotic subject manages its everyday life and routines in an ostensibly autonomous and self-sufficient manner. If the neurotic citizen subject is produced at the intersection of discourses on neoliberalism and terrorism, then perhaps nowhere is its presence more manifest than in London, a city at the forefront of both neoliberalization and the 'war on terror.' The way in which the neurotic subject is governed, and governs itself, through an injunction to eliminate insecurities is particularly evident in urban infrastructures and practices. I will illustrate this by discussing three cultural phenomena that exemplify the contemporary urban poetics of neurosis: the securitization of the home, the militarization of urban space, and citizens' participation in counter-terrorism culture.

LONDON AS A NEUROTIC METROPOLIS

When Londoners wish to search for or advertise rooms or flats, they often turn to *SpareRoom.co.uk*, a website run by the private company Flatshare Ltd. Even the most cursory overview of ads for flatshares in London shows that references to the security of properties abound. This emphasis appears particularly pronounced in adverts for rooms that are located in ethnically diverse boroughs. In these cases, signifiers like *safe* and *secure* are often placed strategically in the headlines. In the Finsbury Park area, for example, a "lovely room in a secure, landscaped development" was advertised in June 2015.[2] The person advertising the room was looking for "a clean and tidy sharer to enjoy this modern, minimalist flat in a lovely new

1 Ahmed uses the term *stickiness* in order to describe "how 'signs' become sticky or saturated with affect" (194-195), thus making particular emotions, figures, or bodies appear indissociable in the public imagination.

2 This and subsequent quotations are all taken from the website www.spareroom.co.uk.

development with entry phone system, concierge service, CCTV and security." Next to minimalist design features, technologies of surveillance have evidently become an asset on the housing market. The emphasis placed on security is especially striking for its priority over ideas surrounding the type of person one would like to share a flat with or the kind of communal life one would like to lead. Another ad for a room in the same area, published in September 2015, lists among the amenities of the flat, besides it being located a "3 minute walk to banks, restaurants (incl. subway and KFC, other Turkish, Chinese, Mexican restaurants)," that it is "fully fitted with various security systems, fire alarms, carbon monoxide alarms, etc." The trend continues in September 2017, with an ad for a "Large Ensuite room in secure apartment building" specifying that said building "requires a fob at the entrance and has security doors on every floor. It also has secure parking."

Although the increasing fortification of private property is surely a widely observable phenomenon, I would like to suggest that the value placed on secure housing is not unrelated to the fear of terrorism. In these three examples, the inclusion of details on available security systems might be motivated by the particular location of the properties in the vicinity of Finsbury Park Mosque. The North London Central Mosque, as it is also called, has been in the headlines for more than a decade due to its reputation as a *Suicide Factory*, as a 2006 book by two *Times* journalists labelled it.[3] The mosque is indelibly associated with the radical imam Abu Hamza al Masri, who preached there until 2003, and symbolizes like few other spaces the 'failed integration' of British Muslims and their presumed fundamentalist inclinations. Despite al Masri's arrest for terrorism offences in 2004 and the appointment of chairman Mohammed Kozbar in 2005, who is widely lauded as a moderating influence, the public perception of the mosque as an icon of radical, unassimilable 'otherness' seems to persist. After a series of assaults on the site with cans of petrol and packages of rotten pork, a van was deliberately driven into a group of worshippers in front of the mosque in June 2017, killing one person and injuring several others. These acts of aggression and extreme violence aside, the place of Islamic worship seems to make for an environment that the neurotic citizen cannot inhabit without uneasiness. The fact that the enumeration of 'ethnic' food places in the second flatshare ad is immediately followed by

3 In *The Suicide Factory: Abu Hamza and the Finsbury Park Mosque*, Daniel McGrory and Sean O'Neill investigate the indoctrination of worshippers that took place under Abu Hamza al Masri's leadership. The sensationalist title of the book clearly indicates the irrevocable associations with extremism that the Finsbury Park Mosque evokes in the public perception.

a list of various security systems points to anxieties surrounding the supposed radicalization of religious minorities, which prompt a refashioning of the cosmopolitan city as a secure enclave. The 'exotic' restaurants and security systems are mutually dependent signifiers: multiculturalism comes with its perks and dangers.

As the nonchalant tone in which technologies of security are mentioned in such advertisements demonstrates, the flat-searching subject addressed by these texts is the prototypically white and middle-class neurotic citizen, who has been trained to observe and manage all kinds of insecurities. Anxieties about cohabitation with cultural and religious 'others' are silently accepted and taken for granted, rather than stemming from or being channeled into paranoid distrust. If paranoid narrative schemes work with suspicion and vilification, as seen in a number of TV series and films revolving around terrorist strikes targeting the 'homeland,' the poetics of neurosis relies on enumeration and repetition, on the accumulation of superfluous detail. The abbreviation "etc." that concludes the list of "various security systems, fire alarms, carbon monoxide alarms" in the second flatshare ad encapsulates the nature of the security consensus as a social contract that need not be spelled out. It seems that security systems and alarms have become such essential accessories in real estate that their provision can almost be taken for granted, whereas their efficacy or necessity is not called into question. They make for essential yet inconspicuous details, shrouded by the etcetera, the ordinary stuff of urban living.

More evidence of the securitization of the home can be located in the incidence of gated housing schemes. Again, this phenomenon may not be immediately attributable to the 'war on terror' context, as, in Britain, the "classic gated development concept [was] introduced from the US in the 1980s" (Norwood), and the gating of certain sections of urban places and squares obviously goes even further back. But the demand for and popularity of "voluntary segregation" doubtlessly increased after 9/11, as reports on the rise in gated communities in the UK published after the 2001 attacks would suggest (see Kelbie). Prominent examples in London include the Lancasters, a luxurious gated development overlooking Hyde Park, or the Bow Quarter in East London, a walled-off complex comprising a gym, restaurant, bar, sun deck, and convenience store, all secured by infra-red surveillance cameras and 24/7 security guards (etc). Geographer Cindi Katz argues that 9/11 provided those urbanites that had secretly desired segregation with "a neat alibi" and calls the subsequent expansion of gated communities an expression of "spatial fetishism" (353). Similar to the libidinal investment in a fetishized object, the neurotic citizen becomes attached to the "fantasy of producing citadels of safety" (Katz 354). Following Peter Marcuse, Katz speaks of the practice of "citadelization," which – and this is a crucial point – "performs security, but so selectively that it reinforces the vulnerabilities it is staged to counter" (353). The injunction to eliminate insecurities engenders ever new safety measures, which paradoxically only serve to enhance the subject's sense of exposure. There is, accordingly, an obsessive element to the practices of fortressing, bunkering, and securing the home. Here, it is crucial to recall Freud's explanation that anxiety is only "screened by the obsessional action" and released immediately upon letting go of the compulsion or the project to which the neurotic subject is immediately dedicated (see *Introductory Lectures* 452). If the safety measures undertaken by the neurotic subject enhance, rather than alleviate, its anxiety, the subject's relationship to the 'neuroliberal' program testifies to Berlant's notion of "cruel optimism," which "exists when something you desire is actually an obstacle to your flourishing" (1). Even if, or precisely because, social life is increasingly structured by and experienced as precariousness, the neurotic subject holds on to its cruel attachments to 'citadels of safety.'

The second example that elucidates the neurotic structure underlying current modes of living and being in the metropolis revolves around the militarization of urban space. Gargi Bhattacharyya, who reviews developments that are indicative of urban militarization in the 'war on terror' context, such as the increase of police presence, argues that these serve to extend "the scope and discretion of state authority," resulting in "a shift in the relation between citizen and state" (77). Here, one could think of the enhanced police presence across the London transport network or the stationing of troops and tanks at Heathrow Airport in response to a heightened terror alert in 2003. Other instances are the increase in stop-and-search arrests, racial profiling, and high-profile raids. Imogen Tyler sees these developments as evidence of the creation of a "'home front,' a battle line behind which the civilian populace is mobilized as a supporting arm of the military" (59). The militarization of everyday life, she goes on to write, "presumes a popular consensus in favour of forgoing democratic freedoms" (59). Doubtlessly, the UK's various Terrorism Acts have curbed civil liberties by widening police powers to stop and search, arrest, and detain suspects – developments that have disproportionately affected ethnic minorities. While anti-terrorism discourses inevitably frame non-white citizens as liable to raise suspicion, the subject position provided to those located on the upper ends of racial and class hierarchies is infused with neurotic anxiety. Within the stark binaries inculcated by the idea of a 'war on terror,' the "(white) originary citizen is in sharp contradistinction to the (dark) naturalized citizen, the dark immigrant or even the dark citizen born of the dark immigrant whose (latent) 'loyalty' is perennially suspect" (Alexander 235).

To reiterate Tyler's foregrounding of the popular consensus surrounding security culture, views of a top-down inculcation of fear and anxiety cannot serve to account for the neurotic subject's active cooperation in the scheme of militarization. Neither the state nor the citizen is engaged in a single-handed paranoid effort to fortify the borders of the home (front) against terrorist incursions from without or within; instead, there is a tacit agreement on the necessity of such measures, and a collective effort is dedicated to their realization. A pertinent example of the neurotic subject's enlistment on the home front is the palpable increase in SUVs (sports utility vehicles). Sales figures of these cars have gone up immensely, particularly in upmarket areas in London, as their nickname 'Chelsea tractors' indicates. This is not incidental. Zygmunt Bauman considers the spread of these "gas-guzzling military monsters" (12) as symptomatic of a politics of 'law and order,' which translates the idiom and practices of warfare into the Western metropolis. The unsuitability of 4x4 vehicles to navigate the narrow streets of London does not seem to deter a certain section of the (upper) middle classes from this increasingly popular purchase decision. This trend has been satirized, for instance, in the BBC's *Catherine Tate Show* (2004-2007), where upper-middle-class characters seem to invariably drive silver Land Rovers. One of the recurring characters in the sketch show, the Aga Saga Woman, memorably drives through 'Totten-ham' in her 4x4 after taking a wrong turn, with a look of panic on her face as if she were driving through mined territory. Indeed, the SUV is "always advertised as a vehicle of war, a machine of escape and velocity in and through the urban jungle" (Eduardo Mendieta qtd. in Gray and Wyly 339).

Providing armor to the civilian navigating the home front of the 'war on terror,' the SUV becomes an element of Mitchell Gray and Elvin Wyly's "Terror City Hypothesis." The urban geographers define the terror city as "a construct that redefines the urban by portraying all cities in terms of their *vulnerability to terrorism or their propensity to breed and harbor terrorists*" (331; emphasis in the original). In the terror city, the permanent sense of anxiety engendered by constructions of the terrorist threat finds an "iconographic and material expression in the urban landscape" (332); examples include "divisions, separations, walls, and checkpoints" (339) next to other practices of urban militarization, such as driving an SUV. As Gray and Wyly state, the (sub)urban "environment now provides a deep reservoir for intensified insecurities in the 'war on terror.' Private alarm and surveillance companies and automakers have been quick to revise their marketing campaigns to emphasize security" (339). Again, the subject's relation to these protective objects can be characterized as cruelly optimistic: rather than factually augmenting the security of neurotic citizens and their families, the SUV contributes to an increase in air pollution, invites rather than repels burglars, and potentially heightens the subject's sense of isolation, of fending for itself in an increasingly atomized social environment. Yet the neurotic mechanism is functioning and stable precisely because, by forming a socially acceptable symptom, it provides a legitimate outlet for the subject's anxious energies. If citizens were to let go of the obsessional action, i.e. the compulsion to secure their bodies, their cars, and their homes, they would have to face a deeper, underlying, existential anxiety that cannot be as easily addressed or redressed.

The example of the SUV throws into sharpest relief the classed nature of the image of the prototypical neurotic citizen evoked in this essay: this subject can only govern itself and be governed through an injunction to eliminate insecurities because it is a privileged participant in the neoliberal market economy, and one with a particular purchasing power. Simply put, the neurotic citizen can 'afford' to worry about assaults by terrorists or criminals. If the wealthy patients of Freud and Jung thus recur in the current shape of middle- and upper-middle-class urbanites, then the frequent critique of psychoanalysis as a bourgeois ideology still obtains. This makes it necessary to acknowledge the limitations of approaches such as the one proposed in this chapter, which inevitably reify middle-class subjectivity in terms of a normative 'citizen subject.' With private alarm systems and SUVs, this subject tends to manage and display its anxieties through high-end consumer products that are certainly not accessible to every inhabitant of the terror city. Those excluded from such practices are, to be sure, the very people against whom neurotic citizens wish to safeguard themselves.

This becomes evident as we move on to the third example, the neurotic citizen's participation in counter-terrorism culture. On Fellows Road, a street in North London that stretches from Swiss Cottage underground station to the fashionable Primrose Hill area, Victorian townhouses and social housing estates sit side by side. The four council high-rise buildings on the street exemplify this social density: as an outcome of the so-called Right to Buy scheme of the 1980s and ongoing processes of urban gentrification, affluent flat owners have come to cohabit with housing association tenants on the ethnically diverse estate. Upon entering Bray Tower, one of the high-rise blocks, visitors are greeted by a placard in a display cabinet that instructs residents on how to detect terrorists. Under the headline, "Terrorism: If You Suspect It, Report It," the poster issued by the Metropolitan Police as part of a nation-wide counter-terror campaign details five areas of suspicious activity: "Terrorists need information," "Terrorists need transport," "Terrorists need to travel," "Terrorists need communication," and "Terrorists use computers."[4] Iconic images of a camera, a silver van, a black trolley, a Nokia phone, and a desktop computer illustrate the plain instructions on identifying terrorist behavior (e.g. "Do you know someone who travels but is vague about where they are going?"). Where terrorist suspects and neurotic citizens mingle, the latter are encouraged to fixate their anxieties on the former and report their suspicious behavior directly to the police, via the confidential anti-terrorist hotline specified on the placard. Although one might detect the seeds of paranoid suspicion in the instruction to be wary of one's neighbors' use of cars, computers, or mobile phones, the explicit invitation to citizens to participate in the policing effort appears predicated on a neurotic mode. Again, the police here figures as a benevolent if paternalistic partner, the well-meaning 'big brother,' rather than the ill-disposed 'big other.' The "If You Suspect It, Report It" poster illustrates particularly well that neurotic anxieties are always already in circulation – otherwise, it could only be read as highly comical or entirely absurd.[5] As was seen in the texts of the flatshare ads, the poetics of neurosis derives from the use of repetition and the enumeration of superfluous details. The five parallel phrases that place 'terrorists' in the subject position converge in an appeal to neurotic anxieties, even though the overall tone of the placard is matter-of-fact and none of the descriptions of suspicious activities uses any signifiers (apart from *terrorists*) that might provoke alarm.

The fact that counter-terrorism discourses presuppose a neurotic subject as their recipient is especially evident on public transport. For instance, a leaflet that was issued by the Association of Chief Police Officers and handed out at busy Tube stations in late 2014 instructs commuters on how to "stay safe" in what is cautiously called a "firearms and weapons attack" (qtd. in Hartley-Parkinson). Again, the flyer works with excessive repetition: beyond reiterating the imperative "stay safe" twice, it urges readers to "leave the area safely" and "find a safe place" in the event of an attack. Keeping up the terror alert by means of these publicity campaigns is an essential practice to maintain neurotic anxiety. Alongside the permanent warnings to passengers to keep their belongings with them at all times and to report any suspicious behavior or unattended bags, such instructions can be read

4 The poster can be viewed via the following link: www.lbbd.gov.uk/wp-content/uploads/2015/11/If-you-suspect-it-report-it-Anti-Terrorism-Poster-pdf.pdf.

5 This is not to suggest that the poster cannot be read in such ways, as indeed the perspective taken here demonstrates. Unsurprisingly, the various posters issued as part of the counter-terror campaign have been highly controversial and triggered a number of spoofs on internet forums. However, as of 2017, the poster in question was still in place at the housing estate on Fellows Road and, doubtlessly, at similar sites.

as articulations of what Katz labels "banal terrorism," that is, the "everyday, routinized, barely noticed reminders of terror or the threat of an always already presence of terrorism in our midst" (350). In response to the perpetually reiterated injunctions to be wary of other passengers, the citizens traversing the metropolis become caught in the state of "'expectant anxiety' or 'anxious expectation'" that Freud attributes to neurosis: "People who are tormented by this kind of anxiety always foresee the most frightful of all possibilities [...] and exploit every uncertainty in a bad sense" (*Introductory Lectures* 446). This 'expectant anxiety' reveals itself in a number of neurotic routines, such as changing the carriage if an Asian-looking man carrying a rucksack gets on board, avoiding certain routes or modes of transport altogether, or getting cabin crews to remove suspicious passengers from airplanes – as happened in connection with growing fears of ISIS at various London airports in 2016.

TOWARDS AN ETIOLOGY OF NEUROTIC CITIZENSHIP

If Tyler is right in claiming that "a major characteristic of neoliberal 'democracies' is that they function through the generation of consent via fear and anxiety, rather than fidelity to national identity" (8), this begs the question where the benefits in fixing anxieties onto the terrorist threat might lie. The reason why such emphasis is placed on terrorism both in the model of governmentality approached here and in the neurotic citizen's routines and behaviors can be explained by illuminating the precise logic of displacement that is at work in the joint project of securitization. The Londoners who mobilize substantial financial and psychological resources to fortify their homes, maintain their watchfulness during their travels, or cast a suspicious eye on fellow passengers and neighbors cannot, or at least not comprehensively, be characterized as rational subjects who make "strategic risk decisions," as Ulrich Beck might put it (6). Taking the psychoanalytical concept of neurosis into account helps clarify to what extent rational assessments are bypassed by neurotic anxiety and highlights the psycho-cultural and political function of acting (out) on that anxiety.

Based on a distinction drawn by Bauman, I argue that the neurotic citizen obsessively invests in safety (symptom), yet perpetually fails to achieve a sense of security (wish). As discussed above, the neurotic symptom can quite neatly reflect the original desire – Freud calls it "a representation, a repetition, of the significant scene" (*Introductory Lectures* 302) – which is doubtlessly the case in the project of securitization. Bauman helpfully differentiates between *security*, which he designates as a genuine feeling of being insured and protected by the (welfare) state, and the surrogate character of *safety*, which he relates to the personal management of potentially infinite threats (see 13). Adapting Freud's model to present manifestations of neurotic citizenship, one can hence determine the first step in the formation of this kind of neurosis: the subject's instinctual wish is not of a sexual nature, but stems from the desire for existential security. This wish cannot be satisfied, not so much because the ego intervenes, but because of obstacles in the present, where neoliberal capitalism has eroded the collective foundations on which the possibility of existential security rests. The original wish for the security that could be – or, according to Bauman, formerly has been – fulfilled if (or when) the subject was held by stable networks, social forms and conventions, a reliable workplace, the experience of social justice, and solid institutions cannot be realized due to the neoliberal exigencies of constant mobility, flexibility, and adjustment. Second, libidinal energies become fixated onto a particular object: the terrorist threat. This fixation provides an orientation for the subject's anxious affects, without fully suturing them, for terrorism, as an object of anxiety, is inherently ill-defined and elusive; there is no knowing if, when, how, where, and why an attack might occur. Third, the conflict between the subject's demand for security and the neoliberal obstacles that prevent this wish from being realized results in the compromise formation of obsessive symptoms, which consist in the series of safety measures that we have encountered across the terror city. In other words, the instinctual wish to be held and secured by social networks and the welfare state finds a thinly disguised expression in the subject's substitutive compulsion to shield itself from threats to itself, its property, and its family. In the chain of displacement from security to safety that sustains the governmental mode of ne(ur)oliberalism, the terrorist threat represents an inexhaustible source of anxiety: if anxiety sticks to objects, as Ahmed suggests, the notoriously slippery object that is terrorism offers its amplification, rather than stabilization. Put graphically, anxiety slips from and re-sticks to terrorism in an endlessly repeated mental effort. The stability of the neurotic symptom is hence guaranteed.

What is more, due to the strong social consensus around the need for securitization and the severity of the terrorist threat, the neurotic citizen's obsessional actions are not conventionally perceived as pathological. Just as Freud writes that the neurotic symptom is, as the outcome of a joint search for a compromise, supported by both the ego and the id, the everyday practices of securitization can be understood as a compromise between citizen and state. The neurotic mechanism, here, fulfils a crucial political function insofar as the citizen, while caught up in a constant displacement of anxiety, will not be able to identify the repressed wish for existential security and, in response, formulate concrete political demands. In turn, the obsessional action protects the subject from having to address its fundamental sense of insecurity and precariousness, i.e. the deep-seated and unconscious permanent anxiety that characterizes neoliberal culture. The subject's competent management of its more mundane anxieties provides the sort of cruel satisfaction, to slightly amend Berlant's concept, that can be experienced by the individual who follows the neoliberal path of self-optimization. Accordingly, the type of neurotic action that ensues is entirely compatible and complicit with the neoliberal paradigm, for it isolates citizens as individualistic consumers of 'safety products' and pits suspicious neighbors and commuters against each other. While the inhabitants of Bray Tower are visually cued to police each others' everyday activities whenever they leave or enter their tower block, they have been kept from scrutinizing the council's neglect of their security: after the devastating fire at Grenfell Tower in June 2017, residents had to be evacuated from the Fellows Road estates overnight, as it appeared that a similar cladding as the one that caught fire at Grenfell Tower had been used to make the high-rises more appealing from the perspective of the neighboring townhouses. As state institutions continue to outsource security – and, in particular, to neglect their responsibility to protect the most vulnerable sections of society – neurotic citizens are expected to take over as the personal managers of their own safety.

Perhaps surprisingly, I would like to conclude on a positive note, for I do not believe that the neurotic citizen is permanently stuck in a mode of anxiety or forced to endlessly carry out compulsive safety measures. Freud says of the healing of neurosis that, "[b]y carrying what is unconscious into what is conscious, we transform the pathogenic conflict into a normal one, for which it must be possible somehow to find a solution" (*Introductory Lectures* 486). The critical value of combining psychoanalytical insights into the structure of neurosis with cultural studies approaches to terrorism and neoliberalism might lie in this prospect of 'somehow' finding a solution. I am thinking here of what Mark Featherstone, Elizabeth Poole, and Siobhan Holohan refer to as "politicizing" the 'war on terror,' when they propose to enable Western "populations to understand that the real root of their undefined feelings of anxiety is not terror, but rather the generalized insecurity [they] have to endure in support of neo-liberal capitalism" (172-173). Hence, by dissecting the displacements that turn safety into the substitutive representations of security, a psychoanalytically informed cultural studies perspective may contribute to formulating resistance to the hegemonic projects of neoliberal privatization, securitization, militarization, and the targeting of ethnic and religious minorities.[6] As the continuing relevance of psychoanalytical models for seeking to explain cultural phenomena suggests, there may lie something in their "virtues of endurance" (Frosh 157) that can be mobilized to counter the surprising endurance of neoliberalism in the face of deepening inequalities (as well as financial and economic crises) and to oppose the tenacity of imperialist modes of violence that have been resuscitated in the 'war on terror.'

LIST OF WORKS CITED

Ahmed, Sara. *The Cultural Politics of Emotion.* Edinburgh University Press, 2004.

Alexander, M. Jacqui. *Pedagogies of Crossing: Meditations on Feminism, Sexual Politics, Memory, and the Sacred.* Duke University Press, 2005.

Bauman, Zygmunt. *Liquid Times: Living in an Age of Uncertainty.* Polity Press, 2007.

BBC News. "Defence Secretary Michael Fallon: Corbyn 'a Risk to Security.'" *BBC News*, 12 Sept. 2015, www.bbc.com/news/uk-politics-34231727/. Accessed 14 Feb. 2018.

Beck, Ulrich. "Critical Theory of World Risk Society: A Cosmopolitan Vision." *Constellations*, vol. 16, no. 1, 2009, pp. 3-22.

Berlant, Lauren. *Cruel Optimism.* Duke University Press, 2011.

Bharucha, Rustom. *Terror and Performance.* Routledge, 2014.

Bhattacharyya, Gargi. *Dangerous Brown Men: Exploiting Sex, Violence and Feminism in the War on Terror.* Zed Books, 2008.

Blair, Tony. *A Journey.* Hutchinson, 2010.

Featherstone, Mark, Siobhan Holohan, and Elizabeth Poole. "Discourses of the War on Terror: Constructions of the Islamic Other after 7/7." *International Journal of Media and Cultural Politics*, vol. 6, no. 2, 2010, pp. 169-186.

Freud, Sigmund. *Introductory Lectures on Psychoanalysis.* Edited by James Strachey and Angela Richards, translated by James Strachey, Penguin, 1981.

---. "Mourning and Melancholia." *On the History of the Psycho-Analytic Movement and Other Works*, edited and translated by James Strachey, The Hogarth Press, 1957, pp. 239-258.

6 In this vein, Mark Schmitt offers an excellent account of the work of such cultural critics as Mark Fisher and Franco Berardi, who propose "counter-strategies that usually entail the need to work with and through mental disorders in order to challenge the capitalist condition and its representational systems" (302).

Frosh, Stephen. "Endurance: Psychoanalysis and Ethical Engagement." *American Imago*, vol. 71, no. 2, 2015, pp. 157-175.

Gray, Mitchell, and Elvin Wyly. "The Terror City Hypothesis." *Violent Geographies: Fear, Terror, and Political Violence*, edited by Derek Gregory and Allan Pred, Routledge, 2007, pp. 329-348.

Hartley-Parkinson, Richard. "'Run, Hide and Tell': Police Hand Out Flyer Telling Commuters What to Do in Terror Attack." *Metro*, 26 Nov. 2014, metro.co.uk/2014/11/26/run-hide-and-tell-police-hand-out-flyer-telling-commuters-what-to-do-in-terror-attack-4963021/. Accessed 14 Feb. 2018.

Hopkins, Steven. "7/7 Bombings: How London Bravely Carried On after a Harrowing Day of Trauma." *Huffington Post*, 7 July 2015, www.huffingtonpost.co.uk/2015/07/07/77-bombings-london-victims-what-happened_n_7612010.html/. Accessed 11 May 2018.

Isin, Engin F. "The Neurotic Citizen." *Citizenship Studies*, vol. 8, no. 3, 2004, pp. 217-235.

Jung, C.G. "The Philosophical Tree." *Alchemical Studies*, edited by Herbert Read et al., translated by R.F.C. Hull, Routledge and Kegan Paul, 1967, pp. 251-349.

---. "Psychoanalysis and Neurosis." *Freud and Psychoanalysis*, edited by Herbert Read et al., translated by R.F.C. Hull, Routledge and Kegan Paul, 1961, pp. 243-251.

Katz, Cindi. "Banal Terrorism: Spatial Fetishism and Everyday Insecurity." *Violent Geographies: Fear, Terror, and Political Violence*, edited by Derek Gregory and Allan Pred, Routledge, 2007, pp. 349-361.

Kelbie, Paul. "Rise in Gated Communities Could Pose a Threat to Public Services." *Independent*, 27 Sept. 2003, www.independent.co.uk/property/house-and-home/rise-in-gated-communities-could-pose-a-threat-to-public-services-581318.html/. Accessed 11 May 2018.

Laplanche, Jean, and Jean-Bertrand Pontalis. *The Language of Psycho-Analysis*. Translated by Donald Nicholson-Smith, Hogarth Press, 1985.

Norwood, Graham. "London Leads Move away from Gated Housing Schemes." *Financial Times*, 31 May 2013, www.ft.com/intl/cms/s/2/9dc593c2-c39e-11e2-aa5b-00144feab7de.html/. Accessed 11 May 2018.

Rygiel, Kim. "Protecting and Proving Identity: The Biopolitics of Waging War through Citizenship in the Post-9/11 Era." *(En)Gendering the War on Terror: War Stories and Camouflaged Politics*, edited by Krista Hunt and Kim Rygiel, Ashgate, 2006, pp. 145-167.

Schmitt, Mark. "Dysfunctional Capitalism: Mental Illness, Schizoanalysis and the Epistemology of the Negative in Contemporary Cultural Studies." *Psychoanalysis, Culture & Society*, vol. 22, no. 3, 2017, pp. 298-316.

Taylor, Diana. "Afterword: War Play." *PMLA*, vol. 124, no. 5, 2009, pp. 1886-1895.

Tyler, Imogen. *Revolting Subjects: Social Abjection and Resistance in Neoliberal Britain.* Zed Books, 2013.

Žižek, Slavoj. *Welcome to the Desert of the Real! Five Essays on September 11 and Related Dates.* Verso, 2002.

Pegida as *Angstneurotiker*

A Linguistic Analysis of Concepts of Fear in Right-wing Populist Discourses in German Online Media

DERYA GÜR-ŞEKER

The *Digital Lexicon of German Language* (*DWDS*)[1] defines *Neurose* (neurosis) as a "functional disorder of the nervous system as a result of abnormal processing of experiences"[2] (*DWDS*). For example "nervous, mental overload, tension lead to neuroses"[3] (*DWDS*). According to the *DWDS* typical connections of the noun *neurosis* in the German language usage are as follows: Neuroses are "traumatic," "sexual," "narcissistic," "hysterical," or "collective." Neuroses can be "dragged," "cured," or "lived" (*DWDS*). The adjective *neurotic* is defined in the DWDS as "based on neurosis, belonging to the neurosis"[4] with typical connections to words such as "Störungen" (disorder), "Symptome" (symptom), "Verhaltensstörungen" (behavioral disorders) or "Persönlichkeitsstörung" (personality disorder) (*DWDS*). Looking at the contexts of *neurosis* within the *DWDS* corpus in 2014, the founding year of Pegida,[5] an article can be found that contextualizes the relationship between politics, migration, and *neurosis*: "The time when Germany was massively recruiting guest workers abroad, but did not

1 *Digitales Wörterbuch der deutschen Sprache*, in the following called DWDS.

2 "funktionelle Störung des Nervensystems als Folge abnormer Verarbeitung von Erlebnissen" (DWDS). All translations from the German are by the author.

3 "nervliche, psychische Überlastungen, Spannungen führen zu Neurosen" (DWDS).

4 "auf Neurose beruhend, der Neurose zugehörig" (DWDS).

5 Engl.: Patriotic Europeans Against the Islamization of the Occident; German: Patriotische Europäer gegen die Islamisierung des Abendlandes.

want to be an immigration country, is long gone. But the relationship between politics and migration is still full of neuroses" (*ZEIT*, 10.01.14).[6]

The term "neurosis" refers in this article to the author's statement that "Germany is struggling with its migrants" (*ZEIT*, 10.01.14).[7] The fact that, in the previous passage, "neurosis" is used in the plural underlines that migration is linked to different contexts. With regard to the refugees arriving in Europe from 2014 on and the associated socio-political consequences for Germany and other European countries, this experience can certainly be described as "tension leading to neurosis." Thus neurosis can also be seen as a fear-induced attitude, leading to the conclusion that a surplus of fear produces neurotic responses. Therefore the assumption can be drawn that Germany's migration-related neuroses are also reflected in the rise of right-wing populist movements such as Pegida, which will be the focus of this article, since "questions and problems concerning the accommodation of refugees [...] directly promoted the emergence of Pegida in autumn 2014" (Vorländer, Herold, and Schäller 6). Furthermore Geiges, Marg and Walter as well as Micus highlight that populism can been seen as an 'upside-down psychoanalysis' (see Geiges, Marg and Walter 186; see Micus 14). Upside-down because, in this perception, populists who know the fears or phobias of people do not try to heal them but use them in order to strengthen or reinforce themselves:

> [Populism] *has an antenna for insecurity and neurotic timorousness*, but it is not concerned with healing, but with *affirming and stabilizing phobias and paranoia*. Populists do not treat, but draw their honey from the ongoing state of suffering of their 'patients.' (Geiges, Marg, and Walter 186; emphasis added) [8]

This means that populists, here right-wing populists, use contemporary neuroses of their societies in order to establish themselves in politics and political discourse. These neurotic fears towards refugees, Islam, and migration in general

---

6 "Die Zeit, in der Deutschland massenhaft Gastarbeiter im Ausland anwarb, aber partout kein Einwanderungsland sein wollte, ist lange vorbei. Aber die Beziehung der Politik zur Migration ist immer noch voller Neurosen."

7 "Deutschland tut sich schwer mit seinen Einwanderern" (*ZEIT*, 10.01.14).

8 "[Der Populismus] hat eine Antenne für Verunsicherungen und neurotische Furchtsamkeiten, aber es geht ihm nicht um Heilung, sondern um Bekräftigung und Verstetigung von Phobien und Paranoia. Populisten therapieren nicht, sondern ziehen ihren Honig aus dem fortwährenden Leidenszustand ihrer 'Patienten'" (Geiges, Marg, and Walter 186).

are deliberately served and reinforced in political statements – as for example the analysis of speeches by Pegida chairman Lutz Bachmann will show. This rhetoric strategy used by right-wing populists will be exploited in the paper leading to Micus' thesis that "populists do not solve problems, they merely exacerbate them, they do not cure resentments by addressing them, but exploit them, radicalize them" (14).[9] With a view to this assumption the main aim of this paper is to document the exploitation of fear reflected in language usage and expose it as a neurotic response to migration.

This paper sets out to explore how neurosis – particularly motivated by narratives of fear – is constituted in public discourse regarding migration issues. The analysis will firstly examine attitudes in public discourse towards Pegida as reflected in the media coverage. In this context, this paper will focus on statements regarding Pegida and its legitimation made by opinion makers such as key politicians as well as comments in media articles which reflect shifts in political perceptions such as after a speech of the Dutch right-wing populist Geert Wilders during a Pegida event. Afterwards, I will take into account comments from supporters and opponents posted on the Pegida Facebook group. On the one hand stated fears will be determined and described by focusing on their contexts. I will turn my attention to contexts in the Facebook corpus that concretely articulate neurosis. As part of the context and collocation analyses performed lexemes such as *fear, neurosis*, and *neurotic* are investigated. Afterwards I will look at four speeches by Lutz Bachmann, Pegida Chairman, and especially at passages which reflect attitudes and fears in society. For this purpose, four selected speeches, which Bachmann held on 21 March 2016, 29 August 2016, 5 May 2016, and 9 January 2017 in Dresden, will be examined. This will eventually demonstrate how Pegida uses the fears of citizens in order to establish itself.[10]

9 "Populisten lösen Probleme also nicht, sie verschärfen sie nur, sie kurieren Ressentiments nicht, indem sie diese thematisieren, sondern beuten sie aus, radikalisieren sie" (Micus 14).

10 The discourse linguistic analysis is corpus-based, focusing on words, word groups, and contexts by using concordance software based on digitalized texts and speeches. The discourse linguistic approach helps to capture regularities of language usage in order to determine attitudes and mentalities regarding a discourse topic in society over time (see Gür-Şeker).

THE DATABASE

The analysis will focus on language data, or more precisely on selected corpus data which can be differentiated into self-built and online databases. The database consists of the following resources:

1. December 2014 to November 2016: *ZEIT* Corpus.
2. December 2014 to October 2015: German online media dealing with Pegida (Pegida News Corpus).
3. October 2014 to January 2015: Pegida Facebook comments Corpus (Pegida Facebook Corpus).
4. April 2015: One political speech by Geert Wilders at a Pegida event in Dresden.
5. March 2016 to January 2017: Four political speeches by Lutz Bachmann at Pegida demonstrations in Dresden.

The complete investigation period spans from October 2014 until January 2017. The Pegida Facebook Corpus collected by Gregor Weichbrodt and Hannes Bajohr can be accessed for free online. The Facebook Corpus contains 282,596 comments and 7,751.654 tokens of anonymized users who express arguments and sentiments for or against Pegida. Additionally, a total set of 13 online media articles or online media sources have been selected by the author to examine how Pegida is presented in the media debate (henceforth called: Pegida News Corpus). The self-built news corpus consists of German online newspapers and news websites such as the online newspapers *Spiegel Online* (*SPIEGEL*), *Welt Online* (*WELT*), *Süddeutsche Zeitung* (*SZ*, online and on paper), *Die ZEIT* (*ZEIT*), *Frankfurter Allgemeine Zeitung* (*FAZ*), *Frankfurter Rundschau* (*FR*), *Focus Online* (*FOCUS*), and the news website *tagesthemen.de* as well as *tagesschau.de*. In this news corpus the focus lies on the analysis of images and statements about Pegida within the media discourse, mainly concentrating on key events and politicians. Additionally one YouTube video showing a Pegida event with the Dutch right-wing populist Geert Wilders which has been criticized in media discourse as well as four speeches by Lutz Bachmann will be examined in order to widen the analysis. This self-built corpus and its analysis are supplemented by the *Digital Lexicon of the German Language* (DWDS), which consists of different digitalized German lexicons and newspaper corpora.

PEGIDA IN THE *ZEIT* CORPUS (DECEMBER 2014 – NOVEMBER 2016)

The *DWDS* not only provides definitions from digitalized lexicons but also includes different media corpora of newspapers. This paper concentrates on the media coverage in *Die ZEIT* (referred to as the *ZEIT* Corpus) which can be retrieved in the *DWDS*. The *ZEIT* Corpus is used in order to describe media coverage regarding core features and attitudes of Pegida especially regarding migrants. By entering the word "Pegida" as a search term, one soon realizes that there are no encyclopedia entries, since Pegida is a newly created acronym, used for the first time in 2014. What one can find by entering *Pegida* as a search term is a wide range of *ZEIT* articles which were published from December 2014 until November 2016, with a total of 2,490 hits (or contexts).[11] The *ZEIT* Corpus only lists short contexts[12] of the search term without further corpus linguistic information such as collocations, frequency of words, or word clusters. The contexts of the search term *Pegida* show not only political statements and positions of the movement, for example regarding migration, but also naming practices in the media. First, the acronym is described and defined at the beginning of almost every article, which can also be interpreted as a semantization of an unknown abbreviation. For example, in the following *ZEIT* article the full title of the movement is mentioned first, followed by its abbreviation: "'Patriotische Europäer gegen die Islamisierung des Abendlandes' (Pegida)" (*ZEIT*, 01.12.14).

But which dominant practices of naming Pegida are used in the *ZEIT* Corpus? This question helps to shed light on the relevance Pegida has in society and how Pegida is classified in public discourse. To begin with, the acronym Pegida is used for naming a new actor. In its early stages, media coverage of Pegida in 2014 labeled it as a "group," "alliance," "movement," or more precisely as a "protest movement" (*DWDS*):

Demonstration of the alliance of 'Patriotische Europäer gegen die Islamisierung des Abendlandes' (Pegida). (*ZEIT*, 08.12.14)

---

11 More specifically, the search included hits from 1 December 2014 to 22 November 2016.

12 The search usually shows one to three sentences.

Demonstration of the initiative of Patriotische Europäer gegen die Islamisierung des Abendlandes (Pegida). (*ZEIT*, 09.12.14) [13]

It should be noted that from December 2014 until July 2015 Pegida is named through composites or adjectives which contextualize Pegida as a movement particularly against Islam. For example, we can find compounds such as "anti-Islam movement Pegida" (*ZEIT*, 09.12.14), "anti-Islamic Pegida" (*ZEIT*, 08.01.15), "movements critical of Islam such as Pegida" (*ZEIT*, 07.01.15), or "anti-Islamic protest movement Pegida" (*ZEIT*, 07.01.15).[14]

The manual review of the search term *Pegida* in the *ZEIT* Corpus shows that from December 2014 until July 2015 *ZEIT* strikingly often described Pegida as a "movement" with critical attitudes towards Islam. This is mainly reflected in adjectives such as "critical of Islam" or "anti-Islamic." During this time span, newspaper coverage rarely described Pegida as "right-wing populist" (*ZEIT*, 20.06.15), "racist" (*ZEIT*, 10.02.15), "Islamophobic" (*ZEIT*, 10.02.15) or "xenophobic" (*ZEIT*, 02.05.15). However, in 2016 Pegida is frequently marked and contextualized as "*xenophobic* Pegida" (*ZEIT*, 09.01.16; emphasis added), "*Islamophobic* Pegida" (*ZEIT*, 06.02.16; emphasis added), "the xenophobic and Islamophobic *protest movement*" (*ZEIT*, 05.05.16; emphasis added), or "the Islamophobic and xenophobic *alliance*" (*ZEIT*, 16.10.16; emphasis added).[15]

The lexicon used in media coverage of Pegida reflects a shift in public discourse between 2014 and 2016 and shows core topics of the movement regarding Islam and migrants, both of whom Pegida is opposing. As a consequence, these topics probably also have a special place in political speeches or Facebook discussions of Pegida and the construction of fear. But first perceptions of

13 "Demonstration des Bündnisses Patriotische Europäer gegen die Islamisierung des Abendlandes" (Pegida) (*ZEIT*, 08.12.14) and "Demonstration der Initiative Patriotische Europäer gegen die Islamisierung des Abendlandes (Pegida)" (*ZEIT*, 09.12.14).

14 "*Anti-Islam*-Bewegung 'Pegida'" (*ZEIT*, 09.12.14; emphasis added), "*anti-islamische* Pegida" (*ZEIT*, 08.01.15; emphasis added), "*islamkritische* Bewegungen wie Pegida" (*ZEIT*, 07.01.15; emphasis added), or "*anti-islamische* Protestbewegung Pegida" (*ZEIT*, 07.01.15; emphasis added).

15 "der *fremdenfeindlichen* Pegida" (*ZEIT*, 09.01.16; emphasis added), "die *islamfeindliche* Pegida" (*ZEIT*, 06.02.16; emphasis added), "die fremden- und islamfeindliche *Protestbewegung*" (*ZEIT*, 05.05.16; emphasis added), and "das islam- und fremdenfeindliche *Bündnis*" (*ZEIT*, 16.10.16; emphasis added).

Pegida in media and politics are of interest in the next section in order to show which core features of Pegida are highlighted in media discourse.

PERCEPTIONS OF PEGIDA IN MEDIA AND POLITICS

Besides the naming of Pegida as a *movement* with anti-Islamic features it is also important to address the image of Pegida politicians presented in the media in order to highlight the notions of fear Pegida exploits, manufactures, or is associated with. The analysis of the Pegida Online Media Corpus of 14 media articles shows that at first politicians were uncertain as to how to deal with the demands of Pegida demonstrators, who apparently articulated existing "fears" and "concerns" (*ZEIT*, 12.12.14). In this context, the media described Pegida as a civic movement. Before the anniversary of Pegida in October 2015, politicians used similar expressions in their statements about Pegida. In the following part of the paper I will look at two main political actors, namely Sigmar Gabriel and Thomas de Maizière, and their changing political statements about Pegida. Their shifting views reflect the broader transformation Pegida underwent in public perception, from a civil movement to an explicitly right-wing populist movement.

Despite the uproar caused by a picture of the Pegida leader Lutz Bachmann posing as Hitler found on January 2015 on Facebook, Sigmar Gabriel, at that time Vice-Chancellor, Minister of Economic Affairs, and chairman of the SPD, decided to visit a Pegida debate. His role during the visit was explicitly defined and limited: He visited Pegida as a so-called 'private citizen' and he only spoke with other 'citizens' at the demonstration – not with the organizers. This seemed to be in line with the argumentation of his political party, the SPD, since SPD General Secretary Yasmin Fahimi, the general secretary of SPD at that time, emphasized that the "Social Democratic Party of Germany rejects discussions with the *Pegida organizers*" (*FR*, 19.01.15; emphasis added).[16] Sigmar Gabriel justified his visit as follows: "[…] but with *the people* who go there and who *have concerns* and who are *angry about politics* – of course you have to speak with them. I mean, what other means do we have in a democracy except to speak with each other?" (*Tagesthemen*, 24.01.15; emphasis added).[17] His participation

16 "Die SPD lehnt nach den Worten ihrer Generalsekretärin Yasmin Fahimi Gespräche mit den Pegida-Organisatoren ab" (*FR*, 19.01.15).

17 "[…] aber mit den Menschen, die dort hingehen und die Sorgen haben und die verärgert sind über die Politik – natürlich muss man mit denen reden. Ich meine, was gibt

is categorized in the media discourse as the "breaking of a taboo" (*Tagesthemen*, 24.01.15).[18] Similarly, Yasmin Fahimi made clear that "it is 'a wrong signal', when Social Democrats lend an ear to *supporters* of the Pegida movement" (*ZEIT*, 27.01.15).[19]

In February 2015 the newspaper *Süddeutsche Zeitung* reported a statement Gabriel had made during an interview with the German magazine *Stern*: he had said that Pegida "obviously" belongs to Germany. Gabriel's statements in *Stern* are cited directly: "There is a democratic right to be a German national" and that there is "[e]ven a right to distribute stupidities such as the alleged Islamization of Germany" (*SZ*, 04.02.15).[20] Two months before Gabriel's statements, *Die ZEIT* published an article with Thomas de Maizière, German interior minister at the time, who expressed similar views. In an article titled "De Maizière is Concerned about Pegida Followers" (2014), the paper cited de Maizière as follows:

> The federal interior minister asks for *the fears of anti-Islam protesters to be taken seriously* [...]. In the ARD, Federal Interior Minister Thomas de Maizière (CDU) declared that, although there were "problematic developments" with regard to the initiators among the participants of the demonstrations, "there are quite many who express their *concerns* to the challenges of our time." (*ZEIT*, 12.12.14; emphasis added)[21]

What de Maizière understood under "challenges of our time" remains vague but apparently it is about existing "concerns" which legitimate the protest. Most importantly, de Maizière is cited directly referring to the results of a survey:

---

es in der Demokratie anderes an Mitteln, außer mit einander zu sprechen?" (*Tagesthemen*, 24.01.15; minute: 00:09:18-00:09:33).

18 "Tabubruch" (*Tagesthemen*, 24.01.15; minute: 00:09:37)

19 "Sie hält es für 'ein falsches Zeichen,' wenn Sozialdemokraten den Anhängern der Pegida-Bewegung ihr Ohr schenken" (*ZEIT*, 27.01.15;).

20 "'Es gibt ein demokratisches Recht darauf, rechts zu sein oder deutschnational,' sagte Gabriel. 'Sogar ein Recht, Dummheiten zu verbreiten wie die angebliche Islamisierung Deutschlands'" (*SZ*, 04.02.15).

21 "Der Bundesinnenminister plädiert dafür, *die Ängste der Anti-Islam-Demonstranten ernst zu* nehmen […]. Bundesinnenminister Thomas de Maizière (CDU) sagte in der ARD, zwar gebe es bei den Initiatoren 'problematische Entwicklungen,' aber unter den Teilnehmern der Demonstrationen 'gibt es doch ganz schön viele, die bringen ihre Sorgen zum Ausdruck vor den Herausforderungen unserer Zeit'" (*ZEIT*, 12.12.14; emphasis added).

De Maizière pointed to a study that showed in his view that a part of the *citizens feel like foreigners in their own country*. "We must take *these concerns* seriously, we have to deal with that." (*ZEIT*, 12.12.14; emphasis added)[22]

In the News Corpus, a variety of articles concentrate on such "concerns" of the demonstrators and contextualize these within a perceived Islamization of Germany (see *FAZ*, 18.11.14) or worries regarding a perceived increase in crime that is connected to migrants or non-Germans (see *FAZ*, 25.11.14). The news website *tagesschau.de* emphasized the comparison to other anti-Islam movements in Germany: "(c)ompared to the Hooligans against the Salafists, '*Pegida*' *acts civil*" (*tagesschau.de*, 01.12.14; emphasis added).[23]

In April 2015 the Dutch right-wing populist Geerd Wilders was invited to speak at a Pegida event in Dresden. Addressing Chancellor Angela Merkel in German, he said "Mrs. Merkel, the majority of your *Volk* is of the opinion that Islam does not belong to Germany" (Wilders).[24] Wilders' participation and the fact that he has been invited not only as a speaker but a "guest of honor" (*WELT*, 13.04.15)[25] can be seen as an important feature leading to a shift in public opinion, since Pegida had not been considered an extremist movement up to this point.

Before the Pegida anniversary celebration in October 2015, which took place in Dresden, the German Interior Minister Thomas de Maizière underlined explicitly his new position regarding Pegida in the German Television channel *ARD* (also cited by *ZEIT* on 18.10.15):

German Interior Minister Thomas de Maizière issued an unusually *clear* warning against Pegida. "*By now*, it has become completely obvious. [Pegida] organizers are *hardcore right-wing extremists*," he said in the ARD. "They call *all asylum seekers criminals, all politicians traitors*. This is far from any democratic consensus." […] "Stay away from

22 "De Maizière wies auf eine Studie hin, die seiner Ansicht nach belegt, dass sich ein Teil der *Bürger wie Fremde im eigenen Land fühle*. 'Diese Sorgen müssen wir ernst nehmen, damit müssen wir uns auseinandersetzen'" (*ZEIT*, 12.12.14; emphasis added).

23 "Im Gegensatz zu den Hooligans gegen Salafisten *treten* die *'Pegida' bürgerlich auf*" (*tagesschau.de*, 01.12.14; emphasis added).

24 "Frau Merkel, die Mehrheit Ihres Volkes ist der Meinung, dass der Islam nicht zu Deutschland gehört." (Geerd Wilders, Quote from a YouTube video, 13.04.15; minute: 10:28-10:36).

25 "Ehrengast" (*WELT*, 13.04.15).

those who inject this *hatred*, this poison in our country." (*ZEIT*, 18.10.15; emphasis added)[26]

In the mentioned *ZEIT* article the Interior Minister is reported to have used clear and explicit markers to underline Pegida's development into a right-wing political organization – in this case reflected by the phrases "unusually clear," "completely obvious," and "hardcore right-wing extremists." By using the metaphor of injecting poison into the country, the last sentence emphasizes the importance of not attending the anniversary celebrations.

Shortly before and after the anniversary date a transformation in the portrayal of Pegida in the media indicated the changing perception of the movement. The image of concerned citizens mainly vanished. Pegida became "a racist movement" (*ZEIT*, 18.10.15), "hard right-wing extremists" (*ZEIT*, 18.10.15), the "islamophobic Pegida movement" (*Spiegel*, 27.10.15), and "the islamophobic and xenophobic Pegida alliance" (*Focus*, 26.10.15).[27] While the *Frankfurter Rundschau* quoted vice-chancellor Sigmar Gabriel sharing the similar sentiment that "'Pegida is a right-wing populist movement and, in some cases, a right-wing radical movement of revolt,'" the paper also qualified his statement with the addition of "says the vice-chancellor *now*" (FR, 20.10.15; emphasis in the original).[28] The adverb *now* signals that the newspaper is aware of Gabriel's shifting position regarding Pegida and is highlighting this change (the title "Gabriel's new sharp tone" foreshadows the change).[29] Gabriel's language reflects the shift in public perception. These examples highlight the change in the media as well as in the public political discourse. Before that shift, however, various politicians

---

26 "Ungewohnt deutlich hat Bundesinnenminister Thomas de Maizière vor Pegida gewarnt. '*Inzwischen* ist es völlig eindeutig. Diejenigen, die das organisieren, sind *harte Rechtsextremisten*,' sagte er in der ARD. 'Sie bezeichnen *Asylbewerber pauschal als Verbrecher*, alle *Politiker als Hochverräter*. Das ist fernab jedes demokratischen Konsenses.' [...] 'Bleiben Sie weg von denen, die diesen *Hass*, dieses Gift in unser Land spritzen'" (*ZEIT*, 18.10.15; emphasis added).

27 "die rassistische Bewegung" (*ZEIT*, 18.10.15), "harte Rechtsextremisten" (*ZEIT*, 18.10.15), "islamfeindlichen Pegida-Bewegung" (*Spiegel*, 27.10.15), and "das islam- und fremdenfeindliche Pegida-Bündnis" (*Focus*, 26.10.15).

28 "'Pegida ist eine rechtspopulistische und in Teilen offen rechtsradikale Empörungsbewegung geworden', sagt der Vizekanzler *jetzt*" (*FR*, 20.10.15; emphasis in the original).

29 "Gabriels neuer scharfer Ton" (Pegida Facebook Corpus, user post 2014-12-10T17:38:07+0000; emphasis added).

have utilized the notion of "fear," thereby lending credibility to assumptions about anxiety fueling the protests.

NEUROSIS AND FEAR IN THE PEGIDA FACEBOOK GROUP

The following section focuses on social media, especially Facebook, and on the discourse of fear and neurosis developed by its users. In this part of my analysis I employ the concordance software AntConc to find patterns in how users understand the name Pegida as well as the attitudes and positions of the movement in the Facebook corpus. In the Pegida Facebook corpus the term *Pegida* can be found 43,597 times. The slogan "We are the Volk"[30] is used 1,480 times. For example, one user wrote about the Pegida demonstrations on 10 December 2014: "Best without big speeches, justifications etc. The mere *presence of people* and the *flags* are the message: *We are the Volk* and *we lay claim to our country!*" (Pegida Facebook Corpus; emphasis added).[31] In this comment the flags are symbolically used to indicate that Pegida is a movement for what Pegida sympathizers understand as the German nation. The colors of the flag of the Federal Republic of Germany – black, red, and gold – dominate almost all Pegida demonstration, becoming a symbol for the participants' identification with national space and soil (see Vorländer, Herold, and Schäller 11-17). The user associates the flag with the country, the "presence of people," and thus with the slogan "We are the Volk."

In other Facebook comments, the use of "We are the Volk" leads to the conclusion that if "We are the Volk," we are also the "state" (Pegida Facebook Corpus). These statements actually reflect the mistrust towards the state and its political representatives and the mistrust of the governed towards their legitimately elected representatives. Over time this key feature of mistrusts culminated in the rejection of leading politicians such as Chancellor Angela Merkel. This rejection can be seen as a key feature of populist movements that oppose established polit-

30 "Wir sind das Volk" (Pegida Facebook Corpus, user post 2014-12-12T12:49). "We are the Volk" has been a popular rallying cry during the 1989 revolution when citizens of the FDR toppled their government through peaceful demonstrations. The phrase articulates the demand for democratic reforms and the claim to popular sovereignty by stylizing the demonstrators as "the people" ("Volk").

31 "Am besten ohne große Reden, Rechtfertigungen usw. auftreten. Allein *die Präsenz der Menschen* und die *Fahnen* sind die Botschaft: *Wir sind das Volk* und *wir erheben Anspruch auf unser Land!*".

ical actors (see Priester) and found expression in the slogan "Merkel has to leave."[32]

The lexeme "Angst" (fear) occurs 5,812 times in the Facebook corpus. Partner words which frequently occur with "fear" are for example: "Islam" (151),[33] "Islamization" (129), "Islamists" (55), "terror" (47), "Muslims" (39), "violence" (39), "Muslims" (34), "foreigners" (31) or "strangers" (30).[34] Other related phrases are "I'm scared," "afraid," "fear and anxiety," or "not afraid" (Pegida Facebook Corpus).[35] Expressions of Islamophobia can be found in various posts. Without being able to list all at this point, only a selection of contexts in which this fear is expressed in connection with the supposed Islamization of Germany is listed below.

But this *increasingly extreme Islamization scares and frightens*. Are we Germans worth nothing in our own country? (Pegida Facebook Corpus; emphasis added)[36]
So I know another stat 54% are *afraid of Islamization* and 27% would march. (Pegida Facebook Corpus; emphasis added)[37]

"Fear" is also contextualized with internal security and immigration as expressed in the following postings.

Are you actually running around blindfolded? Is it okay that *German women have to be afraid* when they are alone on the street? (Pegida Facebook Corpus; emphasis added)[38]

32 "Merkel muss weg."

33 Parentheses show frequency of words.

34 In German: "Islam" (151), "Islamisierung" (129), "Islamisten" (55), "Terror" (47), "Moslems" (39), "Gewalt" (39), "Muslime" (34), "Ausländer" (31), "Fremden" (30).

35 "Ich habe Angst," "Angst haben," "Angst und Bange," "keine Angst" (Pegida Facebook Corpus).

36 "Aber diese *immer extremer werdende islamisierung macht einem Angst und Bange*. Sind wir deutschen denn im eigenen Land gar nichts mehr wert? Mann o mann" (Pegida Facebook Corpus, user post 2014-12-10T16:47:58+0000; emphasis added).

37 "Also ich kenn eine andere stat 54% haben *angst vor islamisierung* und 27% würden mitmarschieren." (Pegida Facebook Corpus, user post 2014-12-18T18:24:51+0000; emphasis added).

38 "Lauft ihr eigentlich mit verbundenen Augen durch die Welt? Ist es in Ordnung *das deutsche Frauen Angst haben* müssen wenn sie allein auf der Straße sind???" (Pegida Facebook Corpus, user post 2014-12-14T06:55:46+0000; emphasis added).

> *Of course I'm afraid*, what would Mrs. Merkel say if she gets pushed down the street by *about 13 Africans* and break her bones? Unfortunately this happened to me a week ago. *I'm terrified.* We need a lot more police presence in and near asylum accommodations. *Peaceful life in Germany is over.* (Pegida Facebook Corpus; emphasis added)[39]

As mentioned above, the corpus not only contains posts from Pegida supporters but also from opponents or critics who pick up on and dissent with Pegida's use of fear.

> How does one come up with the idea that the *Muslims* living quite normally among us want to *take over the "Occident"* (ridiculous expression)? *Here a general fear of the future is channeled towards "foreign fellow citizens" and Islam.*) (Pegida Facebook Corpus; emphasis added)[40]
>
> Exactly 50 meters away from me asylum seekers are housed, in the neighboring house. Nobody is afraid of them here. There are far more attacks on asylum homes than by asylum seekers on Germans. *This hatred of a particular group here in Germany is what scares me*. (Pegida Facebook Corpus; emphasis added)[41]

The first user makes clear that a general anxiety is channeled towards minorities (in the context of Pegida and the Facebook group). The second user reverses the fear formulated by Pegida supporters by projecting them onto Pegida. In both

39 "*Und ob ich Angst habe*, was würde Frau Merkel sagen wenn sie auf der Strasse *von ca. 13 Afrikanern* zu Boden geschubst wird und sich dabei Knochenbrüche zuzieht. Mir leider vor einer Woche passiert. *Ich habe Riesenangst.* Wir brauchen viel mehr Polizeipräsenz vor Asylantenunterkünften und in der Nähe von diesen. *Das friedliche Leben ist in Deutschland vorbei*" (Pegida Facebook Corpus, user post 2014-12-20T21:58:07+0000; emphasis added).

40 "Wie kommt man denn bloß auf den Gedanken, daß die ganz normal zwischen uns lebenden *Moslems das 'Abendland'* (lächerlicher Ausdruck) *übernehmen* wollen? *Hier wird eine allgemeine Angst vor der Zukunft in Richtung* 'ausländischer Mitbürger' und Islam kanalisiert" (Pegida Facebook Corpus, user post 2014-12-16T21:00:57+0000; emphasis added).

41 "Genau 50 Meter von mir entfernt sind Asylanten untergebracht, im Nachbarhaus. Hier hat keiner Angst vor ihnen. Es gibt wesentlich mehr Angriffe auf Asylheime als von Asylanten auf Deutsche. *Dieser Hass auf eine bestimmte Gruppe hier in Deutschland ist das, was mir Angst macht*" (Pegida Facebook Corpus, user post 2014-12-20T22:10:41+0000; emphasis added).

posts and their contexts, Pegida critics indicate that Pegida and their supporters are what they are afraid of.

The analysis of "fear" in the Facebook Pegida Corpus shows that the noun is used 5,812 times and is highly associated with Islam and migration but also with developments within German society. The analysis shows that fear is highly present in the discourse surrounding Pegida both in the media coverage and in social media debates. These discursive constructions of fear lead to neurotic responses to migration reflected in the persistence of Pegida demonstrations in Dresden or the success of the right-wing populist Party Alternative für Deutschland (AfD) which won a number of seats in the German Federal Parliament in the 2017 election.

In the Pegida Facebook corpus, users employ the lexemes "neurosis" (2), the noun "neurotic" (3), and the adjective "neurotic" (7). Complexes with "neurosis" such as "profile neurosis" (6), "social neurosis" (1), and "obsessive-compulsive disorder" (1)[42] are preceded by adjectives like "heavy" and "light," or pronouns like "their own." Without mentioning all contexts, the following use can be noted: Compounds with "neurosis" are used in all contexts to describe a mindset or behavior of a person or group that is connoted negatively or whose opinion the speaker does not share.

However, in the corpus users also qualify Pegida's xenophobic attitudes as neurotic – a perspective which gains particular relevance in this investigation of Pegida as a neurotic response to fear. A negative attitude towards Pegida is expressed in the following post:

> You did not understand anything about the history of 89, and yet you appropriate it *to spill your neurotic, xenophobic crap*, that is sad. Poor Germany. (Pegida Facebook Corpus; emphasis added)[43]

The following example similarly contextualizes xenophobia with neurosis, asking Pegida supporters whether "you *fear-neurotics* know how much your main school meetings [Pegida demonstrations] on Mondays cost?" (Pegida Facebook

42 "Neurotiker," "neurotisch," "Profilneurose," "Sozialneurose," and "Zwangsneurose."

43 "Ihr habt nichts begriffen aus der Geschichte von 89, und dennoch macht ihr euch sie zu eigen *um euren neurotischen, fremdenfeindlichen Mist zu verzapfen*, das ist traurig. Armes Deutschland" (Pegida Facebook Corpus, user post 2014-12-23T00:16:17+0000; emphasis added).

Corpus; emphasis added).[44] The compound "fear-neurotics" implies that Pegida plays with or caters to existing 'fears.' "Fear neurotics" is also an attempt to stigmatize Pegida supporters by drawing attention to the core element of Pegida rhetoric: addressing sociopolitical challenges by fueling fear in order to legitimate the movements' existence. After the selective analysis of the Facebook comments has shed light on determining fears of Pegida supporters, the following section will examine speeches by one leading figure behind the Pegida demonstrations, Lutz Bachmann, to help understand which kind of fears Pegida addresses.

FEAR OF MIGRATION AND ISLAM IN PEGIDA SPEECHES

The speeches of Lutz Bachmann (LB) were transcribed on the basis of YouTube videos in the project "Language and Rhetoric of Right-wing Populism in a Country Comparison" funded by the main research area "Transformation of Contemporary Societies"[45] of the University of Duisburg-Essen (see Gür-Şeker 2017).[46] While Bachmann does not use words like *neurosis* or *neurotic* in these speeches, his rhetoric ties in with formulations of fear and anxieties that have been expressed within the Pegida discourse. Of interest is which fears or worries Bachmann formulates in his speeches and how his language usage characterizes migration. The search term "fear" in the singular could be found in three contexts:

1. An understandable *fear* about losing job, pension, and reputation. (LB, 05.12.16; emphasis added)
2. Almost everything we have been *warning* about has become a *reality*, (.) and that is *scary*. (LB, 09.01.17; emphasis added)

44 "Wisst ihr [Pegida-Anhänger] *Angstneurotiker* was eure *Hauptschulversammlung* [Pegida-Demonstrationen] kostet Montags?" (Pegida Facebook Corpus, user post 2015-01-11T02:06:20+0000; emphasis added).

45 "Die Sprache und Rhetorik des Rechtspopulismus im Ländervergleich: Eine bilinguale und multimodale Medien- und Sprachanalyse rechtspopulistischer Akteure in YouTube- und Facebook-Videos in Deutschland, den Niederlanden und Flandern" gefördert vom Profilschwerpunkt Wandel von Gegenwartsgesellschaften an der Universität Duisburg-Essen.

46 For more information, please visit the project's website which also contains the multilingual Dutch and German corpus: www.uni-due.de/rechtspopulismus.

3. And it is this clear line of reason and common sense (.) that *scares* them, the rulers. (LB, 21.03.16; emphasis added)[47]

Context (1) deals with the fear of civil servants who apparently had written Bachmann in order to share their fears with him. Context (2) deals with Pegida positions regarding postulated consequences of migration and refugee policies, which according to Bachmann had become reality. Context (3) refers to the supposed fear of policy makers regarding Pegida.

The search term *fear* in the plural is used in contexts such as "economic fears" (LB, 21.03.16 and 09.01.17).[48] Bachmann appropriates anxieties about the future by citing the (supposed) experience of an (unnamed) refugee helper:

> *Islam* controls these people down to the smallest ramifications of everyday life (.) And if only a fraction of all refugees thinks this way, (.) *I look with concern to our future.* (.) We still have (.) not understood (.) what is coming our way, (.) neither our laws, (.) nor we are prepared for it. (.) We think that tolerance makes everything possible (.) But someone said: (.) 'Tolerance is the last virtue of *a sinking society.*' (LB, 29.08.16; emphasis added)[49]

The repeated worries about the future and the notion of a society in decline are two narratives which make clear why critics in the Facebook group call Pegida supporters "Angstneurotiker." In contrast to the Facebook corpus, there is no evidence for lexemes such as *neurosis* or *neurotic* in Bachmann's speeches, but contexts can be found in which alleged fears of the citizens or worries about "the country" are formulated. Referring to the chairman of the German police union Rainer Wendt, Bachmann continues:

---

47 "verständlicher *Angst* um Job, Pension und Reputation" (LB, 05.12.16); "Nahezu alles wovor wir *gewarnt* haben ist *Realität* geworden, (.) und das macht einem *Angst*, […]" (LB, 09.01.17); "Und genau diese klare Linie der Vernunft und des gesunden Menschenverstandes (.) macht ihnen *Angst*, den Herrschenden (.)" (LB, 21.03.16; emphasis added).

48 "wirtschaftliche Ängste" (LB, 21.03.16 and 09.01.17)

49 "*Der Islam* hat diese Menschen bis in die kleinsten Verästelungen des Alltags im Griff (.) und wenn auch nur ein Bruchteil aller Flüchtlinge so denkt, (.) *sehe ich mit Sorge in unsere Zukunft.* (.) Wir haben (.) immer noch (.) nicht begriffen, (.) was da auf uns zukommt, (.) weder unsere Gesetze, (.) noch wir sind darauf vorbereitet. (.) Wir denken mit Toleranz geht alles, (.) dazu sagte aber schon jemand: (.) 'Toleranz ist die letzte Tugend *einer untergehenden Gesellschaft*'" (LB, 29.08.16; emphasis added).

4. our country would be (…) exposed to *dangers* (.) *that are always connected with mass immigration*. (LB, 05.12.16; emphasis added)
5. This is how the *dangers* for our country *grow constantly*. (LB, 05.12.16; emphasis added)[50]

In another context regarding refugee policies Bachmann highlights again the issue of danger:

6. So instead of reducing the *danger* in the run-up. (LB; 09.01.17; emphasis added)[51]

In the four Bachmann speeches refugees are labelled as "murderer-refugees," "refugee terror à la Würzburg, Munich, Berlin," "so-called refugees," or alternative designations are used such as "adventurers" for example in his speech on 21 March 2016:

7. The worst part, (---) is that now we even pay for the *invasion* of *these adventurers called refugees*. (LB, 21.03.16; emphasis added)[52]

In context (7) the alternative term "Glücksritter" is used for refugees who are portrayed as adventurers trying their luck. In this context real reasons for flight are deliberately hidden and even ridiculed by using the term "Glücksritter." The fact that these people are seeking protection from instability, war, and destruction is strategically ignored here. Meanwhile, the invasion metaphor reinforces the image of forced immigration which is a key feature of Bachmann's speeches. Bachmann contextualizes flight with the adjective "illegal" (see contexts 8, 9) and highly inflates numbers of migrants in Germany to construct a threat scenario (see contexts 8, 10, 11):

8. Qualitative immigration like the Swiss or Canadian model, instead of currently common *quantitative, illegal mass immigration*. (LB, 09.01.17; emphasis added)
9. rejected asylum *cheater*. (LB, 29.08.16; emphasis added)[53]

---

50 "wäre unser Land auf die *Gefahren*, (.) die mit *massenhafter Zuwanderung immer* verbunden sind (.)" (LB, 05.12.16); "so *wachsen* die *Gefahren* für unser Land beständig" (LB, 05.12.16; emphasis added).

51 "Anstatt also die *Gefahr* im Vorfeld zu reduzieren" (LB; 09.01.17; emphasis added).

52 "Das Schlimme daran ist, (---) dass *wir* diesen *als Flüchtlinge bezeichneten Glücksrittern* jetzt auch noch die *Invasion bezahlen*" (LB, 21.03.16; emphasis added).

Again, the contexts also show that real reasons for flight are hidden. Bachmann speaks of "illegal mass immigration," contextualizing "immigration" with "illegal" and highlighting with the noun compound "mass" a large number of people. Similar strategies can be found in contexts (4), (10), and (11).

10. *Millions of so-called* refugees. (LB, 21.03.16; emphasis added)
11. In the summer of 2015, when you were still diligently dancing a Schuhplatter as a sign of welcome (.) at the Munich Central Station for *hundreds, hundreds of thousands of illegal immigrants.* (LB, 21.03.16; emphasis added)[54]

Overall, Bachmann's speeches are characterized by fear- and hate-mongering attitudes towards immigration processes and a highly exclusionary language against refugees, immigrants, and Islam. He deliberately exaggerates ("mass," "millions," "hundreds of thousands") and excludes legal immigration per se ("illegal immigration," "invasion," "so-called refugees") by also systematically relativizing the human right to asylum ("rejected asylum cheater"). The compound "Angstneurotiker" thus reflects public perceptions about Pegida and its political attitudes, which deliberately present immigration and its consequences for Germany as negative.

CONCLUSION

The paper outlined and examined three perspectives on Pegida. First, the media analysis showed that media and politicians were apparently surprised by the success of Pegida. The number of participants at Pegida demonstrations has been interpreted as a legitimate expression of the existing fear(s) and anger of "the *Volk*." After October 2015, a shift of public attitudes towards the movement occurred that explicitly marked Pegida as a right-wing populist movement. Since its beginning, however, Pegida displayed some of the core features of right-wing populist movements such as its opposition to immigration, which is not only re-

---

53 "Qualitative Zuwanderung, anstatt momentan gängiger *quantitativer, illegaler Massen*einwanderung nach schweizerischem oder kanadischem Vorbild" (LB, 09.01.17) and "abgelehnten Asyl*betrüger*" (LB, 29.08.16; emphasis added).

54 "*Abermillionen sogenannte* Flüchtlinge" (LB, 21.03.16) and "Als ihr im Sommer 2015 noch fleißig den Willkommens-Schuhplatter (.) am Münchener Hauptbahnhof für *hunderte, hunderttausende illegale Einwanderer* getanzt habt (.)" (LB, 21.03.16; emphasis added).

flected in media coverage and discourse but also in how topics such as immigration, migration, and Islam are contextualized in the Pegida Facebook group. Furthermore, slogans and signs at demonstrations in Dresden as well as statements on social media reflect Pegida's resentment towards rising ethnic and cultural diversity in Germany (or Europe) (see Boonen, Gür-Şeker, and Thomcezek). Neurotic perspectives of Pegida sympathizers mainly focus on immigration issues and questions of internal security expressed in fears about the role of Islam and the presumed negative consequences for German society.

As a conclusion of the analysis, it can safely be argued that Pegida instrumentalizes citizens' fears regarding social changes. The analysis could show that Bachmann spreads resentments through specific language usage such as marking immigration or flight as illegal, highlighting exaggerating estimates of migrants present in the country, or hiding reasons for flight. These are only some of the strategies which can be traced in the four speeches – further analysis of the complete speeches particularly in comparison to other right-wing populists' such as Björn Höcke or Frauke Petry remains necessary in order to show the similarities and differences in their language use. In addition, the analysis of Facebook comments could show that Pegida supporters also formulate fears and resentments towards minorities. But the positions of Pegida and its supporters are also systematically criticized by opponents. This criticism is reflected in the stigma word "Angstneurotiker," which underlines and confirms Micus' thesis that populist are not solving sociopolitical challenges or problems but on the contrary radicalize and exacerbate them.

LIST OF WORKS CITED

Boonen, Ute. K, Derya Gür-Şeker, and Philipp Thomeczek. "Partizipation populistischer Akteure im Zeitalter digitaler Medien. Multimodale Perspektiven am Beispiel von Pegida." *Sprache und Partizipation in Geschichte und Gegenwart*, edited by Bettina M. Bock and Philipp Dreesen, Hempen Verlag, in preparation.

Digital Lexicon of the German Language. Berlin-Brandenburgischen Akademie der Wissenschaften, www.dwds.de. Accessed 1 July 2017.

Geiges, Lars, Stine Marg, and Franz Walter. *Pegida: Die schmutzige Seite der Zivilgesellschaft*. Bielefeld, 2015.

Goodwin, Matthew. *Die rechte Antwort: Den populistischen Extremismus in Europa verstehen und dagegen angehen.* The Royal Institute of International Affairs, 2011.

Gür-Şeker, Derya. *Politische Reden rechtspopulistischer Akteure in Deutschland: Transkripte auf Basis von YouTube- und Facebook-Videos veröffentlicht im Zeitraum 2013 bis 2017*. University of Duisburg-Essen, 2017, www.uni-due.de/rechtspopulismus. Accessed 25 Nov. 2017.

---. *Transnationale Diskurslinguistik: Theorie und Methodik am Beispiel des sicherheitspolitischen Diskurses über die EU-Verfassung in Deutschland, Großbritannien und der Türkei*. Hempen Verlag, 2012.

Micus, Matthias. "Das Gespenst des Populismus: Ein Annäherungsversuch." *Göttinger Themenhefte zu Zeitfragen von Politik, Gesellschaft und Sozialkultur: Rechtspopulismus in Europa*, edited by Alexander Hensel, Daniela Kallinich, and Robert Lorenz, Institut für Demokratieforschung an der Georg-August-Universität Göttingen, 2014, pp. 16-18.

Priester, Karin. "Wesensmerkmale des Populismus." *Populismus: Aus Politik und Zeitgeschichte*, vol. 62, no. 5-6, 2012. pp. 3-9.

Vorländer, Hans, Maik Herold, and Steven Schäller. *Pegida: Entwicklung, Zusammensetzung und Deutung einer Empörungsbewegung*. Springer VS, 2016.

Weichbrodt, Gregor, and Hannes Bajohr. *Das Pegida-Korpus*. http://0x0a.li/de/die-sprache-pegidas. Accessed 22 April 2015.

Wilders, Geert. "Rede von Geert Wilders zur Gefahr des Islams bei Pegida Dresden." *YouTube*, uploaded by Malarich, 22 April 2015, www.youtube.com/watch?v=b3_xA50rZAg. Accessed 18 Dec. 2015.

Transcribed speeches of Lutz Bachmann

LB, 21.03.16: "PEGIDA live auf dem Theaterplatz." *YouTube*, uploaded by Lutz Bachmann, 21 March 2016, www.youtube.com/watch?v=n92nMa61Fvs. Accessed 25 Nov. 2017.

LB, 29.08.16: "PEGIDA live vom Neumarkt mit Jürgen Elsässer." *YouTube*, uploaded by Lutz Bachmann, 29 August 2016, www.youtube.com/watch?v=3uTkWSZUdnM. Accessed 25 Nov. 2017.

LB, 05.12.16: "PEGIDA Dresden auf dem Schlossplatz." *YouTube*, uploaded by Lutz Bachmann, 5 December 2016, https://www.youtube.com/watch?v=to41c_qBql0. Accessed 25 Nov. 2017.

LB, 09.01.17: "PEGIDA live vom Altmarkt." *YouTube*, uploaded by Lutz Bachmann, 09 Jan. 2017, www.youtube.com/watch?v=C23Vs6IcfIU. Accessed 25 Nov. 2017.

Pegida News Corpus

Caspari, Lisa. "Sigmar Gabriels verlorene Seele." *Zeit Online*, 27 Jan. 2015, zeit.de/politik/deutschland/2015-01/Pegida-spd-dialog-yasmin-fahimi. Accessed 18 Dec. 2015.

"De Maizière sorgt sich um Pegida-Anhänger." *Zeit Online*, 12 Dec. 2014, zeit.de/politik/deutschland/2014-12/Pegida-maiziere-innenminister-islam. Accessed 18 Dec. 2015.

"De Maizière warnt vor Pegida." *Zeit Online*, 18 Oct. 2015, zeit.de/politik/deutschland/2015-10/pegida-maiziere-innenminister-rechtsextremismus-islamfeindlichkeit. Accessed 18 Dec. 2015.

Doemens, Karl. "Gabriels neuer scharfer Ton." *Frankfurter Rundschau*, 20 Jan. 2015, fr-online.de/Pegida/Pegida--gabriels-neuer-scharfer-ton,29337826,32207018.html. Accessed 18 Dec. 2015.

Eichstädt, Sven. "Seltsame Geschichtsvergleiche des Pegida-'Ehrengasts'." *Welt Online,* 13 Apr. 2015, welt.de/politik/deutschland/article139500556/Seltsame-Geschichtsvergleiche-des-Pegida-Ehrengasts.html. Accessed 18 Dec. 2015.

"'Es gibt ein Recht, deutschnational zu sein'." *Süddetusche Zeitung*, 04 Feb. 2015, sueddeutsche.de/politik/spd-chef-ueber-Pegida-gabriel-es-gibt-ein-recht-deutschnational-zu-sein-1.2336763. Accessed 18 Dec. 2015.

Locke, Stefan. "Spezialeinheit Abendland." *Frankfurter Allgemeine Zeitung*, 25 Nov. 2015, faz.net/aktuell/politik/inland/die-anti-asylbewerber-proteste-gewinnen-an-zulauf-13286097.html. Accessed 18 Dec. 2015.

---. "Von einer diffusen Angst beseelt." *Frankfurter Allgemeine Zeitung*, 18 Nov. 2015, faz.net/aktuell/politik/inland/demonstration-gegen-islamisierung-in-dresden-13273374.html. Accessed 18 Dec. 2015.

Müller, Tom. "'Islam- und fremdenfeindliche Pegida-Bündnis?'" *FOCUS Online*, 26 Oct. 2015, focus.de/politik/deutschland/islam-und-fremdenfeindliche-Pegida-buendnis-migration-kommentar_id_6961573.html. Accessed 18 Dec. 2015.

"SPD will nicht mit Pegida reden." *Frankfurter Rundschau*, 19 Jan. 2015, fr-online.de/Pegida/Pegida-spd-will-nicht-mit-Pegida-reden,29337826,29609620.html. Accessed 18 Dec. 2015.

Tagesschau.de. 1 Dec. 2014, tagesschau.de/inland/Pegida-103.html. Accessed 18 Dec. 2015.

Tagesthemen.de. 24 Jan. 2015, ardmediathek.de/tv/Tagesthemen/tagesthemen/Das-Erste/Video?bcastId=3914&documentId=26067270. Accessed 18 Dec. 2015.

"Wieder Tausende bei Pegida-Demo." *Spiegel Online*, 27 Oct. 2015, spiegel.de/politik/deutschland/Pegida-in-dresden-keine-krawalle-aber-tausende-auf-der-strasse-a-1059703.html. Accessed 18 Dec. 2015.

Ain't It Funny?

Danny Brown, Black Subjectivity, and the Performance of Neurosis

ALEX BLUE V

Our scene opens with a classic US television trope – a shot of the outside of a large home, situated in an idyllic suburban area, surrounded by trees, on a large, well-manicured plot of land. It is the American Dream that we have been told we should all aspire to – life outside of the chaotic, noisy, dangerous urbanity of the city. The show, titled *Ain't It Funny,* is offered with closed captioning, and "in stereo – where available" ("Ain't It Funny"). To the sound of a short musical intro and an off-camera studio audience cheering, we are quickly presented with the tragic subject, Danny Brown, sitting up with a woman in a large bed, in an even larger room. Danny holds a bottle of malt liquor in one hand and smokes a cigarette with the other; the yet-to-be-identified woman smokes as well. As the music quickly fades away, the focus turns to her as she looks vacantly into the distance – not into the camera – and says, "physical attention from older men makes me feel validated" ("Ain't It Funny"). The studio audience reacts with an "aww." As the camera cuts to Danny, he replies "I'm empty inside" ("Ain't It Funny"). Danny's words are met with silence. Suddenly, the camera quickly cuts to the bedroom door; as it opens, a young boy walks through and the audience reacts with an "oooooh." The child puts his hands on his hips, tilts his head to the side, and presents a knowing smile: "Oh, Uncle Danny..." ("Ain't It Funny"). The audience cheers wildly at the utterance of this catchphrase.

The music video for "Ain't It Funny," directed by the actor Jonah Hill, presents a distraught, self-destructive Danny Brown[1] in the context of a late 1980s, early 1990s American sitcom airing on the fictional Religious Values Network. Throughout the troubling video, the viewer is constantly forced to acknowledge Danny – who is Black – in pain and asking for help, only to be ignored by most of the other characters and laughed at by the studio audience, all of whom are white. In particular, there are numerous scenes that show Uncle Danny struggling with substance abuse. At one point in the video, he is essentially treated as invisible while sitting in the living room, completely surrounded by family; he smokes a crack pipe and notes that he has a serious problem, only to be met with laughter. "Ain't It Funny" brings to light issues of neurosis, subjection, and voyeurism. The video joins a growing discourse on the abuse of Black people, identities, and bodies as consumable entertainment and spectacle.

BLACKNESS AS NEUROSIS AND THE VOYEURISTIC GAZE

The term *neurosis* was most famously used by Sigmund Freud and can be understood as emotional disturbances expressed through mental illness, psychological distress, and physical reactions (see Freud 31-65). While the use of neurosis to describe various mental illnesses has fallen out of fashion in the scientific and medical worlds in favor of more specific labels for diagnoses (anxiety disorder, depression, etc), the definitions presented by Freud still provide some useful guidance for understanding the concept. In particular, Freud's understanding of neurosis as expressions of psychological distress occurring as a result of experiences of anxiety is useful for understanding parallels between Black life and neurosis. In *Black Skins, White Masks (1952),* Frantz Fanon, writing about the psychology of Black people, states that a "normal Negro child, having grown up within a normal family, will become abnormal on the slightest contact with the white world" (111). Contact with the white world is what causes a non-white person to understand that they are not white. As the dominant culture in the United States is white, this contact is essentially a cause for anxiety; a person of color learns that they are viewed as less-than by dominant society by being exposed to it. I am primarily interested in the use of the term neurosis as both a label for mental illness, and as metaphor for the conflicted existence and

1 US rapper Danny Brown is the performer of the song to which the music video is set, and he also portrays the main character, "Uncle Danny," in the music video directed by Hill.

doubleness[2] experienced as a Black person in the United States. In the case of "Ain't It Funny," I find that the former is heavily influenced by the latter. In the text that follows, I argue that Danny Brown's "Ain't It Funny" can be interpreted as an audiovisual expression of neurosis, which is further complicated by the category of race, by notions of marginalized Blackness against a pervasive, dominant whiteness.

The tensions depicted in "Ain't It Funny" bring to mind questions of positionality posed by Saidiya Hartman in her book *Scenes of Subjection* (1997): whether we are witnesses, merely confirming the truth of the various representations of suffering, or voyeurs, both positions are "fascinated with and repelled by exhibitions of terror and sufferance" (3). These inquiries raise another pertinent question; whether all participants, voyeur or witness, are complicit in the suffering in similar ways. If someone is watching a film, or reading an account, are they involved in the scene being depicted?

Historically, the existential questions of observation, identity, and participation have been a frequent topic of theorists and philosophers.[3] These issues have also been addressed through the framework of race by a number of Black scholars. Frederick Douglass, for example, wrote an account of the physical beating and subjugation of his Aunt Hester at the hand of her slave master (see 6-8). It was through the observation of this vile act and through the normalization and regularity of such trauma that Douglass understood his identity as Black, and as an enslaved person. Hartman discusses this scene of subjection without reproducing the exact account presented by Douglass:

---

2 W.E.B. Du Bois' *The Souls of Black Folk* famously introduced the concept of "double-consciousness" in 1903, as Du Bois commented on the current and upcoming difficulties of Black people in the US. Du Bois wrote of feeling a constant twoness due to being Black and suddenly being (partially) considered American, the stress of using the dominant culture's rubric to judge one's self, and the resilience of the Black American, able to live with the conflicting worlds of the Black and White US, having to occupy both, being forced to see yourself through the gaze of others, and managing to live daily with this turmoil (see Dubois 3, 8).

3 Many of the most famous philosophical works have dealt with these questions, from Plato's "Allegory of the Cave" (ca. 380 BC) to Descartes positing "cogito ergo sum" (1637). Two particularly pertinent examples come to mind: Louis Althusser's usage of "interpellation" to describe the act of being hailed by the dominant ideology into a subject position (see 174); and Michel Foucault's invocation of the "panopticon," a physical structure that becomes metaphor for the ability to discipline and control subjects (and force them to be the source of their own subjection) through the fear of surveillance that they cannot predict (see 202-203).

> I have chosen not to reproduce Douglass's account of the beating of Aunt Hester in order to call attention to the ease with which such scenes are usually reiterated, the casualness with which they are circulated, and the consequences of this routine display of the slave's ravaged body. Rather than inciting indignation, too often they immure us to pain by virtue of their familiarity – the oft-repeated or restored character of these accounts and our distance from them are signaled by the theatrical language usually resorted to in describing these instances – and especially because they reinforce the spectacular character of Black suffering. What interests me are the ways we are called upon to participate in such scenes. (3)

This positing leads her to investigate the precarity of the blurry line between witness and voyeur.

Fred Moten brings attention to Hartman's refusal to reproduce Douglass's account in his 2003 monograph *In the Break*, noting that in referencing it, she has reproduced it. However, as he notes, "[her] brilliance is present in the space she leaves for the ongoing (re)production of that performance in all its guises and for a critical awareness of how each of those guises is always already present in and disruptive of the supposed originarity of that primal scene" (4). Christina Sharpe's *In the Wake: On Blackness and Being* (2016) engages all of these explicit and implicit reproductions of Black suffering, arguing that they directly shape Black existence in the present day:

> Living in the wake means living the history and present of terror, from slavery to the present, as the ground of our everyday Black existence; living the historically and geographically dis/continuous but always present and endlessly reinvigorated brutality in, and on, our bodies while even as that terror is visited on our bodies the realities of that terror are erased. Put another way, living in the wake means living in and with terror in that in much of what passes for public discourse *about* terror we, Black people, become the *carriers* of terror, terror's embodiment, and not the primary objects of terror's multiple enactments; the ground of terror's possibility globally. (15; emphasis in the original)

These analyses reveal our constant involvement in the lives and regenerations of these accounts of terror, and the inescapability of this reality. The involvement is not equal, it is often reliant on the subject position of the participant – voyeur or witness. While there are a few instances of bearing witness present in the music video (there are characters who confirm the truth of Danny's suffering), I am more interested in the place of the voyeur, those that watch his suffering with fascination and are complicit in the suffering. The place of voyeurism and mental illness in

"Ain't It Funny" can be productively analyzed through the critical race framework set forth by Hartman et al.

To frustrate this issue of Danny Brown as the subject of voyeurism even further, issues of performativity[4] must be taken into account, as rappers are burdened with the task of 'keeping it real,' or maintaining 'authenticity,' rapping about actual lived experience, in a way that many other performers are not. As noted in Michael Eric Dyson's "The Culture of Hip-Hop" (2004) and Jonathan D. Williams' "Tha Realness" (2007), hip-hop remains fascinated and entangled with authenticity, and that is a function of the genre's roots as the cultural expression of African Americans.[5] Daniel Dewan Sewell, commonly known by his stage name Danny Brown, is a rapper from Detroit, Michigan. Brown has often been seen as a 'party rapper,' due in part to his rowdy live performances,[6] his proclivity towards ostentation, his frequent mentions of cocaine, MDMA, and other social drugs in his lyrics and interviews, the hypersexual lyrics in many of his songs, and the timbre of his unmistakably aggressive, strained, high-pitched lyrical delivery. However, over the course of his career, his lyrics have also often addressed mental

4 Performativity, as noted by editor Henry Bial in *The Performance Studies Reader* (2013), is a term layered with multiple meanings, the most prevalent two being "performative" as a variation on the theatrical, and "performative" referring to an utterance that does not truly or falsely express an already-existing condition, but actually performs an action on its own (the utterance of "I do" to perform the act of marrying is a classic example) (see 123). The tension between these two definitions of performativity has been at the forefront of debates about hip-hop for quite some time in the US. As reported by Lily Hirsch (2014) and Amanda Holpuch (2015) in *The Guardian,* a bevy of rappers have had prosecutors attempt – sometimes successfully – to use their own lyrics and album covers as evidence of wrongdoing in court cases.

5 Constant incantations of 'the real' are also used as a way to demarcate the border between black and white (the former grants quick access into hip-hop, the latter must earn it), and the genre and the mainstream – though that border is blurred to the point of being illegible. As Dyson, Williams, Murray Forman, and many other scholars have observed, authenticity is necessary cultural currency within hip-hop. This endless pursuit of realness has been weaponized against performers throughout the history of the genre. As I wrote in the previous footnote, prosecutors have used lyrics as evidence of wrongdoing against defendants, assuming that rappers are *always* performing real depictions of their lives.

6 One of the more extreme examples occurred in 2013, when a young woman in the crowd began to engage in unsolicited oral sex on Danny as he was rapping his song "Monopoly." He continued to perform as if the act was quotidian to his live performances.

health and illnesses such as paranoia, anxiety, and depression; he has also frequently rapped about drug use as a means of self-medication[7] to address mental instability, death, suicide, and constant exposure to trauma as a condition of life within the city of Detroit. In "XXX" the title track from his 2011 album *XXX* – a nod to both his age in Roman numerals, and a means of classifying the album as carrying X-Rated content – Danny Brown references his anxiety over having a successful music career after years of trying, his diminishing mental health, and his struggle with substance abuse:

I never leave the house, ain't slept in three days
Poppin' pills, writin', drinkin' and smokin' haze
Weaving kicks and snares, tryna dodge these hooks
Keepin' it original's something that's overlooked
The way a nigga goin', might go out like Sam Cooke
Or locked up, calling home for money on my books
'Cause if this shit don't work, nigga, I failed at life!
Turning to these drugs, now these drugs turned my life!
And it's the downward spiral, got me suicidal
But too scared to do it, so these pills'll be the rifle
Surpassing all my idols, took the wrong turn
But can't go back now, so let that blunt burn
'Cause now it's my turn if I fuck it all up
It took a while to get here, now I depend on these drugs.
(Brown, "XXX")

In the beginning of "Downward Spiral," the opening track from Brown's 2016 album *Atrocity Exhibition,* he raps "I'm sweatin' like I'm in a rave, been in this room for three days, think I'm hearing voices, paranoid and think I'm seein' ghost-es; oh, shit!" Danny Brown's lyrics and performances have been influenced not only by his personal experiences, cultural understandings, and representations of mental illness, but also by a number of artists – often outside of the hip-hop genre – who have presented varying expressions of mental disorder.[8] As J. Bradford

7 In Brown's lyrics, this self-medication often leads to hallucination and psychosis, which are typically considered separate from neurosis in Freudian psycho-analysis.

8 Danny Brown's album *Atrocity Exhibition* (2016) takes its name from both the Joy Division song "Atrocity Exhibition" (1980) and the novel *The Atrocity Exhibition* by J.G. Ballard (1970). The Joy Division song opens with the lyrics, "Asylums with doors open wide, where people had paid to see inside; for entertainment they watch his body twist, behind his eyes, he says, 'I still exist.'" The book by Ballard is a set of linked

Campbell writes in "The Schizophrenic Solution: Dialectis of Neurosis and Anti-Psychiatric Animus in Ralph Ellison's *Invisible Man*":

> Of course, no textual representation of mental illness or literary engagement with psychiatry is entirely self-contained. Rather, it is inevitably and in staggeringly intricate ways connected to the various discourses – popular, scientific, medical, and otherwise—that seek to condition what mental illness means, to whom it applies, and to whom it belongs. (447)

Throughout his article, Campbell meticulously rehearses the historical treatment of Black subjects in discourses of mental illness and psychiatric care. He finds numerous instances of Black people considered inherently happy and therefore unable to be neurotic subjects, or even considered a solution to white neurosis because of their assumed happy dispositions (see 447-450). Traces of this historical attitude are at the forefront of the music video for Danny Brown's "Ain't It Funny." Consequentially, the video not only serves as an audiovisual expression of neurosis as it is also a representation of the possibility of a neurotic Black subject, and the probability of Black neurosis when constantly subjugated by dominant whiteness and white voyeurism. In the music video, Danny's drug abuse is reactionary, growing more and more the more that he is made a spectacle. He receives no empathy from the studio audience, eventually driving him to view anthropomorphized versions of the substances he is abusing as his friends – these "friends" end up killing him, though constant subjection is arguably the true cause of his death.

Neurosis, as various writings within this volume note, is often predicated on the social understanding that there is a normal state of mind or being, and that *normalcy* allows one to function in an approved manner within society – neurosis is a fracture with this normal state of mind. As a result of social norms, subjects learn what is expected of them in their social interactions. Based on this understanding, the neurotic is one who functions outside of this normalcy, and thus cannot function within social norms without changing, conceding, or bending to gain societal approval. But it seems a daunting task, perhaps even a fool's errand, to define what is normal and what is not – even the most fleeting glance at global history would show the answer is constantly changing. Heinz Ickstadt captures the discomfort in the historical malleability of the term in "The Creation of Normalcy":

stories that are the hallucinations of a mental hospital worker who is suffering a mental breakdown.

> Part of my problem of definition is that the *descriptive* and the *prescriptive* are hopelessly entangled here: the Greeks linked the concept of the "normal" with that of the "natural," thus denoting an ideal state in which the regular and average also merges with the "healthy" and the "good." This intermingling of the descriptive with the normative is a constant in the history of the term – everything else, however, is *not*. For, obviously, Nature is *not* regular – the irregular is *also* natural and therefore "normal." Already here we may get the dizzying sense of sliding on the slippery slope of a total relativism of terms: for even if we do not take the "irregular" but the abnormal, or the pathological, as being the opposite of what is considered "normal," we can well conceive of the pathological as creating its own order of normality. (7-8; emphasis in the original)

Ickstadt's abundant use of quotation marks further illustrates the shakiness of *normalcy* by linking it to value-laden concepts like "health" and "good," terms that are also wildly subjective. Nonetheless, normative constructions of neurosis persist in popular culture. To be neurotic is not just to be outside of normalcy, but to be unsettled and unstable, trying to find some stability in whatever the tacitly-derived normal happens to be. Following Ickstadt's analysis, the constant struggle to force a marginal identity to conform to the mainstream causes anxiety, fear, stress, depression, and other mental traumas.

As the default, 'normal,' dominant state of being in the United States is to be white, other racial identities are treated as either pathological, or always already neurotic; the latter must then find a way to reconcile their societally-imposed sense of abnormality.[9] Discussing the work of Donald B. Gibson, J. Bradford Campbell notes that Gibson illuminates some of the possible shortcomings and risks in psychological studies of race, including the danger of "reading African Americans as *necessarily* pathological and biologically destined to suffer"; he draws attention to the necessity of allowing Black neurotics "the possibility of agency" (446; emphasis in the original). Neurosis is not an inevitability of Blackness; rather, the use of race as a *master category*,[10] a primary organizing force in the United States

9 Many ethnicities that are now considered 'white' in the United States were not initially afforded all of the privileges of Anglo-Saxon whiteness upon emigration to the United States. David Roediger's monograph *Working Toward Whiteness* (2005) chronicles the discrimination faced by white-skinned immigrant groups in the US, noting the pieces of their ethnic identities that had to be shed, and the common resentment towards Black people that had to be adopted, in order to gradually become white Americans. Those with non-white skin have not had this opportunity, yet are still expected to live their lives according to the rule of whiteness.

10 This is asserted by Michael Omi and Howard Winant in *Racial Formation in the United States* (1986 [2015]), who write "*race is a master category* – a fundamental concept

which constantly reinvents and reasserts the normalcy and centrality of whiteness, facilitates the imposition of neuroses onto marginal identities. Though race is often taken as a logical means of organization, and a historically unchanged fact (see McCoskey 3), it is a fairly modern construction; 'white' as a unified category is a complicated construction in and of itself in the United States. As recently as the late nineteenth century in the US, 'white' was a category reserved for the Anglo-Saxon descended, and did not automatically extend to European immigrants who happened to have light skin (see Omi and Winant 25). Blackness was (and continues to be) used as whiteness' foil, as the neurotic outlier to the normalcy of whiteness.[11] It is primarily these lenses of voyeurism, the neurotic/normal binary, and Blackness as neurosis that inform my analysis of the music video for "Ain't It Funny."

Throughout the video, Danny Brown is presented in stark contrast to his surroundings – he is moving when others are still, he is intoxicated when others are sober. Most importantly, he is Black, in pain, and seeking help. Every other character or audience member seen on-screen is white, the family members overwhelmingly ignore him; the all-white studio audience subjects him to their voyeuristic gaze, actively reveling in his suffering. His family is complicit in his suffering, and they essentially encourage the audience's voyeuristic gaze by doing nothing to help Danny. The stark racial difference present in the music video also lends credence to the positing of Blackness as neurosis; Brown's character is forced to carry his psychological distress and substance abuse problems with no hope for relief from the white world he inhabits – in fact, he learns that this world finds pleasure in his suffering.

The methodology I employ for reading and interpreting music videos is heavily indebted to the work of Carol Vernallis. Pertaining to "Ain't It Funny," Vernallis' method is particularly productive because of the separation between lyrics and storyline present in the music video. Vernallis' questions of what draws us into a music video and what constitutes craft and artistry within the genre

---

that has profoundly shaped, and continues to shape, the history, polity, economic structure, and culture of the United States" (106; emphasis in the original). They do not see race as a "transcendent category" (ibid), one that is somehow outside of other categories like class, gender, etc. In fact, they carefully notate the intersectionality of race with other forms of social stratification, noting that it cannot be understood as working completely separate from each other. However, the unique role that race has played and continues to plays in the construction of the United States leads to the assertion that race is a master category of organization.

11 This is certainly true for other non-white identities; I have chosen to focus on the black/white contrast due to the primary subject of my writing.

formed the basis for her inquiry into new modes of analyzing music video as a form *separate* from film (see "The Aesthetics" 153). Vernallis' work examines the relationality of music, image, and lyrics, focusing on the connections that music video directors can establish through a variety of devices, including shaping images to mimic their experiential source while maintaining a syncretic link, and the matching of images with sound through symbolic, indexical, or iconic resemblance (see *Experiencing Music Videos* 175). On the latter device, she writes:

> The semiotic categories of icon, symbol, and index can be useful for understanding the relations among sound, image, and lyrics. To appreciate this approach to video aesthetics, the reader is asked to anticipate that a visual gesture will be mirrored by an aural one. Many music/image correspondences in commercials and films bear this out; for example, in the Roadrunner cartoons, Wile E. Coyote falls from the precipice to the bottom of a canyon, and the pitch drops. (*Experiencing Music Videos* 183)

Providing a meticulous analysis of the music video for Madonna's "Cherish," Vernallis seeks to reconcile musical codes such as melodic contour, lyrics, timbre, and texture, and the ways in which they shape perception of the visual. Her description of musical and visual codes along with her analysis reveal a particular temporal flow that exists in music videos and marks them as a distinct medium from film. In fact, she states that relying on film theory to analyze music videos tends to result in music videos coming off as failed narratives (see "The Aesthetics" 153).

For a multitude of reasons, this method does not work so smoothly for analyzing hip-hop music videos; hip-hop does not always follow the prioritized Western European parameters of musical construction that are present in other forms of popular music, like melodic contour or harmony.[12] In the case of Danny Brown's "Ain't It Funny," the disorientation created by the speedy delivery of lyrics that are *separate* from the storyline presented in the music video – often with subtitles – make it a further challenge to view. Though much of the narrative

12 Music theorists like Kyle Adams in "Aspects of the Music/Text Relationship in Rap" (2008) and "Flow in Rap Music" (2009) along with other music scholars like Adam Krims in *Rap Music and the Poetics of Identity* (2000) have worked to devise new methods of musical analysis for hip-hop, generally focused on rhythm. The typical lyrical delivery in rap music, while containing pitches like speech, is not sung, so it cannot be said to have melodic contour. The accompanying music behind rap lyrics, or beat, can often be analyzed for harmony, but the lyrical delivery generally does not factor into that harmonic analysis (see Adams and Krims).

of the sitcom within the music video does cohere with the song's thematic material, it is nearly impossible to digest both simultaneously. This lends weight to the argument that "Ain't It Funny" can be interpreted as an audiovisual representation of neurosis. The sitcom presents notions of white normalcy that are constantly frustrated and interrupted by Danny Brown as he attempts to find stability. Both the sitcom and the song lyrics present a performance of neurosis within which the simultaneity and collision of focuses force the viewer-listener to decide what is center and what is margin.

AIN'T IT FUNNY?

As the recorded track "Ain't It Funny" begins, the opening credits for the sitcom roll in, introducing the audience to each character as they enter the main doorway one-by-one.[13] Dad walks in holding a briefcase, wearing a cardigan over business attire; he tilts his head to the side, puts his hands on his hips, and offers a knowing smile. Mom follows, wearing a bright windbreaker suit, carrying a large purse; she – much like Dad – smiles, arms akimbo. Daughter enters, wearing a patterned sweater, distressed denim skirt, and tights. She is holding a large telephone to her ear with one hand, her other arm folded across her stomach, while she smacks on a piece of gum, mouth agape, and refuses to look at the camera. Kid appears, in a denim jacket and everyday slacks, wearing headphones. He catches a football tossed to him from off-camera and exclaims "Kids Rock!" as the words animate from his mouth. Lastly, Uncle Danny steps aggressively through the door, in black pants, a white t-shirt, and a leather jacket. Holding a 40oz bottle of malt liquor, he scowls at the camera, performs a couple of hip thrusts, then holds a defiant pose. Next, the video cuts to the whole family sitting on the living room couch, with Uncle Danny in the middle, as they all laugh heartily. The sitcom title appears over their heads: *Ain't It Funny*. Uncle Danny is Black; the rest of the family is white.

13 The cast of characters includes Dad, played by Gus Van Sant, the critically-acclaimed director of *Drugstore Cowboy* (1989), *Good Will Hunting* (1997), and many other films; Mom, played by Joanna Kerns, the celebrated actress most known for her portrayal of Maggie Seaver, the mother in the classic American sitcom, *Growing Pains* (ABC 1985-1992); Daughter, played by Lauren Avery, an heiress and native of Los Angeles who acts and models, but is most well-known for her social media presence; Kid, played by "This Fucking Kid" as noted in the video; Uncle Danny, played by Danny Brown.

From the onset of the video, Uncle Danny (played by Danny Brown) is presented as an outsider, that which does not fit. His Blackness serves as an obvious example of his difference, as it is the most instantly visible sign within a US context. But beyond this phenotypical contrast, Uncle Danny's difference is registered in his transgressive behavior – recall that before the music has started and the characters are introduced, the video began with a prelude of sorts: Uncle Danny in bed with Daughter. As his character is formally introduced, he holds symbols of addiction, and he gestures menacingly and sexually to the camera. These transgressions are exaggerated by the fact that his family is not only white but personifications of archetypical white Americana – a working, breadwinning father, a mother who might work, but primarily exists to support the husband, a teenage daughter, detached and approaching adulthood (and being sexualized in the process), and the young, sporty, inquisitive son, papa's pride and joy.[14] Uncle Danny is absolutely none of that.[15] As Frantz Fanon might argue, Uncle Danny's Blackness in contact with this white sitcom world is likely the source for his behavior. If not the source, it is certainly the catalyst.

But this is also where a massive fracture occurs in the video. The musical track to which this music video is set has only just begun, only partially pulling viewers from the developing sitcom. The music sounds tense, dissonant, and uncomfortable, there is no voice. As the music video features an internal sitcom as its primary narrative, it is clear that "Ain't It Funny" is not merely a set of images meant to showcase a mood, nor is it what is more typical of music videos – performers lip syncing and pantomiming their songs; it is presented as if it could stand alone as a television show. The addition of lyrics that are not represented on

---

14 Mediated representations of the white, suburban, middle-class family skyrocketed to popularity in the 1950s, primarily via television programs like *Father Knows Best* (CBS 1954-1960) and *Leave It to Beaver* (CBS 1958-1959; ABC 1958-1963). However, the trope finds its origin in 1930s American radio programs (see Hayes 97). These formulations of familial whiteness persist on American television to this day. Though contemporary sitcoms appear to have diversified, they are often still rooted in these recycled conventions of television whiteness; when they are not, they generally still participate in the logics of white/nonwhite as an organizing theme (see Khanna and Harris 39).

15 In "Ain't It Funny," director Jonah Hill plays on the trope of the rebel or outsider character that has been deployed for comic relief in a number of US sitcoms, from Fonzie of *Happy Days* (ABC 1974-1984) to Uncle Jesse of *Full House* (ABC 1987-1995) and (Uncle) Gob of *Arrested Development* (Fox 2003-2006; Netflix 2013). The reimagining of this archetype within "Ain't It Funny" is undoubtedly more sinister, but still used for comedy – as evidenced by the laughter of the studio audience.

screen creates a split focus, and viewers must constantly shift between watching the sitcom – which has its own dialogue and subtitles separate from the song's lyrics – and listening to Danny Brown rap.[16] The video returns to the opening scene in the bedroom, with Uncle Danny and Daughter sitting in bed, talking. Because the song to which the music video is set is now audible, their conversations become represented by subtitles.

Daughter*:* [I'm really worried about you, Danny.]
Uncle Danny*:* [I'm fucked up and everyone thinks it's a joke.]

The studio audience is shown for the first time, applauding and laughing hysterically; they are all white. Because of the whiteness of both the audience and the family in the sitcom, the video produces a chilling scene of subjection as a confused and suffering Uncle Danny functions merely as spectacle, and the audience revels in their voyeurism. The audience's enjoyment suggests that they have learned to view and appreciate Black suffering as theater. Writing about Frederick Douglass's recollection of his Aunt Hester's savage beating at the hands of her slave master (and about other reiterated scenes of Black suffering), Sadiya Hartman writes:

> Rather than inciting indignation, too often they immure us to pain by virtue of their familiarity – the oft-repeated or restored character of these accounts and our distance from them are signaled by the theatrical language usually resorted to in describing these instances – and especially because they reinforce the spectacular character of black suffering. (see 4)

The voyeuristic audience sees Black suffering, represented by Uncle Danny's on-screen anguish, not only as spectacle, but as completely familiar. They find joy not only through gazing upon suffering, but through having their expectations fulfilled. In their view, it is Danny's place to suffer.

As the music video proceeds to the next scene, the cameras return to the living room, where Uncle Danny sits nervously on the edge of the couch, leaning forward tensely while the rest of the family (minus Kid) relaxes and reclines back. Though Danny is on the same couch, it is obvious through body language and position that he is apart from the rest of the family; he is crouched forward and closed off, not interacting with anyone. Dad has his arm around Mom, and the video cuts to a close-up of them.

---

16 In the following, I present the subtitles in brackets to give a sense of the general disorientation created by this video.

Dad, to Mom: [I love this show.]
Daughter: [Stop watching TV and pay attention to Danny's illness.]

At this point in the sitcom, Uncle Danny has overtly addressed his mental distress and substance abuse multiple times, and Daughter is the only character interested in acknowledging this at all, though she does nothing beyond telling others to pay attention. The other characters have ignored him, and the studio audience has laughed at him. The video quickly cuts between the coffee table in front of the couch – with a crack pipe resting atop the pages of a small book – Uncle Danny's distraught face, and the smiling faces of an oblivious – or indifferent – Mom and Dad. Uncle Danny picks up the pipe and begins to smoke as Mom and Dad remain unfazed, Kid stands behind, laughing from the staircase, and Daughter sits sulking. It would be simple to label Uncle Danny's behavior as purely self-destructive, but the complete lack of attention and intervention from the family (despite Uncle Danny's requests for assistance), coupled with the laughter of the white audience, paints a picture far more sinister. He is being subjected to the abject gaze of both the studio audience and his family; these white voyeurs are both directly responsible for and complicit in his suffering. Within this environment, there is no way for Uncle Danny to escape his psychological distress.

Uncle Danny: [I have a serious problem.]
Dad and Mom laugh at their television program,
Uncle Danny: [Please stop laughing.]

As the camera turns to the studio audience, an illuminated "APPLAUSE" sign instructs the crowd to cheer and clap, both furthering the intensity of their exploitative voyeuristic gaze and suggesting there is a large, societal structure responsible for engineering and perpetuating the voyeurism.

Afterwards, the video returns to the bedroom, where Uncle Danny is now seated in the middle of the bed, in between Daughter *and* Mom. The very beginning of the sitcom showed Danny in bed with Daughter, heavily implying a sexual relationship between the two. The addition of Mom implies an even more taboo encounter, as she is both married and in bed with her own daughter. She has yet to verbally acknowledge Danny but, presumably, has acknowledged him physically, for her own enjoyment. The women sit completely still, blank-faced, holding cigarettes, while Danny grabs his head in his hands, motions wildly with his arms and performs the song's chorus looking into the camera – this is the first instance when "Ain't It Funny" uses typical music video elements, such as the performer lip syncing the lyrics for the camera. The juxtaposition of still, lifeless characters against a wildly-animated Danny Brown showcases the intense contrast between him and his environment, echoing the video's recurring placement of Danny as separate, outside, and different.

The video then cuts erratically between three scenes. The first shows Uncle Danny in bed between Daughter and Mom. The second one sees Uncle Danny alone in the living room, aggressively screaming into the camera. The last of these three scenes is a grotesque version of Uncle Danny in bed with Daughter and Mom (who are now unconscious), where they are all wounded, and covered in blood as giant, mascot-like versions of a prescription cough syrup bottle and a Xanax tab – indicators of Uncle Danny's self-medication – dance on either side of the bed. The jarring, blood-filled scene represents both the violence of self-harm through addiction, and the potential of physical violence that an addict may inflict on others. Uncle Danny is at the center of every scene, maniacally performing the song's chorus: "Ain't it? Ain't it funny how it happens?" As the video continues to cut between the three scenes and nothing about the scenario has been funny, the question gains a sarcastic tone. Uncle Danny has begged the family and the studio audience for help as he slides further into substance abuse as a means to counter his affliction. With blood-soaked arms, and an unsettling grin, he grabs the camera, shaking it as he gazes through the lens. Through the act of 'breaking the fourth wall,' Danny is directly addressing the video's viewers, forcing them to take part in the scene as witnesses to his suffering and inability to escape the horrific situation.

Suddenly, however, the musical track stops, and as the video returns to the sitcom, viewers are greeted with the sound of a laughing, joyous studio audience as Uncle Danny stands on the couch alone in the living room, his back turned to the camera, urinating on a floral arrangement and some family pictures. Dad enters through the front door. Startled by what he sees, he quickly puts down his coat and briefcase and approaches Uncle Danny.

Dad: "Danny, get down from there."
Dad: "Why are you doing this, Danny?"
Uncle Danny: "I've been destroyed, and if I destroy, maybe I'll feel okay."
Dad: "None of us feel okay."
The audience offers a sympathetic "aww." Kid walks into the room, puts his hands on his hips, tilts his head to the side, and smiles.
Kid: "Oh, Uncle Danny..."

The audience cheers and laughs hysterically while the camera remains on Kid. His eyes suddenly glow red and a disarming low frequency plays underneath the applause. Uncle Danny sighs as the musical playback continues.

In this scene, for the first time in the music video, someone seems concerned enough with Uncle Danny's behavior to have a conversation with him about it. However, the concern is only shown after Uncle Danny is doing damage to family property. By allowing Uncle Danny to harm himself constantly without so much as batting an eye, but choosing to intervene because possessions are being destroyed, Dad is effectively showing Uncle Danny just how little he is valued as a member of the family. The possessions mean more. When asked to justify his actions, Uncle Danny explains that he is attempting to make himself feel better. This can be interpreted as Uncle Danny simply lashing out as a result of the family's inattentiveness; however, when viewed as a neurotic subject, his actions are an attempt to control his environment, a way to find balance. If he destroys the things around him, he will fit into his environment, as a subject also destroyed. While Dad does seem to offer some encouraging words, given the context, this attempt at empathy does nothing for Uncle Danny.

Most startling in this scene is the audience, offering their sympathy and empathy to Dad, a character whose whiteness affords him recognition – the audience identifies with Dad, he's a peer. They have been unwilling or unable to confront Uncle Danny's pain with any kind of sympathy or empathy; in fact, he has been met with derision. Yet Dad's utterance of pain is instantly met with care and concern. His humanity is recognized by the audience in a way that Uncle Danny will never be privileged to know.

The video continues in a fractured manner between Uncle Danny performing the lyrics, linking the rapper Danny Brown and the character Uncle Danny together, and the music taking on a background role while the sitcom dialogue comes into focus via text on screen. Mom and Uncle Danny sit in bed smoking, and the camera cuts briefly to zoom in on the night table, stacked with a lamp, some porcelain, a 40oz bottle of "Danny Brown" malt liquor, a pack of cigarettes, and opened packages of "Danny Brown" branded condoms – a clear indication that a sexual relationship exists between the two of them. The techniques of self-medication to which Uncle Danny frequently turns have become such an integral part of his life that they literally bear his name.

In the final scene of "Ain't It Funny," the video turns to the dining room table, where Danny is standing with the large, anthropomorphic prescription cough syrup bottle and Xanax tab who were dancing in the bedroom; the trio is playing a game of dominoes.

Uncle Danny: [You guys are my only friends. I need you.]
Xanax Tab: [We'll kill you and everyone you love.]

The Xanax tab reveals a knife and stabs Uncle Danny in the abdomen as the cough syrup bottle offers its encouragement and support for the act of violence. As Danny falls to the floor wounded, the audience cheers and laughs. Kid appears closely in the frame and glares directly into the camera.

Kid: [He's DYING and you people are LAUGHING. You DISGUST me.]
Uncle Danny: [I'm glad you found my pain entertaining. Goodbye.]

As Uncle Danny lies in anguish and dies, the studio audience offers a standing ovation.

This scene is a continuation of the theme of Uncle Danny's tendency toward addictive behavior and substance abuse as a means of controlling his psychological distress. The bottle and pill have taken on lives of their own and they are literally playing games with Uncle Danny. He declares his loyalty to them, and even his dependency. He is met with a stark, honest response to his congenial statement, and beyond hypothetical honesty, the Xanax tab has made a pledge to kill Danny. But through his neuroses, Uncle Danny does not view these characters as dangerous. He is willing to do what it takes to find balance, and his desperation and dependency are met with the promise of death. It is surprising that Kid suddenly chastises the audience, as he spends the entirety of the video to that point passing off Uncle Danny's pleas as non-serious and comedic. The scene of subjection has finished unfolding and comes to its logical end, to the delight of the voyeuristic white studio audience. Their reaction suggests that they were purposely ignoring Uncle Danny's pleas because they are actively invested in his death.

Many of the lyrics to Danny Brown's "Ain't It Funny" provide a parallel narrative to the music video. In particular, the third verse echoes many of the scenes depicted in the sitcom:

Ain't it funny how it happen, upcoming heavy traffic
Say you need to slow down, 'cause you feel yourself crashing
Staring in the devil's face, but you can't stop laughing
Staring in the devil's face, but you can't stop laughing
It's a living nightmare that most of us might share
Inherited in our blood, it's why we stuck in the mud
Can't quit the drug use or the alcohol abuse

Even if I wanted to, tell you what I'm gonna do
I'ma wash away my problems with this bottle of Henny[17]
Anxiety got the best of me, so I'm poppin' them Xannies[18]
Might need rehab, but to me that shit pussy[19]
Pray for me, y'all 'cause I don't know what's coming to me
Bought a 8-ball of coke, and my nigga on the way
Got three hoes with him, and they all tryna play
Ain't it funny how it happens, whoever would imagine?
That joke's on you, but Satan the one laughing

Every utterance of the title serves to dig a deeper, more sarcastic hole – it is not at all funny how the descent into self-destruction through substance abuse happens, yet Brown raps about "staring in the devil's face" and being unable to take the encounter seriously. This is due to his addictions becoming so overwhelming that he feels compelled to push his habits to the limit, and to chemically force himself into happiness. Congruent to the interpretation of subjugated Blackness as a conduit for anxiety and depression that J. Bradford Campbell finds in his reading of Ralph Ellison's *Invisible Man* ("The Schizophrenic Solution"), Danny raps about a shared living nightmare that is inherited, a metaphorical neurosis carried by Black Americans from birth. Uncle Danny's turn to self-medication after multiple unanswered pleas for help is reflective of Danny's lyrics, claiming that he cannot drop his vices, despite his desire and effort. Rather than continuing to seek help, he decides to accept the path that he is on, a life of neuroses with no permanent relief.

From a narrative standpoint, the music video for "Ain't It Funny" provides a grim look at a man struggling with addictions that he turns to in an attempt to address the mental health issues that seemingly no one will help him with. He is subjected to a voyeuristic white gaze, fascinated with his suffering and not at all interested in helping to alleviate it. Although subjugated, Uncle Danny is entirely self-aware of his neuroses, and he is aware of the sources of his subjugation. He implores both the audience and the family to stop laughing, a request that goes

17 Slang for Hennessy Cognac

18 Slang for Xanax

19 This is a moment in the song that is somewhat, though not completely, contrary to the music video, and it is indicative of typical notions of Black hyper-masculinity. Throughout the video, Uncle Danny is telling people that he has a problem, and asking for their attention. The lyric implies that to seek help would be antithetical to his performance of masculinity. This is another site of neurosis: the imagined conflict between Black masculinity and mental health issues.

ignored. No one actively helps him – Daughter tells others to help him, and Kid admonishes the audience for reveling in his demise, but neither actually help Uncle Danny. In the context of the sitcom, he is practically invisible. The family almost never recognizes him; he is only acknowledged by Dad when destroying property, only acknowledged by Mom in a sexual setting, misinterpreted by Kid, and half-heartedly engaged by Daughter, who expresses her worry, yet is uninterested in emotional or physical labor. The family is responsible for much of his mental health decline. The studio audience almost always recognizes him through the fetishization of his neurosis, and they climax at the sight of his death. "Ain't It Funny" with its chilling depiction of the voyeurism of Black suffering, is an apt metaphor for the subjugation, doubleness, and neurosis with which Black people live.

LIST OF WORKS CITED

Adams, Kyle. "Aspects of the Music/Text Relationship in Rap." *Music Theory Online*, vol. 14, no. 2, 2008, www.mtosmt.org/issues/mto.08.14.2/mto.08.14.2.adams.html. Accessed 15 Feb. 2018.

---. "Flow in Rap Music." *Music Theory Online*, vol. 15, no. 5, 2009, www.mtosmt.org/issues/mto.09.15.5/mto.09.15.5.adams.html. Accessed 15 Feb. 2018.

Althusser, Louis. *Lenin and Philosophy and Other Essays*. Monthly Review Press, 1971.

Ballard, J.G. *The Atrocity Exhibition.* Johnathan Cape, 1970.

Bial, Henry, editor. *The Performance Studies Reader*. 3rd ed., Routledge, 2013.

Brown, Danny. "Ain't It Funny (Official Video)." *YouTube*, uploaded by xdannyxbrownxVEVO, 28 March 2017, www.youtube.com/watch?v=7-L4JnAuW00k.

---. *Atrocity Exhibition.* Warp Records, 2016.

Campbell, J. Bradford. "The Schizophrenic Solution: Dialectics of Neurosis and Anti-psychiatric Animus in Ralph Ellison's *Invisible Man*." *Novel: A Forum on Fiction,* vol. 43, no. 3, 2010, pp. 443-65.

Douglass, Frederick. *Narrative of the Life of Frederick Douglass: An American Slave.* Published at the Anti-Slavery Office of Boston, Massachusetts, 1845.

DuBois, W.E.B. *The Souls of Black Folk.* 8th ed., A.C. McClurg and Co., 1909.

Dyson, Michael Eric. "The Culture of Hip-Hop." *That's The Joint! The Hip-Hop Studies Reader,* edited by Murray Forman and Mark Anthony Neal, Routledge, 2004, pp. 61-68.

Foucault, Michel. *Discipline and Punish.* 1975. Translated by Alan Sheridan, Penguin Books, 1977.

Forman, Murray. *The 'Hood Comes First: Race, Space, and Place in Rap and Hip-Hop.* Wesleyan University Press, 1997.

Freud, Sigmund. "On the Grounds for Detaching a Particular Syndrome from Neurasthenia under the Description *Anxiety Neurosis.*" *On Psychopathology.* Translated by James Strachey, edited by Angela Richards, Penguin Books, 1987, pp. 31-65.

Gómez-Peña, Guillermo. "Culturas-in-extremis: Performing against the Cultural Backdrop of the Mainstream Bizarre." *The Performance Studies Reader*, 2nd ed., edited by Henry Bial, Routledge, 2007, pp. 287-298.

Hartman, Saidiya V. *Scenes of Subjection: Terror, Slavery, and Self-making in Nineteenth-century America.* Oxford University Press, 1997.

Hayes, Joy Elizabeth. "White Noise: Performing the White, Middle-Class Family on 1930s Radio." *Cinema Journal,* vol. 51, no. 3, 2012, pp. 97-118.

Hirsch, Lily. "The Right to Free Speech Includes Rap: Misunderstanding It Makes Bad Law." *The Guardian,* 30 Dec. 2014, www.theguardian.com/commentisfree/2014/dec/30/free-speech-rap-music-bad-law. Accessed 4 January 2018.

Holpuch, Amanda. "Hip-hop Artists Back Push to Send Rap Lyrics Case to US Supreme Court." *The Guardian*, 21 Dec. 2015. www.theguardian.com/us-news/2015/dec/21/hip-hop-first-amendment-rap-lyrics-supreme-court-killer-mike. Accessed 7 January 2018

Ickstadt, Heinz. "The Creation of Normalcy." *Revue Française D'études Américaines*, vol. 85, no. 1, 2000, pp. 6-22.

Khanna, Nikki and Cherise A. Harris. "Discovering Race in a 'Post-Racial' World: Teaching Race through Primetime Television." *Teaching Sociology* vol. 43, no. 1, 2015, pp. 39-45.

Krims, Adam. *Rap Music and the Poetics of Identity.* Cambridge University Press, 2000.

Lott, Eric. *Love and Theft: Blackface Minstrelsy and the American Working Class.* 1993. Oxford University Press, 2013.

McCoskey, Denise Eileen. *Race: Antiquity and Its Legacy.* Oxford University Press, 2012.

Moten, Fred. *In the Break: The Aesthetics of the Black Radical Tradition.* University of Minnesota Press, 2003.

Omi, Michael, and Howard Winant. *Racial Formation in the United States.* 1986. Routledge, 2015.

Roediger, David R. *The Wages of Whiteness: Race and the Making of the American Working Class.* 1991. Verso, 2007.

Sharpe, Christina Elizabeth. *In the Wake: On Blackness and Being*. Duke University Press, 2016.

Vernallis, Carol. "The Aesthetics of Music Video: An Analysis of Madonna's 'Cherish'." *Popular Music* vol. 17, no. 2, 1998, pp. 153-85.

---. *Experiencing Music Video: Aesthetics and Cultural Context*. Columbia University Press, 2004.

Williams, Jonathan D. "'Tha Realness': In Search of Hip-Hop Authenticity." *CUREJ – College Undergraduate Research Electronic Journal,* University of Pennsylvania, December 14, 2007.

Neurosis as Resilience in Jhumpa Lahiri's Diasporic Short Fictions

ANGELO MONACO

> "I am neurotic. I could never settle down in either the country or the city."
> SYLVIA PLATH, *THE BELL JAR*

THE NEW INDIAN DIASPORA BETWEEN MODEL MINORITY AND SENSE OF LOSS

The 2012 survey on immigrants of Asian origin, provided by the Pew Research Centre, reveals that Asian Americans are "the highest-income, best-educated and fastest-growing racial group in the United States" (Pew 2013). Asian Americans embody the neoliberal success of model minority migrants conforming to the new opportunities of the post-1965 immigration laws.[1] Asian Americans tend to be highly educated (61% of the adults aged 25-64 have at least a bachelor's degree); they exceed white American adults in median annual household income ($66,000 *versus* $49,800); and, finally, "they place more value than other Americans do on marriage, parenthood, hard work and career success" (Pew 2013).

1 The 1965 Immigration and Naturalization Act abolished the quota system which had previously ruled the American immigration policy, introducing technical skills and expertise as prerequisites for visas. New ethnic communities, coming from South Asian middle-class backgrounds, started to settle in the country and they constituted a brain drain of specialized professionals (doctors, engineers, scientists, university professors, and doctoral students) who crossed the American border in search of material and financial success, seeing the United States as a place of better opportunities. For further details, see Chin and Villazor 2015.

Unlike other Asian American subgroups (Chinese, Filipino, Korean, Vietnamese and Japanese), Indian Americans have higher shares in education and income and they rate parenthood highly, but they are less likely to see themselves as 'typical' Americans. Yet, they say that they can carry on a conversation in proficient English very well and, together with Filipinos, they are more inclined to define themselves as a successful "model minority"[2] in comparison with other ethnic groups (see Pew 2013).

Through emulation of white Americans, Asian Americans try to fill in the gap between their migrant status and the desire to adjust to the host society by embracing the fluid movements of accumulation and self-realization that define capitalist orthodoxy. With their flexibility, they exemplify a model of "reproductive citizenship" that, borrowing from Susan Koshy (2013), "harnesses heterosexuality to the productivity of knowledge work to enhance national competitiveness in a globalizing economy" (351). A perceived obsession with the pressure of accumulating economic resources and passing on human capital to future generations leaves a gap in the affective and filial dynamics of Asian American families. The myth of the Asian Tigers veils insecurities and contradictions that immigrants of Asian descent experience in their ordinary lives, particularly in maintaining affective and family ties. Intergenerational conflicts are stronger when second generations disrupt their parents' expectations such as accruing economic success and neutralizing biases against minority status. According to Koshy, the subjection of daughters and sons to the pressures of their families entails a "filial gothic" form that shows how "the simultaneous idealization and instrumentalization of filial duty in the model minority family creates intense pressure to succeed on parental terms and creates a schism between the subjective experience of filial coercion and the benevolent image of filial love" (358).[3] At

2 The term was coined by the sociologist William Petersen who, in a 1966 article in *The New York Magazine*, described how Japanese Americans were able to overcome racial discriminations thanks to family cohesion and hard work.

3 Koshy (2013) expands the concept of "marital gothic" proposed by Michelle Massé who identifies "a genre of fiction in which the women protagonists become insane or kill themselves because their roles as wives or mothers have become unbearable to them" (357). According to Koshy, Lahiri's stories demonstrate how familial structures and generational conflicts may generate pain and vulnerability in migrant characters. Though gothic motifs (tombs, urns, wild natural environments and severe weather conditions) permeate Lahiri's stories, particularly in *Unaccustomed Earth*, I find Koshy's idea of the gothic too bleak and limitative. Not all the tales end in conflict and

what personal cost is such a neoliberal model reproduced and who bears its counter effects?

To answer the question, I look at fictional representations of Asian American immigrants in the throes of problematic assimilation into the American society of economic productivity and entrepreneurship.[4] By mapping the configurations of neurosis, trauma theory and diaspora studies, in this essay I shall focus on the narrative and rhetorical devices aligning Jhumpa Lahiri's short stories with the aesthetics of signifying neurosis. If neurosis is a way "of defending oneself from the pressures of intersubjective life" (Rosson 118), my hypothesis is that in diasporic literature this defensive strategy conjures up neurotic tensions that plunge into nostalgia and melancholia. At the heart of Lahiri's fiction there is a vision of neurosis that emerges from the failure to assimilate. Her characters seem to challenge narratives of wholesomeness, generating empathy in the reader's affective response. On one hand, Lahiri exposes neurotic symptoms of vulnerability in characters who face paralysis, mutism, repetition compulsion and depression, thus offering no hope of redemption. On the other, her macrotext charts the potential benefits for those who linger over the in-between, shuttling physically and imaginatively between two worlds. Lahiri's fiction retains the wounds of a "homeland trauma" (Mishra 153) which triggers divergent responses to the sense of homelessness. The prospect of the model minority is a source of anxiety for some of her fictional immigrants who face psychological dilemmas, whilst others, capable of adjusting to the host land, tend to dwell in the interstices of cultures. Lahiri's tales, therefore, juxtapose vulnerability and resilience in everyday life, bringing to the fore an aesthetics of neurosis as a way to criticise socio-economic pressures.

I shall, first, discuss how "suburban neurosis" (Taylor 759) discloses the controversial assimilation of the new Indian diaspora[5] into the American competi-

---

when tensions remain unresolved endings are open, leaving the reader to figure out the outcomes of the narratives.

4 While 'integration' is typically viewed as incorporating individuals from different groups, I argue that 'assimilation' offers a better way of understanding how Lahiri's characters embody a condition of mimicry of certain American values. My use of the term invokes the connotations of imitation and it carries "a referent to which immigrants and/or their offspring can become *similar*" (Schneider and Crul 2).

5 Vijay Mishra (2007) draws a distinction between "old" and "new" Indian diaspora. The first migrant wave was oriented towards the colonial areas of Fiji, Malaysia, Trinidad and Suriname, where migrants were employed in sugar, tea and rubber plantations between the end of the nineteenth century and the post-war period. The "new"

tive society. Mrs. Sen, the eponymous protagonist of Lahiri's story in the 1999 collection *Interpreter of Maladies* – which won the Pulitzer Prize for Fiction – babysits an American eleven-year-old boy in her suburban flat while experiencing a repetition-compulsion that fractures her *ego*. By examining the dynamics between the narrative and "suburban neurosis," I argue that metonymy is the master trope of Lahiri's poetics of neurosis in "Mrs. Sen's" since it figures the presence of the past and the persistence of a deep sense of nostalgia. Metonymy, according to Lacan, represents the impossibility of achieving unity between signifier and signified because it displaces meaning (see Wilden 241). I shall turn, then, to explore the maladjustments of Amit Sarkar, the hero of "A Choice of Accommodation," a story in Lahiri's second collection *Unaccustomed Earth* (2008). Amit's problematic accommodation results in a melancholic exposure to pain, in which metaphor and prosopopoeia become the central tropes. Metaphors, a transfer of "one word for another" (Lacan 157), condensate meaning, while prosopopoeia, "the trope of address" (De Man 76), confers a human voice to a non-human speaker, a figurative choice that challenges the centrality of the subject. I finally maintain that Lahiri's stories rely on performance rather than representation. In presenting the effects and causes of neurotic behaviours, Lahiri's poetics of neurosis that I will briefly sketch here privileges performativity through contiguities, associations, substitutions and chronological disarray over resemblance and diegesis, evoking the performative power of emotions.[6]

THE LANGUAGE OF "SUBURBAN NEUROSIS" AND CULINARY NOSTALGIA IN LAHIRI'S DIASPORIC WOMEN

In a 1938 *Lancet* article that described the anxieties and depressive states of women dwelling in suburban estates, Doctor Stephen Taylor launched the term "suburban neurosis." According to Taylor, the symptoms of the affliction were insomnia, backache and loss of breath. Two major factors were deemed to be re-

diaspora, instead, came with capitalism and hypermobility. It was triggered by the 1955 Indian Citizen Act that granted the double citizenship to those who emigrated to Europe, the United States and Canada in search of more qualified jobs.

6 My reference is to Sara Ahmed's discussion of emotions as performative acts that do not simply exist, but also "do things" (*Cultural Politics of Emotions* 13-26). Emotions, then, should be viewed not for what they are, but for what they do and their circulation allows for the construction of intersubjective relationships, joining the self with the other.

sponsible for this neurotic disorder: first, isolation and lack of kinship; second, suburban English women, or "Mrs. Everyman" as Taylor ironically dubs them, were suffering from being victim of "false values" (Taylor 760), such as housewares, electronic equipment, and ready-made food and clothes that left them with plenty of spare time. Suburban neighbourhoods, in addition, did not allow for comradeship nor did they offer amenities and services. Linked to diaspora, this connection between the stories of "Mrs. Everyman" and the migrants' experience of domestic alienation opens new lines for studying Lahiri's poetics of neurosis.

In the aftermath of the 1965 Immigration and Naturalization Act, suburban isolation came to affect the mental health of South Asian women who had followed their husbands in search of better professional opportunities in the United States. For Lahiri's female characters suburban homes operate as prisons: the lack of transportation available and the inability to drive generate a sense of alienation in the bored existences of the immigrant women of suburbia. Lahiri's fiction holds many examples of female immigrants as being tied to notions of domesticity and home and, as Dutt-Ballerstadt (2010) notes, while "the men come to America as intellectual migrants and work as professors, librarians and company executives," the women "join their husbands as housewives and depend on their spouses to introduce them to America" (66). Like the protagonist of Sylvia Plath's *The Bell Jar*, a woman who tries to escape growth through neurotic indecision, "wanting two mutually exclusive things at one and the same time" (76), Mrs. Sen yearns for assimilation but constantly gazes back to the past.

In this section, I investigate "suburban neurosis" in the Asian American diaspora and I specifically consider how the linguistic trope of metonymy governs "Mrs. Sen's," a tale about the loss of ethnic, cultural and identity ties. Displacement is a *leitmotif* in Lahiri's *œuvre* beyond gender differences and urban geographies. Mrs. Sen's dislocation may be connected to other characters in *Interpreter of Maladies*, such as Mala in "The Third and Final Continent" or Shukumar and Sanjeev, the male protagonists of "A Temporary Matter" and "This Blessed House" respectively. Both Shukumar and Sanjeev are portrayed as nurturing husbands performing traditionally female housekeeping duties, such as organizing the cooking and vacuuming the floor. Lahiri, therefore, challenges the traditional stereotype of the kitchen as the place where only women are relegated. For Mrs. Sen, for instance, food and kitchenware signify the loss of the homeland. The taste of Indian food transports Mrs. Sen back to Calcutta through a culinary nostalgia that displaces her suspended affiliation. By weaving together culinary memories and neurotic disorder, Lahiri's story foreshadows a melancholic gap of identification: this space of loss and grief, for Mrs. Sen, is repeatedly amplified by metonymy and repetitions that, on one side, evoke the original loss, while, on the other, stage the sense of void of the Indian woman.

Mrs. Sen lives in a clean and warm "university apartment located on the fringes of the campus" (Lahiri, *Interpreter of Maladies* 112). Like Taylor's Mrs. Everyman, the eponymous protagonist of Lahiri's story is a woman in her thirties, married to an Indian professor of mathematics who uprooted her from her native Calcutta. The expatriate woman, thus, is a victim of the post-1965 brain drain and her abiding resistance to accommodate is epitomised by the refusal of getting a driving license and by a scrupulous clinging to Indian cuisine. The tale narrates how Mrs. Sen, who experiences loneliness in the suburban environment and faces marital problems with a man who embodies the "productive citizenship" of model minorities, builds an unexpected connection with Eliot, the eleven-year-old American boy whom she starts babysitting in her suburban flat. In spite of the differences in age and ethnicity, both Mrs. Sen, whose first and birth name is unknown, and Eliot share the same sense of isolation. Even though the Indian woman does not suffer from insomnia or backache, her pathological distress echoes the symptoms of suburban neurosis. Her homesickness for the community left behind in Calcutta is symbolically displayed by the way her apartment is neatly furnished. From Eliot's perspective, which is the narrative focus of the story, the daily rituals of his new babysitter entail a traumatic neurosis reminiscent of her ethnic origins. Every afternoon, she "took whole vegetables between her hands and hacked them apart: cauliflower, cabbage, butternut squash. She split things in half, then quarters, speedily producing florets, cubes, slices, and shreds" (114). While the "daily procedure took about one hour" (115), Eliot, who is given food and comics to read, observes his babysitter's inability to regulate moods. Euphoria and creativity in the kitchen are interspersed with agonizing moment of loneliness and acute nostalgia when Mrs. Sen is unable to prepare a proper meal. The woman repeats rituals that seem to come from outside the self, a form of neurotic enactment the *ego* cannot offer any resistance to. As Eliot notes, "[i]t was her custom to check the mailbox" (121), buy fresh fish, apply "a fresh stroke of scarlet powder" (117) on her eyebrows and prepare dinner in a kitchen where "brimming bowls and colanders lined the countertop, spices and pastes were measured and blended" (117) every evening. Cooking Indian food is the only way of reconnecting with her past, but it also triggers an automatic and unconscious neurotic mechanism against anxiety: even if the recreation of these past experiences generates wounds, it enables, as Freud explains in "Beyond the Pleasure Principle," to recover "an initial state from which the living entity has at one time or other departed and to which it is striving to return" (38).

Following Freud in "The Ego and the Id," we can say that Mrs. Sen exposes herself to a repetition compulsion that revolves around "the antithesis between the coherent ego and the repressed which splits off from it" (17). The dialectic of coherence and repression produces an emotional turmoil hosted in Mrs. Sen's ego. Whereas Indian recipes represent a vehicle for preserving the ego's coherence, they also activate a sense of loss that emerges in manifestations of passivity and alienation. Once the moment of euphoria has passed, Mrs. Sen seems to plunge into depression: she "refused to practice driving," "the blade never emerged from the cupboard," and she "did not call the fish store" (Lahiri, *Interpreter of Maladies* 128-129). Her neurotic behaviours illustrate the tension between the real and the ideal *ego*, a conflict that, as John Russon (2003) argues, represents "some sector of a person's behaviour [that] stands as a hindrance to achieving this normal selfhood" (85).

Though Mrs. Sen's story foregrounds her sense of loss, the search for solidarity and mutual care interrupts the vulnerable strands of the plot, particularly from Eliot's silent perspective. Albeit a visual observer, Eliot functions as a naïf and innocent narrative witness to Mrs. Sen's neurotic behaviour. By using Eliot as the narrative focus, a second storyline emerges behind Mrs. Sen's tale of suffering, a counter-narrative that leaves a significant impact on Eliot. Despite his young age, the boy seems to possess an awareness of his babysitter's search of care. Eliot shares Mrs. Sen's loneliness: he lives in suburbia, he does not know his father and his mother is almost absent. Unlike his mother who is accustomed to ordering pizza, Eliot seems to realize the importance that food plays in Mrs. Sen's life. While experiencing new tastes, he acts as an observer and a translator of the Indian woman's cultural conundrum but, since he lacks the rigidity of maturity, his perception of the differences is more fluid and nuanced. As Michael Cox (2003) suggests, Eliot may provide a "largely judgment-free perspective" (121) that enables him to develop a liking for his new babysitter, not only because "Mrs. Sen's apartment was warm" (Lahiri, *Interpreter of Maladies* 114), but because the woman offers solidarity and care which he himself craves. In her house, Eliot undergoes a gradual transformation, becoming more aware of his needs as we can infer when Mrs. Sen asks him: "'Do you miss your mother, Eliot, these afternoons with me?' The thought had never occurred to him" (122). By reading the plot through his eyes and senses, the reader may encounter a possible way out of the paralysing neurosis of the Indian woman, thus envisaging a transformative process of self-discovery. Since linguistic exchanges are limited between Eliot and Mrs. Sen, food and domestic rituals becomes the arena for their interaction and for a reposition of their identities in the world.

Eliot is particularly attracted by two elements: a blade and the agonising wait Mrs. Sen endures upon receiving letters from her Indian relatives. The blade and the letters are metonyms of India and the boy realises that "when Mrs. Sen said home, she meant India, not the apartment where she sat chopping vegetables" (115). The tidy and warm American apartment, therefore, is only a shadow of the original home that looms like a ghost throughout the narrative. Likewise, a sense of neurotic disorder permeates his babysitter's reading of the letters: "[a]s she read, her voice was louder and seemed to shift in key. Though she stayed plainly before him, Eliot had the sensation that Mrs. Sen was no longer present in the room with the pear-colored carpet" (122). The metonymic analogy between the letters and India is the rhetorical device that provides access to the signified "[e]verything is there" (113). The implied allusion to India in the deictic reference, during the first conversation between Mrs. Sen and Eliot's mother, indicates the sense of loss that haunts the Indian woman in her new American house.

Lahiri encompasses anxiety and desire at the same time through metonymic associations. Lacan equates desire with metonymy: in his words, desire is caught in "the rails of metonymy" (518). Metonymy indicates the pursuit of a lost signified since the original object is replaced by a substitute which creates a metonymic chain of desire. In Lacanian theory, desire stands between *jouissance* and anxiety, the latter being a signal that there is a lack and "if desire is the metonymy of the want-to-be, the ego is the metonymy of the desire" (623). Desire, hence, can be understood as a continuous displacement from one signifier to another, while anxiety reveals a gap. Those who suffer from obsession, like Mrs. Sen, are confronted with anxiety since they fail to stop this chain. Inspired by the distinction drawn by linguist Roman Jakobson, Lacan argues that while metaphors operate at the paradigmatic level through similarity and substitution, metonymies carry the signified across the syntagmatic axis through contiguity and associations. Metonymies, hence, displace emotions and desires from the original object to substitute ones: because "there is no connection between word [signifier] and thing [signified] in the way metonymy operates, the signifying function in language is metonymy" (Walden 241). Studying this linguistic opposition from a psychological perspective, Lacan says that metonymy "installs the lack of being in the object relation, using the value of reference-back possessed by signification in order to invest it with the desire aimed at the very task it supports" (274). The logic of metonymy follows a horizontal line that defers desires from one object to another and Mrs. Sen reads food items and kitchenware as metonymic signifiers of a culinary nostalgia charged with profound dislocation. Mrs. Sen's blade, "that curved like the prow of a Viking ship, sailing to battle in distant seas" (Lahiri, *Interpreter of Maladies* 114), is a metonymic reminder of India and of the sense of gendered community that the kitchen utensil epitomises:

> "Whenever there is a wedding in the family," she told Eliot one day, "or a large celebration of any kind, my mother sends out word in the evening for all the neighborhood women to bring blades just like this one, and then they sit in an enormous circle on the roof of our building, laughing and gossiping and slicing fifty kilos of vegetables through the night." (115)

The sense of lack spells desires that are continuously deferred, reappearing in other guises. Mrs. Sen's daily ritual of chopping cabbages, potatoes and cauliflowers may symbolically be read as an attempt to reduce the distance between the United States and India, the representation of a desire she cannot fulfil. Lack and desire give shape to the memories of diasporic subjects and, in "Mrs. Sen's" culinary idiom, food emerges as metonymic vehicle of ambivalence.

Culinary nostalgia bears witness to the complex processes of diaspora and migration that recreate the homeland as a contradictory space, limiting and emancipatory at the same time. Culinary fiction, as Anita Mannur contends, "occupies a seemingly paradoxical space – at once a site of affirmation and resistance" (7). This ambivalence can be traced in Lahiri's fiction and similarly evokes Svetlana Boym's double vision of nostalgia as both restorative and reflective. In "Mrs. Sen's," restorative nostalgia, a strategy that, borrowing from Boym, "puts emphasis on *nostos* and proposes to rebuild a lost home and patch up the memory gaps" (41; emphasis in the original), structures the Indian woman's obsession with order and culinary practices. Mrs. Sen's re-enactments become a means of installing a sense of the self: having lost her previous self, connected to her life in India, Mrs. Sen seeks to reassure herself of the authenticity of her life and Indian food embodies the most genuine strategy of engaging with her condition. The textual fixation on kitchenware, such as "pots and mugs" (Lahiri, *Interpreter of Maladies* 112), "plastic bowl[s]" (115), "plates, glasses, napkins and silverware" (117) and the insistence on household chores, like vacuuming the floor, doing the shopping and preparing dinner, slow down the temporality of the text, contributing to a sense of paralysis and numbness.

In the eyes of Eliot's mother, a career woman who clings to ready-made food, Mrs. Sen's apartment looks like a small-scale reproduction of Indian tastes, where "[h]er profile hovered protectively over her work, a confetti of cucumber, eggplant, and onion skins heaped around her" (115). Mrs. Sen's neurotic daily rituals of cleansing utensils, chopping and drying vegetables are incomprehensible to Eliot's mother, while for the Indian protagonist they stand for a compulsive restoration of lost traditions. When the American woman picks up her son from Mrs. Sen's apartment, she notices the evidence of Mrs. Sen's routine: "[t]he blade was scrubbed, rinsed, dried, folded, and stowed away" (117). Thus, Lahiri intensifies Mrs. Sen's habits through Eliot's mother's perspective, producing an effect of strangeness.

Loss and lack dominate the story and Mrs. Sen's cross-cultural neurosis defers desires that emerge in representations of loss and lost objects. Readers are not allowed to know the name of the Indian woman. Lahiri's heroine, the representative of a community with a plenty of names, South Asians, Asian Americans, *desi* and brown folk, is nameless. The woman's namelessness is counterbalanced by a plethora of Indian references that invade the American apartment. Not only tastes and letters, Mrs. Sen also listens to the tape where the voices of her relatives, speaking Bengali, resonate across the suburban house: "[o]ne day she played a tape of something she called a raga; it sounded a little bit like someone plucking very slowly and then very quickly on a violin [...]. Another day she played a cassette of people talking in her language [...]" (128). Without a name and with a gap between her teeth, that may be read as a further sign of absence that physically characterises her, Mrs. Sen compensates the identity conundrum by restoring her daily routines in the new American flat, though the missing genitive in the title illustrates the lack of a sense of home. Lahiri ironically reinforces loss and lack through the difficulty in finding ingredients for her cuisine: "[i]t's very frustrating [...] [t]o live so close to the ocean and not to have so much fish" (123). Mrs. Sen regrets the lack of fish she would always have in Calcutta where "people ate fish first thing in the morning, last thing before bed, as a snack after school if they were lucky" (123) and her obsession with cooking fish, as a sign of cultural belonging, elicits Eliot's mother prompt reply, "[t]ry the supermarket" (123), a position that expands the distance between the United States and India. The fish is, once more, a metonymic motif charged with nostalgia and neurosis that animates everyday practices. Lahiri's female characters, therefore, are unable to change habits.

As Russon puts it, identity is based on habits and neurosis means "to find that one cannot control one's behavior in areas that, according to the narrative of normalcy, should be areas in which the free ego has an uninhibited ability to exercise choice" (86). Neurotic behaviours restore a memory of who we are, "the memory of those patterns of recognition through which, and as which, we were made familiar with other people" (94). The question of memory leads to nostalgic yearning for cultural roots, a central theme in Lahiri's prose: restorative nostalgia and neurosis entangle Mrs. Sen's desires, shedding light on the vulnerability of diasporic subjects over the myth of the model minority.

Even though Mrs. Sen's struggle to find her own place is stylistically performed in the text through the adaptation of metonymic solutions, suburban neurosis resurfaces through anxiety and distractions while she tries to drive Mr. Sen's car. Ignoring his advice to pay attention to road signs, Mrs. Sen seems to be incapable of adjusting to the rules of the road: "the same stream of cars made her knuckles pale, her wrists tremble, and her English falter" (Lahiri, *Interpreter of Maladies* 121). At the end of the story, in a final attempt to seize her chance to cross the border from neurosis to 'normalcy,' Mrs. Sen drives her husband's car with Eliot. In search of a halibut for a special Indian recipe, she embarks on an errand to the fishmonger's but a minor accident occurs. Although neither Mrs. Sen nor Eliot are hurt, the episode functions as a reminder of the ambivalent assimilation of South Asians into the United States. When the woman returns home, she stows back the blade and throws away the vegetables she had already sliced, offering Eliot "a plate of crackers with peanut butter" (134). Though the conclusion introduces a crisis, it also provides the reader with a change of culinary habit. The perpetual evocation of Indian food leaves space to an American snack, a solution that seems to reactivate temporality and open up to the future, at least for Eliot. Eliot's mother realises that the boy is old enough to stay on his own and takes him away from Mrs. Sen's care, putting an end to the solidarity between the babysitter and the boy. The story, therefore, concludes with the South Asian woman trapped in her suburban flat, crying for the impossibility to find her own place in the United States, and opting for American food as a sign of failure and change. By the end of the story, both characters have experienced change. While Eliot has come of age with a new intercultural awareness, Mrs. Sen's sense of loss seems to prevail. And yet, the American snack she finally serves conjures up a possible transformation: in this view, the Indian woman might achieve freedom from her neurosis through the renunciation of her past culinary habits. Lahiri, in conclusion, turns Mrs. Sen's metonymic activities into a performative space that serves as an example for the migrant's experience of nostalgic neurosis.

TROPES OF "RACIAL MELANCHOLIA" AND DEFERRED DESIRES

In his *Seminar X*, Lacan suggests that desires create conflicts and split individual subjectivity between the "I" and the "ideal-I," generating neurotic anxiety and a sense of loss. He argues that desires are always in motion and, like language, they are always deferred. Desires, Lacan explains, enhance an "incessant sliding of the signified under the signifier" (502). Following the French psychoanalyst, we can say that those who suffer from obsessional neurosis endure conflicts between the self and the external world, a tension that Freud categorized as "melancholia." In his seminal essay "Mourning and Melancholia" (1917), Freud sees melancholia as pathological mourning that results in "cessation of interest in the outside world, loss of the capacity of love, inhibition of all activity" (244). The melancholic position stems from the idealization of a lost object and "racial melancholia" generates "a cleaving of the psyche" (Eng and Han 675) in ethnic minorities that aspire to accommodate. In their study, Eng and Han pinpoint how assimilation into mainstream American culture for South Asians means adopting a series of norms and how failures to integrate produce melancholic feelings which affect Asian Americans' suspended assimilation. In this light, "melancholia describes an unresolved process," an inability to assimilate entailing that "for Asian Americans, ideals of whiteness are continually estranged. They remain at an unattainable distance, at once a compelling fantasy and a lost ideal" (671).

Taking these assumptions as a starting point, I claim that Lahiri's second-generation migrants epitomise the psychic splitting generated by mimicry and assimilation to whiteness. Extending Homi Bhabha's concept of "mimicry" to racial issues, Eng and Han maintain that "Asians Americans are forced to mimic the model minority stereotype in order to be recognized by mainstream society – in order *to be* at all" (677, emphasis in the original). By imitating western norms and ideals, Asian Americans are exposed to haunting melancholia because they inherit losses from the first generations that lead to intergenerational conflicts. From such a perspective, the stories in *Unaccustomed Earth*[7] reveal Lahiri's engagement with the politics of racial melancholia. In the process of signifying melancholia, two tropes come into play, metaphors and prosopopoeia, that create a poetics in which every event refers back to the recollection of an impossible desire, condensing loss into narratives saturated with exposure to vulnerability. Lahiri's five stories, and one novella, chart the ordinary lives and daily rituals of Bengali American migrants who, in the wake of the 1965 Immigration and Naturalization Act, experience marital and filial conflicts in the "unaccustomed earth" of the American dream, split between the model minority paradigm and the neurotic disorders it produces.

7 The title of the collection, winner of the Frank O'Connor International Short Story Award, is inspired by a quote from Nathaniel Hawthorne's preface to *The Scarlet Letter* (1850).

In "A Choice of Accommodation," Lahiri explores the complex dynamics of marriage across racial differences between Amit Sarkar, a second-generation Asian American, and his white wife Megan. The story chronicles Amit and Megan's trip from New York to Langford, where they are attending the wedding ceremony of Pam, Amit's friend on whom he had a crush from their time at Langford College. The couple wishes to spend a romantic weekend in the countryside, but Amit's decision to book a room in a pricey hotel "in the middle of nowhere" (Lahiri, *Unaccustomed Earth* 86), rather than staying at Langford with the other guests, hides his repudiation of Langford. The miscommunication and the silences between husband and wife are metaphorically rendered through the pine tree that obstructs the view from the balcony of their hotel room. Amit's college infatuation with Pam is an instance of the sense of detachment between husband and wife: though Amit thinks that since Pam had "never been his girlfriend there had been nothing to explain" (88), Megan, as the narrator remarks, "was insecure about Pam, defensive the one or two times they'd met" (88). Impediments, silences, incidents and pouring rain are thus used to narrate the sense of haunting obsession that looms over the story: while the room is dark and the place is "without character" (84), the partners discuss whether to change room since "Amit and Megan had a tradition, in their relationship, of switching hotel rooms" (87), a habit that exposes the difficulties in making choices in their conjugal relationship and the need to find a proper accommodation. Lahiri juxtaposes the bleak description of the place with the thoughts running in Amit's mind: the reader learns that he "was plagued by his daughters' vulnerability, both to illness and to accidents of all kinds" (90) and that he "was still haunted by an incident in the cafeteria of the Museum of Natural History" (90) when his older daughter had choked on a piece of apricot.

Through metaphors and prosopopoeia Lahiri problematises the search of both physical and symbolic accommodation of her Asian Americans characters. The use of metaphors in the story allow a latent readability of the unconscious to emerge. The language of loss and vulnerability, of desire and fear, casts a special light on the neurotic content, unveiling its hidden meaning. The title incorporates two motifs, 'choice' and 'the process to adjust,' and it clearly resonates with irony since Amit seems unable to make choices and find a suitable accommodation, even when booking hotel rooms. Therefore, the metaphorical meaning of the title carries traces of a condensation that reveals a return of the repressed, in an echo of Lacan's equivalence between metaphors and condensation (see 160). Metaphors manifest unarticulated or deferred desires and because the world in Lahiri's story is replete with condensation, spaces are metaphors structuring Amit's unconscious. Langford itself, for instance, functions as a metaphor in the life of the protagonist: as the narrator explains, "there was nothing to remind him of those years of his life" (Lahiri, *Unaccustomed Earth* 86) in a place where he was the only Indian student, "crippled with homesickness, missing his parents to the point where tears often filled his eyes" (97). The place gives us glimpses of the wounds from which the story emerges since Amit's recollection of Langford is an eruption of his unconscious. His anger, directed at his parents who had sent him to the college, manifests itself as a physical disability limiting his freedom, as clearly indicated by the verb "cripple."

In the same vein, the Langford days are intensely metaphorical, as place and language are used metaphorically. Though born and raised in the United States, Amit seems dissociated from himself. His deep sense of loss emerges from the struggles with his parents' expectations and with the aloof adolescence spent at Langford, in a WASP environment, where his mates complimented him on his accent, assuming that "he'd been born and raised in that country [India] and not in Massachusetts" (97). Like many other characters in Lahiri's fiction, Amit searches for identity and recognition externally, in relationship to others. Disregarding his parents' expectations, he does not become a doctor, like his father, and he does not marry a Bengali woman. Both Megan and Pam are white, which suggests tensions between Amit's desire and the Bengali habit of arranged marriages. Megan, who is a doctor and comes from a WASP family, represents a seething dissatisfaction for his parents who are already disappointed about Amit's decision of dropping the medical studies in order to apply to a school of journalism. The trip to Langford, hence, is not a peaceful homecoming. In contrast, Amit associates the place with the lack of a stable sense of the self and with the first appearance of grey hair:

> It was here, at Langford, that it had begun, when he was in the sixth form. At first it was just a few strands, well concealed in his black hair. But by the time he was a junior at Columbia it was the black hairs he could count on one hand. He'd read it was possible, after a traumatic experience, for a person's hair to turn grey in youth. But there had been no sudden death he could point to, no accident. No profound life change, apart from his parents sending him to Langford. (93)

Again, Amit recalls the sense of loss for being left alone in Langford, whilst his parents had returned to India. His obsessional neurosis is conveyed through the recollections of the days at college that metaphorically seem to spoil his appearance. Strikingly, the past surfaces as a kind of disabling disease that not only physically limits Amit's vital strength, it also spoils his youth. Though Amit's mental disorder is not diagnosed in medical terms, the narrative portrays the effects of trauma. Amit's return to Langford reactivates the persistence of traumatic memories blurring the border between past and present. The flashback, which foregrounds Amit's sense of exclusion and suffering as a student at Langford, is an instance of Freudian *Nachträglichkeit*[8] that stretches to the limits the temporality of traumatic memory. Although Amit himself denies to have undergone any traumas, I would say that traumatic temporality is relevant since Amit is caught in the recollection of a returning past that leaves consequences on his psyche.

Among the metaphorical wounds in the protagonist's melancholic life, linguistic fragmentation comes at the top of the list. By evoking his journey to relatives in Delhi, Amit recalls his "broken Bengali [being] of no use in that city" (96). On one side, the man yearns for a sense of accommodation that Lahiri depicts through a ghost language that inhabits the protagonist's mind; on the other, Amit cannot come to terms with India and he misses the tranquillity of his American hometown. Lahiri's protagonist straddles the boundary between paralysis and agency. The linguistic state of loss underlines Amit's vulnerable side and ties in with Kristeva's insights on melancholia and linguistic representation. The melancholic buries his sense of loss in a sort of mental crypt, a trajectory that is translated into the failure to use language properly. The Kristevan version of melancholia is grounded on language pathology since "melancholy persons are foreigners in their maternal tongue. They have lost the meaning – the value – of their mother tongue for want of losing their mother" (53). While Mrs. Sen's English falters when she is confronted with American habits, Amit's limited mastery of Bengali is a metaphor for the loss of his origins, a template for his search of cultural and physical accommodation.

As described above, the man is obsessed with fears about his daughters who are staying with his in-laws while he is at Pam's wedding with his wife. Having studied surgery for some years and inured to the body's "inherent fragility" (Lahiri, *Unaccustomed Earth* 90), Amit is conscious of human vulnerability. While reading about accidents on newspapers, he is obsessed with the idea of the death of his daughters: "he imagined a wave at Jones Beach, where he had been taking them once a week during the summer, dragging one of them down, or a pile of sand suffocating them as he was flipping, a few feet away, through a magazine" (91). Though the two young daughters never make an appearance in the story, their absence summons the most vulnerable side of Amit's mind. The narrator

8 The term that Laplanche has translated as "afterwardsness" (263) refers to Freud's observations on trauma. The memory of a traumatic experiences becomes traumatic only at a later stage, when it is revivified with a belated understanding.

presents Amit as a split and fragile subject, torn between the desire to adjust and the fear of losing connections to his ethnic roots. His quest for a proper accommodation is interspersed with the fear of losing his origins, a threat that the two daughters embody in their physical features since both "Maya and Monika had inherited Megan's coloring, without a trace of Amit's deeply tan skin and black eyes, so that apart from their vaguely Indian names they appeared fully American" (94). The fact bothers Amit who, however, feels a connection to his daughters, dreaming catastrophic scenarios that "could toss his existence over a cliff" (91). Amit's fears reveal his acute alienation and the metaphor of throwing away his own life is a symptom of his mental disturbance.

In the metaphoric line, signifiers tend to be substituted with others, while the signified, in Lacan's terms, "crosses the bar" (164) of repression that separates it from the signifier, achieving a witnessing function and giving voice to what it previously refused to convey. With its metaphoric condensation of the place and of the experiences in the college, the short story discloses its narrative force and, by crossing the bar of resistance, the signified is made visible, determining the signifier. Amit's tunnelling drags his unconscious out into the light, an evocative power that Lahiri also elicits through prosopopoeia, a figurative linguistic device providing non-human entities with discourse.

By linking a poetics of narrative neurosis to pathological memory, "A Choice of Accommodation" tends to resist silence through prosopopoeia, a new narrative energy that, by making Amit's neurosis visible and audible, serves as a testimony and conveys his need of recovery – conveyed in particular by Amit's failed attempt to find a phone booth to talk to his daughters. Slightly tipsy, he leaves the college where the wedding ceremony has just started, but the search of a phone booth collapses into a solitary wandering across the dark fields around Langford. In his stumbling through the natural landscape, Amit's melancholic mood and cultural conundrum are intensified by the haunting "serenade of the frogs" (Lahiri, *Unaccustomed Earth* 117), an uncanny sound he had already heard in his dormitory as a student:

> It was a sound he had forgotten, one that had haunted him and kept him awake his first nights in a Langford dormitory, at the end of another August when he was fifteen years old. All the incoming students heard it as they slept in their new rooms, in their strange beds, missing their parents, their homes; they were told at their first assembly that the frogs were calling for their mates, defending their territory by the water's edge before burying themselves under mud for the winter. (117)

Such a soul-stirring effect signals Amit's awareness of the things he cannot grasp. Not only does the eerie concert played by the frogs break the silence of the countryside, but their hoarse and "deafening" (117) croaks also vocalize his unvoiced obsession with death. If, as Paul de Man (1984) states, prosopopoeia is "the trope of autobiography" (76), a rhetoric representation of the self, in Amit's case, his inner silences are thus couched in the croaking of the amphibians. Furthermore, the frogs' movement downwards starkly contrasts with the outward process materializing in Amit's mind: while for the amphibians the aquatic burial is a symbol of shelter and comradeship, Amit's psychological tunnel leads him to paralysis and solitude, forcing him to deal with his controversial "accommodation" to America. Furthermore, the Hindi etymology of his name, 'boundless,' is at odds with his inability to adjust. Whereas boundless means 'without limit,' Amit seems to be paralysed, a passivity clashing with the restlessness of his parents who, after their departure to India, first move to Switzerland and finally settle down in Saudi Arabia. Their transcontinental migrations are opposed to the paralysis which metaphorically limits Amit's 'boundless' potentiality. Through paradoxes and reversal, prosopopoeia, like a Janus-faced trope, awakens Amit, making him aware "of everything in the world that teemed beyond his vision" (Lahiri, *Unaccustomed Earth* 117). At the same time, the performative logics of prosopopoeia gestures towards the end of the story, by indicating a path away from the past.

The story ends with Amit's awakening in the late morning in the hotel, where he finds Megan waiting for him. Before going back to New York, they return to Langford for the wedding brunch but they are late and find shelter from the rain in a dorm room where Amit finds the courage to confess that Pam was "nothing" (125) to him and the recollection of his erotic fantasy about Pam arouses him. "A Choice of Accommodation" ends with Amit and Megan having sex on a bed in the dorm room, a place bereft of any romanticism but that ultimately makes space for Amit's precarious accommodation into the American soil.

CONCLUSION

The poetics of neurosis I have engaged with here offer a way for neurosis to develop fully, allowing ontological vulnerability to emerge. Lahiri's short fictions depict forms of disorder and fragility that problematise the status of the South Asian model minority paradigm, animating a mode of embracing the wounds. From this point of view, the exposure to neurosis as nostalgia and melancholia portrays characters driven by contradictions and ambiguities which challenge the "promise of happiness" (see Ahmed, *Promise of Happiness*) that migration ought to entail. As Sara Ahmed explains, "even if happiness holds its place as the object of desire, it does not always signify something, let alone signify the same thing" (201). Ahmed focuses on what happiness can do, exploring the ways happiness can generate affect. In other words, emotions have a performative quality, "creating a political and personal horizon that gives us an image of the good life" (*Cultural Politics of Emotions* 14), and what constitutes happiness is the ability to do things. Both Mrs. Sen and Amit epitomise examples of the kind of "melancholic migrants" embodying, in Ahmed's words, existences that "cannot be wished away with happiness" (*The Promise of Happiness* 159). Ahmed criticises the imperative of happiness, a grief that the stories analysed here clearly expose: if the promise of happiness entails becoming a model minority, Lahiri's short fiction reveals the gap between the myth of model minority and a more complex reality: the migrants, like Mrs. Sen and Amit, who are unable to do things, such as driving a car or booking a hotel room, do not fit into this notion of 'normalcy' and find themselves at loss. What is at stake in Lahiri's stories is the myth of the model minority, a sense of achievement that for immigrants means "telling a certain story about your arrival as good" (158). Thus, when the stories are not positive, they involve silence and fragility, stretching the force of narrative representation to the limits.

As I have tried to underline in my analysis, Lahiri's poetics of neurosis features a preference for linguistic tropes, such as metonyms, metaphors and prosopopoeia that alert the reader to the situations of vulnerability and awareness of her migrant characters. If we return briefly to Russon's exploration of neurosis, we may remember that he sees neurosis as "a memorial, bodily comportment, primarily realized as a way of having a world of objects – a place, a home" (94) and both Mrs. Sen and Amit imaginatively occupy multiple spaces in the attempt to find a sense of belonging. The fact that both short stories do not allow for closure may be interpreted as a possible way out of the neurotic content the narratives rely on. Whereas neurosis foregrounds a promise to realise happiness, the characters' unhappiness alludes to the persistence of an emotional turmoil. And yet, the hidden meanings of the tales, accessed via metonyms, metaphors and prosopopopeia, unveil a resilience of the subject that, in his/her neurosis, is however caught in a web of connectivity and interdependence. This leads me to a final point that I find extremely relevant for Lahiri's fiction, which gives visibility to the disrupted memories of the past constituting the core of neurotic states. By focusing on everyday life and traumatic memories, Lahiri makes literature a privileged site for addressing neurosis and the search of care and solidarity.

LIST OF WORKS CITED

Ahmed, Sara. *The Cultural Politics of Emotions*. Routledge, 2004.

---. *The Promise of Happiness*. Duke University Press, 2010.

Boym, Svetlana. *The Future of Nostalgia*. Basic Books, 2001.

Chin, Gabriel J., and Rose Cuison Villazor, editors. *The Immigration and Nationality Act of 1965: Legislating a New America*. Cambridge University Press, 2015.

Cox, Michael. "Interpreter of Cultural Difference: The Use of Children in Jhumpa Lahiri's Short Fiction." *South Asian Review*, vol. 24, no. 2, 2003, pp. 120-132.

De Man, Paul. "Autobiography as De-Facement." *The Rhetoric of Romanticism*. Columbia University Press, 1984, pp. 67-81.

Dutt-Ballerstadt, Reshmi. *The Postcolonial Citizen: The Intellectual Migrant*. Peter Lang, 2010.

Eng, David L., and Shinhee Han, "A Dialogue on Racial Melancholia." *Psychoanalytic Dialogues*, vol. 10, no. 4, 2000, pp. 667-700.

Freud, Sigmund. "Beyond the Pleasure Principle." *Beyond the Pleasure Principle, Group Psychology and Other Works*, edited and translated by James Strachey, The Hogarth Press, 1956, pp. 1-64.

---."The Ego and the Id." *The Ego and the Id and Other Works*, edited and translated by James Strachey, vol. 19, The Hogarth Press, 1956, pp. 12-66.

---. "Mourning and Melancholia." *On the History of the Psycho-Analytic Movement, Papers on Metapsychology and Other Works*, edited and translated by James Strachey, vol. 14, The Hogarth Press, 1956, pp. 243-258.

Koshy, Susan. "Neoliberal Family Matters." *American Literary History*, vol. 25, no. 2, 2013, pp. 344-380.

Kristeva, Julia. *Black Sun: Depression and Melancholia*. Columbia University Press, 1989.

Lacan, Jacques. *Écrits*. Edited by Alan Sheridan, Tavistock Publications, 1977.

Laplanche, Jean. "Notes on Afterwardsness." *Essays on Otherness*, edited by John Fletcher and Jean Laplanche, Routledge, 1999, pp. 260-265.

Lahiri, Jhumpa. *Interpreter of Maladies*. Houghton Mifflin Harcourt, 1999.

---. *The Namesake*. Harper Perennial, 2003.

---. *Unaccustomed Earth*. Bloomsbury, 2008.

Mannur, Anita. *Culinary Fictions: Food in South Asian Diasporic Culture*. Temple University Press, 2010.

Mishra, Vijay. *The Literature of the Indian Diaspora: Theorizing the Diasporic Imaginary*. Routledge, 2007.

Peterson, William. "Success Story, Japanese American Style." *The New York Times*, 9 Jan. 1966, pp. 20-21.

Plath, Sylvia. *The Bell Jar*. Faber and Faber, 1963.

Russon. John. *Human Experience: Philosophy, Neurosis, and the Elements of Everyday Life*. State University of New York Press, 2003.

Schneider, Jens, and Maurice Crul. *Theorising Integration and Assimilation*. Routledge, 2012.

Taylor, Stephan. "The Suburban Neurosis." *The Lancet*, vol. 231, no. 5978, 1938, pp. 759-761.

"The Rise of Asian Americans." *Pew Research Centre*, 19 June 2012, www.pewsocialtrends.org/2012/06/19/the-rise-of-asian-americans. Accessed 26 March 2017.

Wilden, Anthony. "Lacan and the Discourse of the Other." *The Language of the Self: The Function of Language in Psychoanalysis*, edited by Anthony Wilden, Johns Hopkins University Press, 1968, pp. 159-311.

Allegories of Pathology

Post-War Colonial Expatriates and Imperial Neurosis in F. Scott Fitzgerald's *Tender is the Night* and Derek Walcott's *Omeros*

Sneharika Roy

In his seminal essay "The Negro and Pychopathology" (1952), Frantz Fanon calls upon us to "investigate the extent to which the conclusions of Freud or of Adler can be applied to the effort to understand the man of colour's view of the world" (141). A deeply personal response to his experiences of racism as a black Martinican in Lyon, Fanon's affirmation of the "man of colour's view of the world" was consonant with the radical developments of the time, notably the Bandung Conference (1955) and the Tricontinental Conference (1966) that gave political voice to representatives of Asia, Africa and South America.[1] Today, however, – more than half a decade after the publication of Fanon's *Black Skin, White Masks* (1952) – the postcolonial subject has been firmly established in scholarly discourse. It is time to reimagine new possibilities for Fanon's exhortation. To do so, we need to rebalance Fanon's binary distinction and shift some of the focus back to the so-called 'white man.' Postcolonial studies tend to focus ei-

1 Held in 1955 during the Cold War, the Afro-Asian Conference or the Bandung Conference was an international platform from which delegates from Asian and African nations publicly and collectively articulated their condemnation of colonialism and neocolonialism as well as their solidarity as nations aligned neither with the US nor with the Soviet Union. Extending this Afro-Asian solidarity to the Americas, the 1966 Tricontinental Conference, also known as the Solidarity Conference of the Peoples of Africa, Asia and Latin America, brought together delegates representing national liberation movements in thirty-five countries in the non-western world.

ther on the oppressed subaltern or the privileged postcolonial expatriate writer. The experience of the 'white man,' particularly the colonial administrator and Christian missionary, is often used in dialectic opposition to the colonized individual or postcolonial subject. As for the condition of the 'white postcolonial,' an expatriate living in the formerly colonized, now-independent country, it has only recently attracted the attention of scholars. Highlighting the extent to which "whiteness itself remains a largely unexamined category" in relation to colonialism and its aftermath, Alfred J. López pointedly asks, "*What happens to whiteness after empire?*" (4; emphasis in original).

The ramifications of this question being too vast to explore in the space of an essay, I will focus on the trope of the war injury as a means to problematise the white experience of postcolonial expatriation. In line with Fanon's insights into the psychopathology of colonialism, I examine the links between empire, war and neurosis from the prism of the post-war expatriate situation. I therefore counterpoint the experiences of three radically different post-war expatriates: the eponymous Odysseus, the archetypal expatriate; Nicole Warren, the extremely privileged American expatriate heiress of the Jazz Age in F. Scott Fitzgerald's *Tender is the Night* (1934); and Major Plunkett, the British expatriate living in the former British colony and now independent island-state of Saint Lucia in Derek Walcott's *Omeros* (1990). The latter two texts, in particular, are structured around the typically postcolonial strategy of the personal and national allegory as conceptualised by Fredric Jameson (see 69).[2] The international dimension of expatriation allows me to extend these critical categories into the domain of "transnational allegory" (Ramazani 1997). In *Tender is the Night* and *Omeros*, pathological disorders constitute an allegory of the white expatriate's sense of spatial and psychological dislocation. Having underlined this significant convergence between American expatriate writing and postcolonial aesthetics, I will underscore what I believe to be the fundamental point of divergence and the specificity of postcolonial literature: its preoccupation with time and historiography.

2 While I see the Jamesonian national allegory as typical of postcolonial poetics, I do not see it as necessarily limited to postcolonial literature. However, I do share Jameson's sense that the interpenetrating relationship between the libidinal and the political is explicitly thematized and staged to a degree uncommon to other bodies of literature.

POST-WAR NARRATIVES

The central importance of the figure of the expatriate in *Tender is the Night* and *Omeros* signals their intertextual affiliation to the *Odyssey*. All three narratives are set in a post-war context. The *Odyssey*, set in the aftermath of the Trojan War, follows Odysseus as he wanders around the Mediterranean before successfully returning to Ithaca. George de F. Lord helpfully summarises existing interpretations of the epic by dividing them into two categories: the allegorists, from the Augustan Heraclitus to Roger Ascham, who see in it a moral allegory of reason's triumph over temptation, and the realists including C.S. Lewis, who see it as an adventure story in which events are 'accidental,' 'external,' and devoid of ethical significance. To the realists one may add Eric Auerbach. In his famous study of Odysseus's scar (recognized by the old housekeeper Euryclea but concealed from Penelope), Auerbach posits that Homeric epic represents phenomena as "fully externalised" so that "nothing remains hidden and unexpressed" (23). As Euryclea washes Odysseus's feet, Homer describes the scene thus:

The scar: he had forgotten that. She must not
handle his scarred thigh or the game was up.
But when she bared her lord's leg, bending near,
she knew the groove at once.
An old wound
a boar's white tusk had inflicted, on Parnassos
years ago. (XIX.456–462)

The back-story of Odysseus's scar is presented as a narrative digression on par with other narrative events, and not as, say, a psychological flashback that Odysseus could have had. This "Homeric style knows only a foreground, only a uniformly illuminated, uniformly objective present" (Auerbach 7). In contrast, George de F. Lord, writing almost a decade after the devastation of World War II, subscribes to Denton J. Snider's reading of the poem. For Snider, the *Odyssey* recounts the "estrangement" and "spiritual restoration" of Odysseus, "the wise man, who, through his intelligence, was able to take Troy, but who now has another and greater problem – the return out of the grand estrangement caused by the Trojan expedition" (qtd. in Lord 409).

Unlike Odysseus, whose exile is involuntary, Nicole Warren in *Tender is the Night* and Major Plunkett in *Omeros* are expatriates by choice. Like Odysseus, both are linked to visible, external signs of bodily penetration. A bloodstained bedspread in a Parisian hotel triggers a seemingly irrational outburst of horror on the part of Nicole. After having helped her husband Dick move the corpse of a black man to another room, she locks herself in the bathroom. When Dick enters to check on her, she exclaims,

> "it's you come to intrude on the only privacy I have in the world – with your spread with red blood on it […] don't come into the bathroom, the only place I can go for privacy, dragging spreads with red blood on them and asking me to fix them." (125–126)

We learn that such outbursts are part of a recurrent pattern of behaviour. Witnessing Nicole's breakdown in the hotel bathroom, the young actress Rosemary recalls a previous episode: "now she knew what Violet McKisco had seen in the bathroom at the Villa Diana" (126). Finally, in *Omeros*, Major Plunkett, a retired British army officer, is still haunted by traumatic memories of World War II, during which he sustained a serious head wound. When serving under General Bernard Montgomery in the North Africa campaign of the Second World War, Plunkett is wounded in the head as he witnesses the death of his "chums, companions. Comrades-in-arms":

> They crouched, hands on helmets, while the Messerschmitt's gun
> stitched, in staccato succession, miniature palms
>
> along the top of a trench. He shot up. Again
> Tumbly pulled him down. "Just keep your bleedin' 'ead low!"
> Scott was running to them, laughing, but the only thing
>
> funny about him was the fact that one elbow
> didn't have the rest of the arm. (27)

Plunkett's suffering is compounded by his wife's inability to have a son. As a British expatriate who has relocated to the idyllic island of Saint Lucia, he becomes obsessed with the island's colonial history, in particularly the Battle of the Saintes, which inaugurated Britain's supremacy in much of the West Indies. Plunkett researches this battle extensively in an attempt to find meaning to war and the life he has devoted to it. In this sense, his expatriate location initially does not allow him to distance himself from imperial discourse. On the contrary, his nostalgic desire to reinscribe himself within a glorious imperialist narrative deprives him of lucidity. The causes of his neurosis are therefore multiple, linked to his traumatic experience in World War II, the loss of Britain's colonial grandeur and a resulting obsession with Eurocentric history, and the couple's childlessness.

The *Odyssey*, *Tender is the Night* and *Omeros* thus present three very different expatriate 'types.' Odysseus, the war veteran of classical antiquity, frequently draws attention not only to the physical suffering he endured, but also to the alienation of exile: "Where shall a man find sweetness to surpass / his own home and his parents? In far lands / he shall not, though he find a house of gold" (IX.38–40). A far more explicit link between geographical expatriation and existential expatriation from the self is established in *Tender is the Night.* Nicole, in a moment of free indirect discourse, muses, "there was no home left to her, save emptiness and pain" (159). Moreover, as an 'American expatriate' in Europe moving in the glittering world of lavish parties and insouciant escapades, she would seem to share little in common with a 'postcolonial expatriate'[3] like Major Plunkett, whose life of ease in St Lucian society is the direct result of Britain's colonial domination of the island. Still, in *Tender is the Night*, there is a distinctly colonial dynamic in the economic relationship between the rich expatriate Americans in France and the native French, who appear almost exclusively in the role of subalterns as cooks, waiters, maid-servants, valets and hotel personnel. Their resentment against America's capitalist hegemony is particularly evident in the confrontation between Dick and Augustine, the maid-servant, who accuses him of being a "disgusting American" with "the voice of the commune" (286).[4] While the historical situations of an 'American expatriate' like Nicole and a 'postcolonial expatriate' like Plunkett are undeniably distinct, I argue that they are nonetheless comparable, specifically through the depiction of their experiences as narratives of neurosis.

3 Plunkett may also be called a 'colonial expatriate' by virtue of his connection to Britain, the former colonizing power in Saint Lucia. Yet, Walcott focuses on Plunkett's experiences as a white Britisher in a *postcolonial* context. Though he enjoys economic privileges bestowed by the disparities created by the colonial system, he also experiences cultural alienation as a resident who *wants* to be considered St Lucian but is not fully integrated in St Lucian society.

4 A proletariat uprising in 1871 in Paris. It resulted in a short-lived government – the Commune – that promoted radical socialism.

PHYSICAL AND PSYCHOLOGICAL WOUNDS

Unlike the purely physical manifestation of Odysseus's scar that appears not "out of the darkness of an unilluminated past" but is "set in full light," Nicole's and Plunkett's wounds are, to borrow Auerbach's terms, "mysterious and 'fraught with background'" (15). In *Tender is the Night*, the bloodstain becomes the visible manifestation of underlying psychological trauma. At the centre of the narrative is the act of incest between Nicole Warren and her father. This painful childhood experience constitutes the root cause of Nicole's neurosis. The traumatic origin of her psychic discomfort is displaced to a bedspread, presumably because of its association with the bedsheet of the original scene of incest. Nicole's doctors recognise that she has also dealt with her trauma through the classic psychoanalytic strategy of transference. She redirects her feelings vis-à-vis her father to another father-figure, the young doctor Dick Diver. As Nicole begins to improve, her doctor Franz Gregorovious exclaims to Dick: "It was the best thing that could have ever happened to her [...] a transference of the most fortuitous kind" (134). Dick subsequently marries the wealthy Nicole because he is attracted to her, but also in order to medically treat her during her outbursts of neurotic behaviour. Reflecting on how the transference began yielding a positive change in Nicole's behaviour, Franz says to Dick, "[r]eally, it had become your case" (133). While Franz candidly acknowledges that his unit is "a rich person's clinic" (133), Fitzgerald nonetheless inserts an authorial comment of validation by describing it as "a refuge for the broken, the incomplete, the menacing, of this world" (135).

Omeros, too, follows a psychoanalytic story-arc of trauma, neurosis, identification of the disorder and treatment. Plunkett is treated in an army hospital for his head wound sustained in the North African campaign, but he must still recover morally. He tries to find meaning to war, but is increasingly disillusioned. Reflecting on the Latin expression "*[p]ro honoris causa*" or "for the sake of honour," he asks himself, "but in whose honour did his head-wound graduate?" (25; emphasis in the original). Plunkett's head-wound is part of the reason he has moved to St Lucia with his wife: "They'd been out here / since and the war and his wound" (25). However, Plunkett is haunted by the couple's inability to produce a child. Once in St Lucia, Plunkett finds new purpose through a kind of transference, born of a happy coincidence. As he researches St Lucia's history, he stumbles upon a namesake: a nineteen-year-old Dutch midshipman also named Plunkett who died during the Battle of the Saintes in 1782. This sea battle marked a key victory for the English, enabling them to definitively consolidate their colonial possessions in the Caribbean. The midshipman thus represents a patriotic sacrifice that served a purpose, as opposed to the horrific slaughter of World War I, notably the Battle of the Somme, in which Plunkett's father lost his life (see 87). While Plunkett never articulates this contrast between the Battle of the Saintes' patriotic finality and the Battle of the Somme's futility, the chilling reference to his father in a description of a genealogical tree Plunkett is having drawn up is telling: "One pod was the Somme's. / It burst with his father's lungs" (87). Major Plunkett sees in this midshipman a glorious version of himself as well as the son he never had. His newfound passion for history becomes a neurotic compulsion as he pours over details concerning cannons, ships, wind direction and other aspects of the "battle's numerological poetry" (91). Like Nicole, Plunkett initially seeks refuge in a false 'cure' through an unhealthy transference. While Plunkett transfers his desire for a son to the young midshipman, Nicole resorts to a transference of feelings from one father-figure (her biological father) to another (Dick). Indeed, the father-child relationship is a major structural principle of both narratives. The leitmotiv of "Daddy's girl" and failed fathers is central to *Tender is the Night* (see Prigozy; Ullrich) while the replication and reversal of father-son genealogies proliferate across *Omeros* (see Hamner 54–58, 62).

THE WOUND OF WAR: PERSONAL ALLEGORIES OF CIVILIZATIONAL DISORDER

Nicole's and Plunkett's neuroses are also symptomatic of broader social crises. The shadow of World War I is never far from the dazzling party-life of expatriate hedonism. For example, Nicole's father uses his clout to bring her to Europe for treatment on an American battle-ship during World War I; earlier in the novel, Rosemary, the young starlet, and Dick, along with others, visit the site of the Battle of the Somme. E.W. Pitcher succinctly foregrounds the convergences between Nicole's life and World War I:

> Her father brings her to Europe on an American battleship in November of 1917, and she is committed at Dohmler's clinic in February 1918. In October-November of 1918 there is a favourable crisis in her malady (the Armistice is negotiated in Europe), and early in 1919 she is ready to be demobilized with the rest of those who have been to war. Of course, Nicole's 'war' is internal, but the parallels are too striking to be coincidental. (76)

Nicole's psychological disorder is thus symptomatic of the collective trauma of American expatriates in Europe living in the aftermath of the First World War.

Moreover, she is born in 1901 and is thus "the representative of the twentieth century, the child of the modern age" (76). Such temporal 'coincidences' between Nicole's private life and the American Century recall those in postcolonial works such as Rushdie's *Midnight's Children* (1981), in which Saleem Sinai is born at the midnight-hour of India's independence. Moreover, the roots of Nicole's disorder can be traced to an act of incest occurring at the same time as the outbreak of the war. David Ullrich sees a revealing parallel between Nicole's 'betrayal' by her father and the collective 'betrayal' of the idealistic young men sent to the battlefield by the older generation: "A young girl being seduced by her father at home in Lake Forest, Illinois, in 1914 is the equivalent evil of a young boy being seduced by his patriarchs into being slaughtered in his homeland in trench warfare" (61–62). The fact that Nicole's father brings her to Europe on an American battle-ship also links the psychological violence of incest with the collective violence of the war.

Nicole's initial recovery is clearly connected to the Armistice of World War I, as reflected in the kinds of letters she wrote Dick: "The letters were divided into two classes, of which the first class, *up to about the time of the armistice*, was of marked pathological turn, and of which the second class, running from thence up to the present, was entirely normal" (135; emphasis added). As Ullrich eloquently explains, "Fitzgerald merges interpersonal and political dramas; the act of sexual violence in its most malignant form, incest, is equivalent to political violence in its most evil form: war" (60-61). For Ullrich, incest is a psychosexual 'metaphor' for pathological political violence.

I would like to expand Pitcher's and Ullrich's lexicons of symbolical 'representative' and 'metaphor' by linking them to the postcolonial concept of national allegory as theorised by Fredric Jameson (1986). "Third-world texts," Jameson famously argues, "necessarily project a political dimension in the form of national allegory: *the story of the private individual destiny is always an allegory of the embattled situation of the public third-world culture and society*" (69; emphasis in the original). However, Nicole's mixed parentage (her father is American, her mother European) makes her a personification not only of the American nation, but of the American expatriate location. Similarly, her neurosis is less an expression of American national experience than one of transatlantic violence and trauma, particularly the complications of America's entanglements abroad. As Judith Kitchen puts it, "the recent war [...] had devastated most of Europe and taken the lives of countless American soldiers. America's history, now, was implicated in European fate" (51). Nicole's symbolic significance, therefore, is not limited to that of a "national allegory," but in fact becomes what Jahan Ramazani has called a "transnational allegory" (412) when describing the trope of the wound in *Omeros*. Transnational allegory, Ramazani posits, disrupts the "unproblematic referentiality" of nationalist politics and realist poetics, both of which tend to focus on "the particular historical experience of a particular race in a particular part of the world" (412). Transnational allegory "widen[s] rather than purif[ies] what might be called the dialectic of the tribe" (410). In this sense, *Tender is the Night* expands the scope of Jameson's famous postulation that "[t]hird-world texts, even those which are seemingly private and invested with a properly libidinal dynamic – necessarily project a political dimension in the form of national allegory" (69). Fitzgerald's representation of American expatriates shows that allegorical dynamics fusing the political and libidinal can also be found in a 'first-world text.' A modernist narrative of expatriation can already contain within it the transnational impulse that would find fuller expression in later postcolonial texts.

The key point of intersection of the private and public in *Tender is the Night* is encapsulated by the wound imagery, specifically that of stained sheets and rugs. In the opening of the book, the narrator uses a strange metaphor to describe the French Riviera beach: "its bright tan prayer rug of a beach" (11). This immaculate holiday beach contrasts sharply with the bloody beach of Thiepval where soldiers died in the beginning of the Battle of the Somme. Expatriate paradise and bloody battlefield interfuse through the shared imagery of the rug as Dick describes the massacred soldiers on the ground at Thiepval as "a million bloody rugs" (67). The blood imagery finally erupts in the more intimate space of a hotel bedroom when Nicole has a nervous breakdown on beholding a blood-stained bedspread at the scene of a murder cited earlier in this paper. It is as much as the memory of the incestual bedsheet as the intrusion and interpenetration of the personal and the political that so appals Nicole. It is also noteworthy to point out that the person murdered is a black man named Jules Paterson involved in a complicated saga of mistaken identity. Furthermore, Paterson's role is compared in the text to "the position of the friendly Indian who helped the white" (119). While the brief appearance this character makes is caricatural, if not racist, it is significant that the narrative engages to different degrees with multiple levels of victimhood and suffering – of the World War I soldiers, of the increasingly emancipated post-war woman, of the post-war generation, but also of the marginalized racial others.

World War I is thus more than the defining narrative event of *Tender is the Night*, it is also the book's preeminent and multidirectional metaphor. Nicole is not the only psychologically 'wounded' character to be allegorically linked to World War I. Dick Diver, her therapist-husband, has also been scarred by war. Ironically, as an Oxford Rhodes Scholar, he does not participate in the war since "he was already too valuable, too much of a capital investment to be shot off in a gun" (129). Yet, Fitzgerald's recurrent imagery of broken shells (a deliberate polysemic play on war shells and egg shells) serves to highlight complex, invisible psychological wounds, linked to his guilt about not serving in the war and living off Nicole's wealth as well as his frustration about not having realized his potential to become a great doctor. In a lucid moment of self-understanding following "a long dream of war," he writes "the half-ironic phrase: 'Non-combatant's shell-shock'" (198).

Furthermore, though Dick is responsible for her therapy, he is irresistibly attracted to two virginal young women: a "beautiful shell" (134) like Nicole and the budding young actress Rosemary Shields. The pathological dimension of this father-daughter complex is evoked symbolically, through references to streets names like *rue des Saint-Pères* and popular culture. Nicole is associated with the song "Why Do They Call Them Babies?" (150) while Rosemary is systematically linked to the film that has brought her stardom, *Daddy's Girl*. Dick is "enough older than Nicole to take pleasure in her youthful vanities" (153). As he watches *Daddy's Girl* beside Rosemary, "a lovely shot of Rosemary and her parents united at the last in a father complex" makes Dick "winc[e] for all the psychologists" (80), but perhaps also subconsciously at his own fascination for 'daddy's girls.' Emphasising the idealisation of womanhood in the Hollywood films and musicals of the 1920s, Ruth Prigozy argues that Dick represents American audiences "of all ages and by the millions [who] were willing dupes" of this ideal of girlish innocence that Fitzgerald ironically exposes as a hollow "artifice" of popular culture (214). In addition, the constant allusions to World War I, generals, as well as physical and psychological violence foreground an allegorical correspondence between Dick's and Nicole's psychological battles to master their pathological drives, on the one hand, and civilization's struggle to control its propensity for violence and destruction, on the other. While Dick and Nicole seem blinkered by their expatriate locations, Fitzgerald, the epitome of the American expatriate (he spent much of the 1920s shuttling between the French Riviera and Delaware) clearly articulates a dual perspective on American culture, seen both from home and abroad.

Fitzgerald's use of the trope of the wound as a site of painful personal and historical trauma is both magnified and multiplied in *Omeros*. The book opens with a powerful allegory established between the felling of trees and a European massacre of the native Arawak tribe. The Caribbean fisherman Philoctete prays before he "wound[s] the first cedar" (3). The trees are described as "bearded elders [who] endured the decimation / of their tribe" (6). This genocide anticipates references in the poem to other examples of colonial violence in North America (the Wounded Knee Massacre) and Africa (the atrocities of the transatlantic slave trade, particularly the voyage from Africa to the Americas, known as the Middle Passage). The most striking example is Philoctete's ankle wound which, he believes, "came from the chained ankles / of his grandfathers" (19). His injury thus associates him with the suffering endured by his forefathers during their forced transportation from their African homeland to the West Indies.

However, the power of the wound imagery in *Omeros* derives not from its potential as an instrument to merely critique colonialism, but in its assertion of the universality of historical trauma. Not all the characters who bear scars are victims of colonial oppression. As pointed out earlier, the white expatriate Plunkett is also morally scarred. The linking of his head-wound with the "fatal wound" (86) sustained by the eighteenth-century midshipman in the Battle of the Saintes associates Plunkett with European colonialism. However, Plunkett's head-wound also makes him the colonial double of the St Lucian Philoctete who bears an ankle injury. Moreover, as a colonial expatriate, Plunkett is an inverted reflection of the poet-narrator, a postcolonial expatriate.

A St Lucian living in America, the poet-persona is, in fact, a fictionalised version of Walcott himself. In a metaleptic moment, the narrator, referring to Plunkett's head-wound, explains, "This wound I have stitched into Plunkett's character." He adds, "affliction is one theme / of this work" (28). Even the narrator is not exempt from the trauma of colonialism, though his dilemma is more existential and linguistic. His simultaneous allegiance to native creole and the English language, to St Lucian performative traditions and the western form of Homeric epic also brings pain. He thus speaks of "the wound of a language I had no wish to remove" (270). By having characters as diverse as Plunkett, the midshipman, Philoctete, and the poet-narrator bear wounds, Walcott emphasises the distinct but nonetheless permeable nature of historical suffering across divides of race, culture and class. Fitzgerald's and Walcott's locations as expatriates perhaps make them particularly sensitive to both the singularity of individual experience and the simultaneous necessity for solidarity across forms of borders.

At this point, it is relevant to address the problematic nature of an endeavour that uses a postcolonial lens to examine the experiences of white characters. To suggest, as I do, that the white expatriate is akin to the postcolonial subject; that he or she is another in-between figure straddling two countries, cultures and imaginaries, is to run the risk of transforming the 'persecutor' into a kind of 'victim.' Such a reading, it may be contended, undermines the oppositional thrust of the postcolonial project, which seeks to challenge white imperial and post-imperial hegemony. However, Walcott's transnational allegory powerfully illustrates the fact that Walcott is "[r]epudiating a separatist aesthetic of affliction" by "turn[ing] the wound into a resonant site of interethnic connection [...], deconstructing the uniqueness of suffering" (Ramazani 406). It is this deconstruction of the "uniqueness of suffering" that creates a "transnational allegory" of affliction. A similarly interconnected allegory of affliction links the privileged Nicole, the debonair Dick, the dead black man, the dead soldiers of World War I and the decadent Lost Generation through the motif of the bloody rug. In this sense, the postcolonial technique of transnational allegory resonates deeply with the epistemological imperative of postcolonial studies which seeks not only to destabilise master-narratives such as imperialism and race but also to reveal their contrived nature as constructs or narratives per se.

CURE

As expatriate white subjects, Nicole and Plunkett also experience psychoanalytic arcs of transformation – from psychological trauma and its resulting neurotic tendencies to self-awareness and treatment. Nicole's ultimate cure is to rid herself of her emotional and psychological over-dependence on Dick by facing up to her psychological disorder. Significantly, her moment of cure is described in explicitly militaristic terms:

> [F]or this inner battle, she used even her weaknesses – fighting courageously with [...] the empty receptacles of her expiated sins [...]. And suddenly, in the space of two minutes she achieved her victory [...] cut[ting] the umbilical cord forever. (Fitzgerald 324)

Yet, Nicole's 'cure' is curiously similar to her 'disease.' As Milton Stern observes, her psychosexual liberation from her father was facilitated by a first sexual transference to Dick, while her emancipation from her over-dependence on Dick is orchestrated by a second transference to Tommy Barban, a self-professed mercenary who becomes her lover and second husband. Nicole's personal cure, however, does not automatically herald an unproblematic fresh start, nor does it necessarily betoken a facile form of broader civilizational healing. Stern notes that the consummation of Nicole and Tommy's relationship is syncopated with a US battleship firing its guns to call its sailors on shore-leave back on board on the ship (see 107). The implications of the boisterous sailors' violence and promiscuity during their leave dramatically underscore the pathological persistence of the life- and death-seeking drives on personal and societal levels.

A similar sense of uncertainty hovers over the major healing sequences in *Omeros*. Plunkett's compulsive need to compensate for the lack of a son through his neurotic obsession with history comes to an end when his wife Maud dies (yet another 'wound' for him), succumbing to an imperialism that spares few: the "empire of cancer" (260). Maud's death brings home the reality of the absence of a son, a fact Plunket has, until this point, been unwilling to accept by imagining the nineteen-year old midshipman as his son: "He forgot the war's / history that cost him a wife and a son" (309). While the Battle of the Saintes did indeed result in the loss of the life of the midshipman (his 'son'), Walcott also underscores the emotional toll Plunkett's obsession with history took on his relationship with Maud. Nonetheless, Maud's literal death allows her husband to come to terms with the figurative 'death' of his absent 'son.' Instead of searching for self-validation in a self-aggrandising imperial past, Plunkett is able to follow his late wife's lesson by living in the present. He begins to appreciate the natural beauty of the island (Maud was an avid gardener, like the poet-narrator): "He learnt how to pause / in the shade of a stone arch watching the bright red / flowers of the immortelle" (309). He also starts seeing the Saint Lucians as individuals, not pawns of history: "he began to speak to the workmen / not as boys who worked with him, till every name / somehow sounded differently" (309).

Similarly, Philoctete's ankle-wound, linked to the ancestral trauma of the Middle Passage, is cured through a mystic concoction from a root carried by a swift from Africa whose flight across the Atlantic repeats the transatlantic routes of the slave trade. Finally, the poet-narrator faces a cultural conundrum – that of being a poet desirous of celebrating the St Lucian people from whom he feels alienated as an anglicised, economically privileged expatriate. Only a hallucinatory Dantean descent to the underworld, represented by the sulphur springs of St Lucia, guided by Omeros, liberates him from "Pride in [his] craft" through a rite of "exorcism" (293-4). His 'cure' is being self-critical of "the hypocrisy / of loving them from [the] hotels" in which he stays each time he revisits his native island (228). He will continuously re-experience this estrangement and, at the same time, attempt to bridge this distance.

In *Omeros*, but also in *Tender is the Night*, the wound thus seems to take on a "homeopathic" power through a "mirroring relation between injury and remedy" (Ramazani 413). The cure lies in a continuing re-exposure and reproduction of pain in order to come to terms with it. In Plunkett's case as well as Nicole's, the merging of injury and remedy also suggests that there is no one-shot solution; that the cure is a continuous, ongoing process, marked by a proactive desire to confront and periodically "exorci[ze]" (Walcott 294) the ghosts of the past. While open to charges of resorting to contrived 'happy endings,' the fact is that both Fitzgerald and Walcott check their utopic allegorical impulses by accepting that "[t]his was history. I had no power to change it" (217). Plunkett may have come to terms with an "empire's guilt" (263) on a personal level, but St Lucian society as a whole remains "besieged / by the lances of yachts" (310), metonyms of the onward march of the tourist sector and neocolonial capitalism. Nicole may have achieved her "victory" (324), but the neurotic impulses of civilization, ominously reiterated by the sounds of naval artillery when she and Tommy make love, foreshadow the onslaught of fresh violence to be brought on by World War II (albeit unwittingly since the book was published in 1934). The figurative sophistication and political resonance of transnational allegory thus lies as much in its celebration of the possibilities of transformation and healing as in an unsentimental appraisal of an allegory's limits in the context of historical and contemporary violence that beget further tribulation and trauma.

As I near my conclusion, I will now offer a belated answer to the question raised at the beginning of the article. Can expatriate writing, whether written in the modernist or postcolonial period, be said to have a specifically postcolonial poetics? The convergences between the expatriate and postcolonial conditions are multiple – varying degrees of spatial, psychological and cultural dislocation, resulting in a renewed need for self-definition. Of most relevance to this paper is the idea that both expatriate and postcolonial narratives also function as political allegories. Warren Susman's definition of expatriate writing applies equally well to postcolonial writing: "a cultural mechanism available to the intellectual whereby he can attempt to turn his personal problems into public issues" (171). Yet, Nicole's expatriation remains fundamentally different from Plunkett's, transnational allegories notwithstanding. While Fitzgerald's Lost Generation appears to be in denial of the shattering psychosocial effects of the Great War, the diverse inhabitants of St Lucia in *Omeros* are haunted by historical events that have shaped their contemporary lives such as the Middle Passage and the Battle of the Saintes. Nicole and her fellow elite expatriates are, above all, travellers across *space*, aimlessly drifting from one European resort to another. Major Plunkett demonstrates the postcolonial preoccupation with *time* and history, attempting to replace his war service and his dying empire at the centre of a master-narrative that he and his nation no longer master. Nicole and Plunkett also serve as important reminders that there are several white experiences (male/female, wealthy heiress/a soldier who has risen through the ranks, Anglo-American/British), just as there are multiple 'postcolonial' locations.

CONCLUSION

To conclude, I would like to return to the *Odyssey* and bring this study full circle. Intertextual references to Homer's epic appear in both *Tender is the Night* and *Omeros*. Dick is systematically associated with the martial tradition and generals, particularly Ulysses Grant, in *Tender is the Night* (see 121, 132, 338). In addition to the eponymous bard Omeros who shares similarities with Odysseus, Plunkett's desire for a son is described as a doomed quest for his Telemachus in *Omeros* (see 263). Yet, Odysseus never experiences the psychological trauma that Nicole and Plunkett do. Admittedly, he suffers – though his theatrical insistence on the pain of exile reflects a propensity for exaggeration and a desire to manipulate his listeners (see Emlyn-Jones). It can also be argued that Homer's epic style leaves no room for the psychological analysis of a post-Freudian world. Nonetheless, it reflects, above all, an understanding of war that is fundamentally different from our own: one of war as simultaneously a source of tragic death and of eternal life through glory (*kleos*). Tragedy is present in this equation – but neurosis is not. The erosion of a martial aristocracy, the rise of individualism and the emergence of pacifist protest render the unequivocal epic glorification of war impossible for the modern post-war expatriate. Both *Tender is the Night* and *Omeros* suggest as much – the morally scarred Nicole and Plunkett are parodic doubles of the psychologically unscathed Odysseus: the wars to which they have been witness can no longer be presented as personal and moral victories but as ethical and civilizational failures. Their redemption lies not in their homecoming but in the difficult task of being at home in a disturbed and disturbing world.

LIST OF WORKS CITED

Auerbach, Eric. "Odysseus's Scar." *Mimesis: The Representation of Reality in Western Literature.* 1953. Princeton University Press, 2003, pp. 3-23.

de F. Lord, George. "The *Odyssey* and the Western World." *The Sewanee Review*, vol. 62, no. 3, 1954, pp. 406-427.

Emlyn-Jones, Chris. "True and Lying Tales in the *Odyssey*." *Greece & Rome*, vol. 33, no. 1, 1986, pp. 1-10.

Fanon, Frantz. "The Negro and Psychopathology." *Black Skin, White Masks* 1952. Pluto Press, 1986, pp. 141-209.

Fitzgerald, F. Scott. *Tender is the Night.* 1934. Penguin, 2001.

Hamner, Robert. *Epic of the Dispossessed: Derek Walcott's* Omeros. University of Missouri Press, 1997.

Homer. *The Odyssey*. 1961. Translated by Robert Fitzgerald, Farrar, Straus and Giroux, 1998.

Jameson, Fredric. "Third-World Literature in the Era of Multinational Capitalism." *Social Text*, vol. 15, 1986, pp. 65-88.

Kitchen, Judith. "F. Scott Fitzgerald's *Tender is the Night*." *Oxford Encyclopedia of American Literature*, vol. 1, edited by Jay Parini and Phillip W. Leininger, Oxford University Press, 2004, pp. 48-52.

López, Alfred J. Introduction: Whiteness after Empire. *Postcolonial Whiteness: A Critical Reader on Race and Empir*e, by López, State University of New York Press, 2005, pp. 1-30.

Pitcher, E.W. "*Tender Is the Night*: Ordered Disorder in the 'Broken Universe'." *Modern Language Studies*, vol. 11, no. 3, 1981, pp. 72-89.

Prigozy, Ruth. "From Griffith's Girls to Daddy's Girl: The Masks of Innocence in Tender is the Night." *Twentieth Century Literature*, vol. 26, no. 2, 1980, pp. 189-221.

Ramazani, Jahan. "The Wound of History: Walcott's *Omeros* and the Postcolonial Poetics of Affliction." *PMLA*, vol. 112, no. 3, 1997, pp. 405-417.

Rushdie, Salman. *Midnight's Children*. 1981. Random House, 2006.

Stern Milton R. "*Tender is the Night* and American History." *The Cambridge Companion to F. Scott Fitzgerald*, edited by Ruth Prigozy, Cambridge University Press, 2002, pp. 95-117.

Susman, Warren. "A Second Country: The Expatriate Image." *Texas Studies in Literature and Language*, vol. 3, no. 2, 1961, pp. 171-183.

Ullrich, David W. "Reconstructing Fitzgerald's Twice-Told Tales: Intertextuality in This Side of Paradise and *Tender Is the Night*." *The F. Scott Fitzgerald Review*, vol. 3, 2004, pp. 43-71.

Walcott, Derek. *Omeros*. 1990. Farrar, Straus and Giroux, 1992.

Contributors

Blue V, Alex, is a doctoral candidate in Ethnomusicology at University of California - Santa Barbara. He is interested in the intersections of sound, race, technology, and space, and his research on these topics has been published in Current Musicology and presented at a multitude of conferences across the United States and Europe. His dissertation illuminates the use of hip-hop as a radical tool for spatial reorientation and reimagining, as a medium for alternative forms of community organization, as a strategy for subverting and decolonizing maps drawn through systemic racism, and as an emergent counter-archive and counter-narrative in contemporary Detroit, Michigan.

de Waal, Ariane, is a post-doctoral researcher in English Literature and Culture at the University of Innsbruck. Her current research project examines the medical and cultural history of skin in 19th-century Britain. A monograph based on her PhD thesis, which addresses the interconnections between terror(ism) and subjectivity in British plays after 9/11, was published with De Gruyter as Theatre on Terror: Subject Positions in British Drama (2017). Some of her previous publications dealt with urban biopolitics, travelling terrorist assemblages, and post-traumatic theatre.

Furlanetto, Elena, earned her PhD in American Studies from the Technical University of Dortmund and currently works as a researcher at the University of Duisburg-Essen. She is the author of *Towards Turkish American Literature: Narratives of Multiculturalism in Post-Imperial Turkey* (2017). Her research interests include American and Postcolonial Literatures, Orientalism, Comparative Empire Studies, and poetry.

Gür-Şeker, Derya, has studied German Linguistics, German Literature, Media Studies and Political Sciences in Düsseldorf and Reading (UK). She is a postdoctoral researcher at the Department of German Linguistics at the University of Duisburg-Essen (Germany). Within her doctorate she analysed the EU constitutional debate using qualitative and quantitative methods for exploring lexical, metaphorical and argumentative phenomena in a multilingual discourse. Her research interests focus on Text and Corpus Linguistics, language in media and politics.

Meinel, Dietmar, currently works as a postdoctoral researcher in American Studies at the University of Duisburg-Essen. He has published in English and German, his articles have appeared in the *European Journal of American Culture* and *NECSUS: European Journal of Media Studies*. He is also the author of *Pixar's America: The Reanimation of American Myths and Symbols* (Palgrave MacMillan 2016). Together with Laura Bieger he co-edited *Black, White & In-Between* (2008).

Monaco, Angelo, is completing his PhD in English Literature at the University of Pisa. His dissertation investigates nostalgia and melancholia in Jhumpa Lahiri's *oeuvre* through the critical convergence of postcolonialism, trauma studies, and ecocriticism. He has published and given conference talks on melancholia, diasporic identities and postcolonial conflicts, focusing on such authors as Jhumpa Lahiri, Amitav Ghosh, Monica Ali, Kiran Desai, Hanif Kureishi, and William Trevor.

Munteán, László, is assistant professor of Cultural Studies and American Studies at Radboud University Nijmegen, the Netherlands. His publications have focused on the memorialization of 9/11 in literature and the visual arts, photography, urban culture and architecture, and cultural heritage. In a broader sense, his scholarly work revolves around the juncture of literature, visual culture, and cultural memory in American and Eastern European contexts. He is co-editor of *Materializing Memory in Art and Popular Culture* (Routledge 2017).

Roy, Sneharika, is assistant professor of Comparative and English Literature at the American University of Paris. Her research focuses on comparative approaches to epic that bridge classical and postcolonial theoretical paradigms. Her chapter for the MLA volume *Approaches to Teaching the Works of Amitav Ghosh* is in the final stages of review. She is also a contributor to the French encyclopaedic project *Dictionnaire des littératures indiennes* (*Dictionary of Indian Literatures*).

Wegner, Jarula M.I., received a B.A. in Chinese Studies and an M.A. in English Studies and German Studies from Goethe University in 2015. He was Visiting Scholar at Columbia University (USA), at the University of the West Indies, St. Augustine (Trinidad and Tobago), and at the University of Warwick (England). He is research assistant in the project "Migration and Transcultural Memory: Literature, Film and the Social Life of Media" at Goethe University and currently working on the PhD project "Transcultural Memory Constellations in Caribbean Carnivals: From Literature to Performance." Furthermore, he is co-speaker of the Interdisciplinary Memory Studies Group at the Frankfurt Humanities Research Centre.

Index

A

B

C

D

E

F

G

H

I

J

L

M

S

T

U

V

W

Cultural Studies

Gundolf S. Freyermuth
Games | Game Design | Game Studies
An Introduction
(With Contributions by André Czauderna, Nathalie Pozzi and Eric Zimmerman)

2015, 296 p., pb.
19,99 € (DE), 978-3-8376-2983-5
E-Book: 17,99 € (DE), ISBN 978-3-8394-2983-9

Andréa Belliger, David J. Krieger
Network Publicy Governance
On Privacy and the Informational Self

February 2018, 170 p., pb.
29,99 € (DE), 978-3-8376-4213-1
E-Book: 26,99 € (DE), ISBN 978-3-8394-4213-5

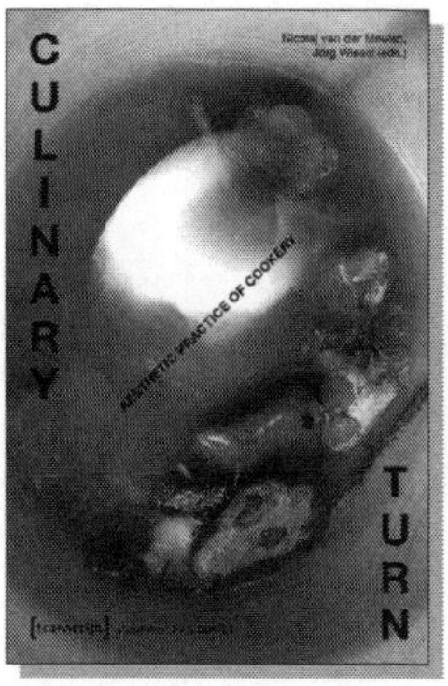

Nicolaj van der Meulen, Jörg Wiesel (eds.)
Culinary Turn
Aesthetic Practice of Cookery
(In collaboration with Anneli Käsmayr and in editorial cooperation with Raphaela Reinmann)

2017, 328 p., pb., col. ill.
29,99 € (DE), 978-3-8376-3031-2
E-Book available as free open access publication
ISBN 978-3-8394-3031-6

All print, e-book and open access versions of the titles in our list are available in our online shop www.transcript-verlag.de/en!

Cultural Studies

Martina Leeker, Imanuel Schipper, Timon Beyes (eds.)
Performing the Digital
Performativity and Performance Studies in Digital Cultures

2016, 304 p., pb.
29,99 € (DE), 978-3-8376-3355-9
E-Book available as free open access publication
ISBN 978-3-8394-3355-3

Suzi Mirgani
Target Markets –
International Terrorism
Meets Global Capitalism in the Mall

2016, 198 p., pb.
29,99 € (DE), 978-3-8376-3352-8
E-Book available as free open access publication
ISBN 978-3-8394-3352-2

Ramón Reichert, Annika Richterich,
Pablo Abend, Mathias Fuchs, Karin Wenz (eds.)
Digital Culture & Society (DCS)
Vol. 3, Issue 2/2017 – Mobile Digital Practices

January 2018, 272 p., pb.
29,99 € (DE), 978-3-8376-3821-9
E-Book: 29,99 € (DE), ISBN 978-3-8394-3821-3

All print, e-book and open access versions of the titles in our list are available in our online shop www.transcript-verlag.de/en!